DATE			

HOT BIRDS & COLD BOTTLES

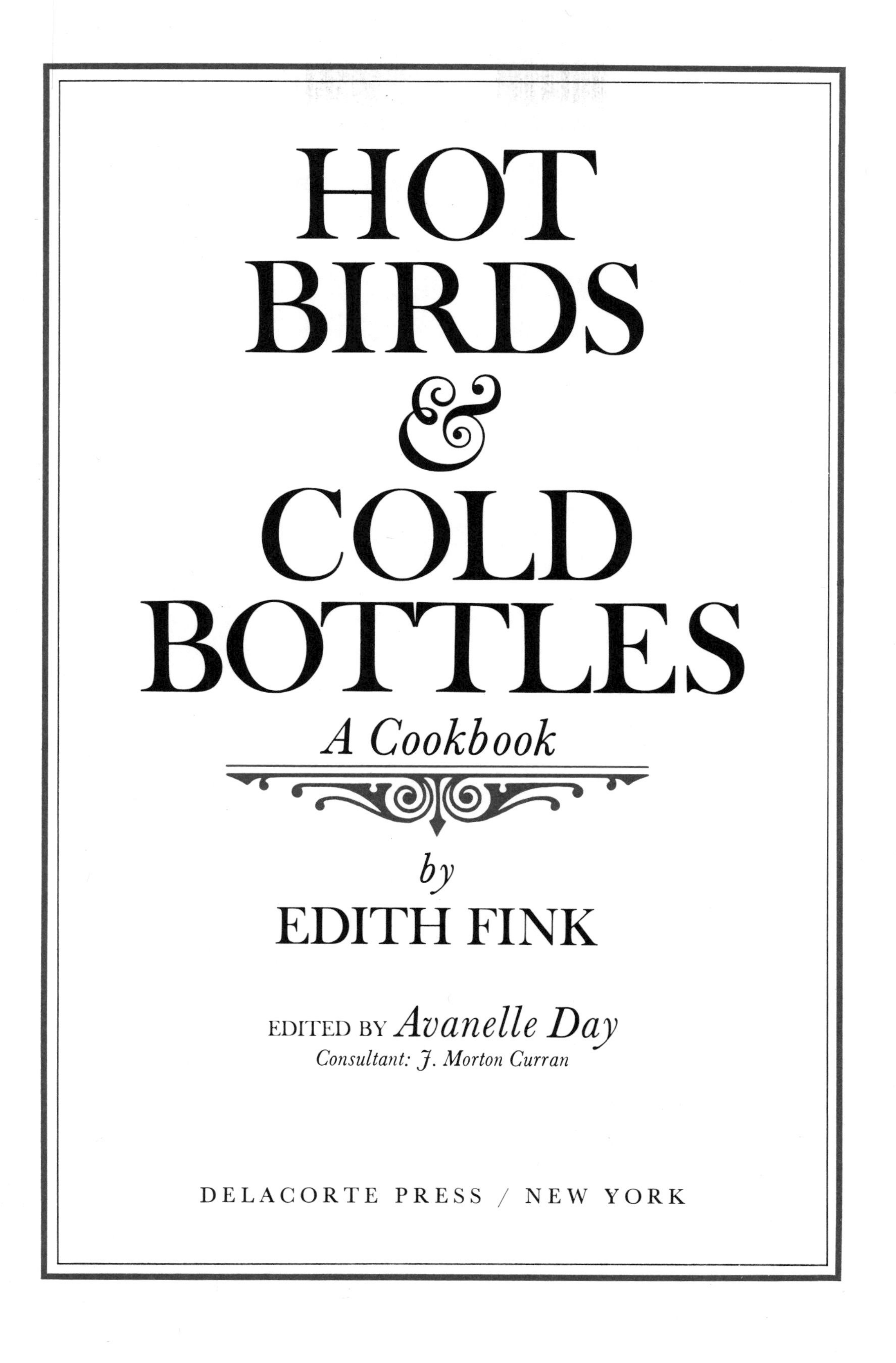

HOT BIRDS & COLD BOTTLES

A Cookbook

by

EDITH FINK

EDITED BY *Avanelle Day*

Consultant: J. Morton Curran

DELACORTE PRESS / NEW YORK

Library of Congress Catalog Card Number: 70–178724
Manufactured in the United States of America
First printing

Library of Congress Cataloging in Publication Data

Fink, Edith, 1917–
Hot birds & cold bottles.

1. Cookery (Poultry) 2. Cookery (Game) 3. Wine and wine making. I. Title.
TX749.F47 641.6'6'5 70–178724

The author would like to express her gratitude to Mr. Michael Dorn and Mr. Bernard Wolfe for their encouragement in writing this book and to Jurgensen's Grocery Company, Mrs. Ella Wepman, and Mrs. Irene Rubin for their generosity in contributing their prized recipes.

CONTENTS

ix Foreword
xiii Preface

1 THE BIRDS

3 Domestic Birds
5 *How to Stuff and Truss a Bird*
6 *Stuffing for Poultry*
7 *How to Roast Chicken or Turkey*
8 *How to Cook Giblets*
8 *How to Make Giblet Gravy*

10 Wild Birds: General Cleaning and Cooking Rules
14 Roasting Timetables for Domestic and Wild Birds
17 Chicken
77 Doves and Squabs
92 Duck
145 Goose
162 Grouse
167 Guinea Fowl
183 Partridge
189 Pheasant
211 Quail
223 Rock Cornish Hen
233 Turkey
260 Woodcock

267 THE BOTTLES

269 Wine Through the Ages
271 Types of Wine
273 General Information About Wine
276 Vintage Wine Chart
279 Categories of Wine
280 Imported White Wines
281 Domestic White Wines
282 Imported Red Wines
284 Domestic Red Wines
284 Domestic Rosé Wines
286 What is Champagne?
287 Imported Champagne
288 Domestic Champagne and Sparkling Wines
291 Index of Recipes

FOREWORD
by Bernard Wolfe

There are few things more depressing than listening to New Yorkers talk about the gastronomic wasteland that is Los Angeles. When I moved to Los Angeles some years ago I kept away from the moaners and groaners—I was busy trying to locate a few eating places serving something that could be designated as more than roughage or, if you will, silage.

In the end I stumbled on an easy and extraordinarily tasty solution to the problem, one I recommend wholeheartedly to enterprising travelers—get invited to dinner at Edith Fink's house in the Northridge section of the San Fernando Valley. It is safe to say that in my first days of exile I was the gastronomic hobo down and out on cookery's Skid Row, until I met Edith.

When she loomed on my horizon, all four-foot-eleven of her, she was identified not as a great cook but as a prolific author. That is to say, people told me about this dynamo in the Valley who ran a spic-and-span house for her biochemist husband Bob and also spent hours at the typewriter batting out fiction in the vein of Henry Miller. I was impressed by this description of her because it was given to me by Henry Miller. When Henry suggested that it might lighten my days in Los Angeles to know his friends the Finks, I said fine—Henry's taste in people is at least on a par with his taste in vintage wines.

I met the Finks. I found them thoroughly simpático. I began to frequent their split-level. We were intensely literary. Night after night we talked about books, books, books, their sizes and shapes, the care and feeding of. Then one night Edith began to observe me closely. She said I looked a bit pale, maybe peaked. Was I perhaps a little off my feed?

I tried to hint, without offending whatever local patriotism they might have, that this was indeed the case, and that with the kind of feed available in these parts, it was the better part of self-preservation to be as far off it as possible.

Twenty minutes later we were sitting down to a meal of *Poularde aux Truffes,* the kind of thing Edith Fink often threw together at the last minute, in between batting out her novels.

I knew from the evidence of my own eyes how competent Edith was on the typewriter. I now discovered from the evidence of my own palate what a goddess she is on the kitchen range. *Poularde aux Truffes* did indeed turn out to be chicken with truffles, which I'd had many times, but never with this heavy whipped-cream overlay and bold traces of Cointreau and brandy running through. It wasn't exactly a parfait but neither was it like any winged animal I'd been near before. The long languishing trencherman in me sat up and took notice, then seconds, then thirds.

Well, I could go on and on, as my eating at the Finks' subsequently did. I could, for example, tell you about the *Suprêmes de Volaille Maurice,* which I was treated to the following week and discovered to be boned breast of chicken with stuffing of spinach, egg, onion, and garlic crumbs, the whole stunning concoction aromatic from vigorous bastings of sherry.

Then I was introduced in rapid succession to *Canard Côte d'Or* (duck stuffed with lobster meat) ; *Suprêmes de Caneton aux Noix* (duckling breast meat, sautéed walnuts, lemon juice) ; Goose Piccadilly (honey, almonds, lemon, stuffed apple) ; Eloise's Stuffed Pheasant (sage sausage-meat stuffing, garnish of liver and sausage and bacon slices wondrously amalgamated, served with sliced pineapple, cherries, unpeeled sliced oranges, all laced, or perhaps the word is embroidered, with Curaçao).

The point of this is that Edith is as much at home on the typewriter as on the range. It finally registered on some of her appreciative guests that Edith might sit down at her typewriter and detail her adventures on the range.

She balked at the idea at first. The typewriter,

she figured, was for literature, the range for cooking, and to bring the two together, to try to make literature out of cookery, no matter whose, would be a contradiction in terms. We tried to explain to her that you can find some literature on any street corner, but a nonpareil meal like those of Edith's is rare.

In the end Edith consented to put her secrets, her techniques for whipping up these culinary sensations, between covers. So now we can save ourselves in the gastronomic wasteland that is Los Angeles or almost any other American city you care to name. Now we can all eat the way Edith and Bob eat, which is to say, like kings. In this book you will find clear recipes for creations of art. Anybody who loves good food will find solace and achievement here.

This cookbook is about birds and the wines that go with them. This is only one of the areas of cookery in which Edith Fink excels, but it's one that corresponds to my tastes. In this age of wholesale cholesterol in the cuisine, when saturated fats are the rule rather than the exception, it is a relief to be brought back to those wonderful birds that are not drenched in clinging greases and oils, whose tender lean flavors blend with, but do not overwhelm, the less boisterous wines. I can't tell you definitively, any more than the doctors can, that a cholesterol-heavy diet will drop you in your prime, but I can guarantee you this, if you leave a lot of room on your dinner table for these fine birds Edith so magnificently tells you how to prepare you'll develop a keen interest in living for a long time.

Bernard Wolfe

PREFACE

Over a period of twenty-seven years I have had an exciting and rewarding experience accumulating these recipes from all parts of the world and then developing liberal variations on them to suit the evolving tastes of my family and friends. I will call these nice people "followers," only in the sense that they have been following me around for some years requesting more and more insistently that I gather my recipes together and make them available in book form. So here, finally, they are—let your respective palates be the judges.

I've tried to emphasize variety and avoid routine cookery. I believe none of the recipes is especially elaborate or hard to follow. Good food does not have to be complicated—superb food is often superbly simple.

I have limited this book to poultry and game birds because the variety of preparation is endless, the birds are easy to prepare, they are low in fat content and very high in protein and usually inexpensive. Most of the birds are available all year round, thanks to the miracle of freezing.

A tough chicken, duck, goose, or turkey is a rare bird indeed since the advent of scientific poultry-raising. Chicken is so plentiful and such a good buy most of the year that we purchase it for large dinner parties, barbecues, and cook-outs of all kinds. We have the choice of chickens whole, cut-up, and halved; or we can purchase legs, thighs, wings, and breasts separately. There is a whole world of cooking with chicken alone.

The small turkeys that are available are a boon for the small family. They are tender and succulent without needing treatment with a tenderizer. The exciting thing about poultry or game birds is their variety. Duck, for instance, has rich dark meat all the way through, and give thanks again, it may be purchased, frozen, all year round.

The poultry we buy in markets is the most carefully chaperoned in the world. Since January, 1959, virtually all birds have had to pass a rigid processing-plant inspection by the U. S. Department of Agriculture. All water and equipment used in processing must also be officially checked. Today, poultry is one of our safest, most carefully supervised foods.

The wonder of those tiny Rock Cornish hens! The plump-breasted, all-light-meat delights were originated in 1950 at Idle Wild Farm in Pomfret Center, Connecticut, by Therese and Jacques Makowsky. These delicious birds, a cross breed of pure Cornish game hens (descended from East Indian jungle birds) and our familiar Plymouth Rock hens, are not a self-perpetuating cross. The breeding must be carefully controlled each year. They, too, are now available, frozen, all year round.

Turkey, once king of the holiday season, is now king all year round, available whole or in parts, frozen or fresh, stuffed or unstuffed.

Is there a hunter in the family? Does he triumphantly return home bearing gifts of partridge or pheasant? Prepare his prize, choosing any one of the game bird recipes. Is there no hunter in the family? There are game birds available, frozen and ready to cook, at specialty shops in every large city, and as close as your telephone.

A bird needs a bottle, a bottle cries out for a bird, and there are myriad lovely ways of bringing them together. I have tried to provide those ways. I hope they give you pleasure.

To invite someone to dinner
is to take charge of his happiness
during the time he is
under your roof.

—Jean-Anthèlme Brillat-Savarin
(from *Physiologie du Goût*)

The
BIRDS

DOMESTIC BIRDS

The term domestic birds includes chicken, duck, goose, guinea fowl, pigeon, and turkey. The two most popular forms of marketing uncooked poultry are fresh chilled and frozen, both of which are fully dressed and ready to cook. These birds are federally or state inspected to insure the consumer that they have met strict standards for wholesomeness, proper preparation, and labeling. The age of the bird indicates how tender it is and determines how it should be cooked. A young bird has a flexible breast, smooth skin which tears easily and shows signs of pinfeathers, and evenly distributed fat.

Poultry is perishable. It should be displayed properly in the markets so that the consumer can obtain top-quality birds. Fresh chilled, ready-to-cook poultry should be enclosed in an unbroken, transparent wrapper and displayed in refrigerated cases. Frozen poultry should be solidly frozen and displayed in freezers at zero degrees F. or lower. The wrapper should be neither torn nor broken.

Once the bird is in the home, proper cleanliness in handling and storing is very important. Raw poultry is particularly susceptible to food-poisoning bacteria. Fresh chilled, raw poultry should be unwrapped. If the bird is whole, remove giblets from the body cavity—wash thoroughly, pat dry, put in a bowl, cover loosely, and store in the coldest part of the food compartment of the refrigerator. Giblets should be cooked within twelve hours. They also may be cooked immediately, cooled, and refrigerated. Place the raw bird on a large tray or platter, cover loosely with waxed paper, aluminum foil, or plastic wrap. Place it in the coldest part of the refrigerator. Use whole birds within twenty-four hours.

Frozen uncooked poultry should be stored at zero degrees F., or lower, in the moisture- and vapor-proof wrapper or container in which the bird was packaged for the market. Frozen poultry is usually defrosted before cooking. Keep it frozen solid until ready to cook, allowing sufficient time for defrosting. Follow the thawing directions on the package or use one of the following methods:

Thawing in Cold Water: Leave bird in the original wrapper and place it under cold running water. Time required will be about one hour for small birds and six to eight hours for a large turkey. Once bird is thawed, remove giblets from body cavity and cook it as you would a fresh one.

Thawing in the Refrigerator: Leave the frozen bird in the original wrapper and place it on a tray or platter. Put the bird in the food compartment of the refrigerator and let it stay one or two days; the time depends upon the size. A turkey weighing eighteen pounds or over may require three days to defrost.

Do not thaw commercially frozen stuffed poultry before cooking. Cook it according to the directions on the label, and remember that a frozen unthawed bird requires a longer cooking time.

Poultry is a protein food and should be cooked at a low temperature so it will be tender, juicy, and uniformly cooked to the bone. Young, tender, plump birds are suitable for barbecuing, broiling, frying, and roasting. Lean, mature birds are best cooked by moist heat. They may be braised, stewed, baked and used in casseroles, and for salads. Old birds need long, slow cooking in water or steam. These birds make excellent, full-flavored soup.

If the wrapper in which the bird is packaged has cooking directions printed on it, follow them for computing the roasting time, or use the roasting guides for domestic birds in this book. Remember that the cooking-time periods are approximate and it may be necessary to decrease or increase the time due to the differences in the individual bird.

If a meat thermometer is used, insert it in the center of the inside thigh muscle or in the thickest part of the breast, being sure that the bulb does not touch a bone. The bird is done when the temperature reaches 180 to 185°. The center of the stuffing should register 165°.

HOW TO STUFF AND TRUSS A BIRD

Trussing a bird before it is roasted compacts it to permit even browning. In addition, the bird is more attractive when it is served on the platter, and is easier to carve.

Rinse the bird in cold water, drain well, and pat dry. Rub the neck and body cavities lightly with salt and ground black pepper. If the bird is to be stuffed, spoon the stuffing lightly into the neck and body cavities to allow room for the stuffing to expand while cooking. Stuff the neck cavity first. Pull the neck skin to the back, fold the end of the skin under neatly, and pin it to the back skin with a skewer. Turn the bird breast-side up and spoon the stuffing loosely into the body cavity. Close the opening by inserting three or four skewers through the skin at the edge of one side of the opening and passing them over the opening and through the skin on the opposite side. Then draw the edges of the skin together by lacing string around the skewers as in lacing shoes. Tie the ends of the string together at the bottom of the opening and fasten to the tailpiece. Press the drumsticks and thighs closely against the body of the bird. Tie the ends of the drumsticks together with a cord and fasten to the tailpiece. If the bird is not stuffed and there is a band of skin across the opening to the body cavity, push the ends of the legs under it. This holds the legs in place. Now, lift each wing, fold the tip under, and press it against the back—akimbo style. This method eliminates the use of skewers for holding the wings in place and gives the bird a base on which to rest in the roasting pan and platter. Remove all skewers and string before serving.

STUFFING FOR POULTRY

The base for poultry stuffing is usually dry breadcrumbs, flaky cooked rice, or mashed potatoes. The base may be seasoned with salt, black pepper, dried or fresh herbs, or chopped vegetables such as onion, celery, and green pepper. Melted butter, margarine, or poultry fat may be added for richness and flavor.

For a moist stuffing, add to the other ingredients the broth in which the giblets were cooked. Add the broth a tablespoon or two at a time to prevent the stuffing from becoming too wet. Remember that the stuffing absorbs moisture from the bird during the roasting period.

Other ingredients—chestnuts, pecans, walnuts, oysters, sausage, dried and fresh fruit, olives, or sauerkraut—may be added to the base to vary the stuffing.

APPROXIMATE AMOUNT OF STUFFING FOR READY-TO-COOK POULTRY

KIND OF POULTRY	READY-TO-COOK WEIGHT IN POUNDS	APPROXIMATE AMOUNT OF STUFFING
CHICKEN		
Broilers or Fryers	1½ to 2½	1 to 2 cups
Roasters	2½ to 4½	2 to 5 cups
Capons	4 to 8	5 to 7 cups
DUCK	3 to 5	2 to 4 cups
GOOSE	4 to 8	3 to 6 cups
	8 to 10	6 to 8 cups
WHOLE TURKEY:	3½ to 5	4 to 6 cups
(*halves, and half-breasts*)	5 to 8	6 to 8 cups
	8 to 12	2 to 3 quarts

WHOLE TURKEY:

Allow 1 cup stuffing for each pound ready-to-cook turkey. For example, to stuff a 12-pound ready-to-cook turkey, make 3 quarts stuffing.

HOW TO ROAST CHICKEN OR TURKEY

After the bird is stuffed and trussed, rub the skin thoroughly with melted or softened butter, margarine, chicken, duck, or goose fat, or cooking oil. Place the bird, breast up, on a rack in a shallow roasting pan, about 2 inches deep. If a V-shaped rack is used, place bird breast down. To eliminate basting and to help the bird brown uniformly, cover it with a fat-moistened, double-thickness of cheesecloth large enough to cover the top of the bird and drape down loosely on all sides, being sure that the edges hang inside the pan. (Do not wrap the bird in the cloth.) Place the bird in a preheated slow oven (325°). Roast birds according to individual timetables (pp. 14–16).

HOW TO TELL WHEN A BIRD IS ROASTED:

1. Press the thickest part of the drumstick between the fingers, protected with a paper towel or napkin. The meat is very soft when done.
2. Move the drumstick up and down; the leg joint should move easily or twist out of joint.
3. If a meat thermometer is used, it should read 180° to 185°. Remove the bird from the oven and allow it to stand twenty minutes. It will be easier to carve.

CARE OF COOKED POULTRY:

Never allow cooked poultry, stuffing, or gravy to stand outside the refrigerator after the meal is served. Remove all stuffing from the bird, put it in a bowl, and refrigerate. If there is only a small amount of meat left on the carcass, remove it and refrigerate in a separate covered bowl. If only one side has been carved, wrap the entire bird in plastic wrap or waxed paper and refrigerate at once. Refrigerate gravy in a covered bowl. Crack the carcass, cover, and refrigerate. Many of the dishes in this book may be prepared ahead of time or partially prepared. This is not considered good practice unless the poultry is thoroughly cooked, quickly cooled and refrigerated until time to finish and serve the dish. If this is not done, bacteria can grow and food poisoning may ensue.

HOW TO COOK GIBLETS

Giblets include the gizzard, heart, and liver of poultry. The neck is also usually included with ready-to-cook whole birds. Wash giblets thoroughly and place them in a saucepan. Add 1 teaspoon salt, 1 rib celery (cut up), 1 small onion, 2 whole black peppers, and cold water to cover. Simmer, covered, 10 to 15 minutes or until the liver is tender and loses its red color. Remove liver and continue simmering the remaining giblets until they are easily pierced with a fork—about 20 minutes if giblets are from a young bird; about 50 minutes if they are from a mature bird; about 1¾ hours if they are from a large turkey or old bird. Remove giblets from the broth and chop and reserve them for use in the giblet gravy. Strain and reserve broth to use for the liquid in the gravy. If a larger amount of broth is desired, purchase additional gizzards and necks. Cook them with the giblets that are included with the whole bird.

HOW TO MAKE GIBLET GRAVY

INGREDIENTS	FOR 2 CUPS GRAVY	FOR 4 CUPS GRAVY
Pan drippings	*3 tablespoons*	*6 tablespoons*
Flour	*3 tablespoons*	*6 tablespoons*
Broth, water, or milk	*2 cups*	*4 cups*
Salt or seasoned salt	*to taste*	*to taste*
Ground black pepper	*to taste*	*to taste*
Chopped giblets	*½ cup*	*1 cup*

Allow 1/4 cup gravy for each person.

1. When bird is done, remove it from the roasting pan to a heated platter.
2. Pour the drippings from the roasting pan into a small bowl, leaving the browned bits in the pan.
3. Measure the amount of pan drippings needed for the gravy and return it to the roasting pan.
4. Add the amount of flour needed and blend it with the measured drippings until the mixture is smooth.
5. Stir and cook the mixture over low heat until it is bubbly.
6. Remove pan from the heat, add broth, water, or milk, or a combination of broth and water or broth and milk. (A little heavy cream may be added for extra richness.) Mix well.
7. Cook, stirring, until the gravy is uniformly thick and smooth, scraping up the browned bits from the bottom of the pan.
8. Season to taste with salt or seasoned salt and black pepper. Add chopped giblets. Serve piping hot.

WILD BIRDS
GENERAL CLEANING AND COOKING RULES

Game birds are always plucked but seldom skinned. Remove wings at joint nearest body, and legs at first joint above feet. Pull out all larger feathers near wings and tail and pick bird roughly. Paraffin and water will do a fine job of removing feathers. For example, for six ducks, place three twelve-ounce cakes of paraffin in a pot with six quarts of water. Bring to a boil and remove from heat. The melted paraffin will float on top of the water. Immerse birds one by one in water so that a coating of paraffin adheres to the feathers. Set birds aside to cool. When paraffin has hardened, small feathers and down may be easily removed by scraping down the bird with a small knife. The paraffin may be used many times and heated for future birds. If no paraffin is available, pluck the birds and clean them; then singe them, removing the remaining down.

Game birds should be drawn at the earliest opportunity, especially in warm weather. To remove entrails, make a cut starting just to the rear of the breastbone and around the vent. This allows easy removal of entrails, including large intestine, gizzard, heart, lungs, and liver. The empty cavity should be cleaned thoroughly, preferably by wiping out with a cloth soaked in hot water and wrung almost dry. The heart, liver, and gizzards are well worth saving to be used cooked and chopped in stuffing or gravy. They should also be wiped thoroughly. Don't wash by dipping in water or under running water. It may take away some of the flavor.

If there is no time to do a thorough job of drawing the birds soon after they are shot, it is wise to remove the craw and the intestines, at least. This can be done by making a small opening at the neck and another at the anus. A buttonhook or a wire bent into a hook can be pushed into the opening to withdraw intestines. Removal of the craw and intestines will go a long way toward insuring good keeping qualities for your game. Any game taken with shotguns will have pellets penetrating the abdominal cavity and the intestines. The fluids from the intestines have a tremendous degenerative effect on body tissue, so the quicker you can remove the entrails from the bird and get it aired out and cooled, the better. In warm weather I would suggest with the larger birds, like wild geese, that as soon as you get the bird back to the blind, take your knife and cut the jugular vein, draw the bird, keep the vent open so air can circulate.

All game birds should be allowed to hang at a temperature just above freezing for ten days to two weeks before they are cooked.

Feathers should be left on birds that are to be hung immediately or to be shipped without refrigeration in ordinary ice. When shipping game in this manner, it is best to stuff the body cavity with dry grass or clean crumpled paper. However, birds should be plucked before they are frozen as it is more difficult to pluck a bird that has been frozen and allowed to thaw. When shipped with dry ice, the birds should be cleaned, plucked, and frozen before they are shipped.

Freeze your bird well-wrapped in plastic wrap. Be sure your bird is wet when you wrap it. The final wrapping is freezer paper, two layers. It is not recommended that the bird be soaked in vinegar water or soda or salt water. If anything, soak in cold water. Put some ice cubes in it. You might also take time to remove any pellets and blood clots. The proper care of game has so much to do with making it palatable!

Pheasant, grouse, prairie chicken, quail, Hungarian partridge, dove, turkey, chukar partridge, and many other species all require the same treatment in the field. Dress them out as soon as possible; carry them on a game hanger so the air circulates around them. They'll come through much better than if you put them in an airtight canvas pocket. Birds stacked one upon the other have a tendency to heat up and spoil.

There's a debate among hunters as to whether our upland birds should be picked or skinned. Each person must decide for himself. Pheasant, quail, and Hungarian partridge can be scalded and picked. But some birds–ruffed grouse, for example—have very thin and tender skin, which makes the chore difficult. Some wild-game cooks insist the skin be left on, since fat is deposited just under it and that has a lot to do with imparting a more delicate flavor to the meat. Skinning a bird is rather simple. Start at the breast, peel the feathers off; cut off the legs at the knee joint. Take off the wings too. When the job's done, soak the bird in cold water. Prepare for eating or freezing in the manner described above.

When testing game birds to identify those that are young and tender, the stiffness of the bill is a good guide. If pheasant and grouse, for example, can be lifted by the lower jaw without breaking it, they are mature birds whose jaws are set. They will not be as tender as the younger, less developed birds and will require longer cooking, perhaps moist cooking, such as braising.

Young pheasants' spurs will be pliable. The breastbone of a young partridge will break easily, and the leg will be plump close to the foot. The claws of a young bird of any kind are sharp. The claws of an older bird are blunter at the tip. If the bird is old, a commercial tenderizer will be of help. Follow the package directions, but use the tenderizer in the cavity, not on the surface of the bird.

To truss the bird, place it on its back and fold the tail upward; insert a skewer to hold the tail in place, then tie the legs over the tail with twine. Turn the bird on its breast and fold the wings against the backbone. Tie the wings, leaving the breast clear of twine.

To carve the bird, place it on its back. With a sharp knife, cut the legs at the thigh and remove them to a platter. Then cut the joints from the thighs. Cut off the wings and set aside. With the bird on its back, split it lengthwise and cut it away from the backbone, which may be discarded if desired. Quarter the two sections of the body or cut into small sections.

If the bird is large, such as a turkey or goose that has a meaty breast, remove one of the legs and thighs and put aside. With the meat away from you, carve long slices of breast meat with a sharp knife. If you carve only as much meat as you need, the remaining meat on the carcass will not dry out.

As for how many you can serve with your bag, that depends partly on the recipe. If the bird is to be stuffed, braised with accompanying vegetables, or cooked in a potpie, a single bird will go farther. In general, however, a pheasant will serve three or four, a partridge one or two if it's very large. With quail and woodcock, count on one bird for each serving.

ROASTING TIMETABLES *for* DOMESTIC *and* WILD BIRDS

STUFFED CHICKEN
(At 325°)

KIND	READY-TO-COOK WEIGHT IN POUNDS	APPROXIMATE ROASTING TIME (HOURS)
Broilers*	1½ to 2½	1¼ to 2
Fryers*	1½ to 2½	1¼ to 2
Roasters*	2½ to 4½	2 to 3½
Capons	4 to 8	3 to 5
Rock Cornish Hens	1 to 2	1 to 1½

* If broilers, fryers, and roasters are unstuffed, increase oven temperature to 400° (hot) and roast broilers and fryers for ¾ to 1½ hours and roasters for 1½ to 2¾ hours.

STUFFED TURKEY
(At 325°)

READY-TO-COOK WEIGHT IN POUNDS	APPROXIMATE ROASTING TIME (HOURS)
6 to 8	2 to 2½
8 to 12	2½ to 3
12 to 16	3 to 3¾
16 to 20	3¾ to 4½
20 to 24	4½ to 5½

When buying turkey, if ready-to-cook weight is less than 2 pounds, allow 3/4 pound to 1 pound per serving. If over 12 pounds, allow 1/2 to 3/4 pound per serving. Cold cooked turkey yields more servings per pound than hot cooked turkey.

Roast an unstuffed wild turkey in a preheated oven at 350°, allowing at least 20 to 25 minutes per pound roasting time.

All recipes for turkey may be prepared with domestic or wild birds. Roast a stuffed wild turkey in a preheated 325° oven for 20 to 25 minutes per pound, or until the thickest part of the thigh is easily pierced with the tip of a knife and the juices have no red tint.

UNSTUFFED GOOSE
(At 325°)

READY-TO-COOK WEIGHT IN POUNDS	APPROXIMATE ROASTING TIME (HOURS)
4 to 6	2 3/4 to 3
6 to 8	3 to 3 1/2
8 to 10	3 1/2 to 3 3/4
10 to 12	3 3/4 to 4 1/4
12 to 14	4 to 4 3/4

If goose is stuffed, increase roasting time of a 4- to 8-pound goose 30 minutes; for 9 to 14 pounds increase 20 minutes.

Following are roasting guides for the other birds, both stuffed and unstuffed.

DUCK

To roast an unstuffed duck, place in a preheated slow oven (325°). Roast 2 1/2 to 3 hours, or until the skin is crisp and brown and the meat on the drumsticks is soft.

If duck is stuffed, increase cooking time 30 minutes.

Allow one duck, weighing 4 to 5 pounds, for 4 servings.

Roast an unstuffed wild duck at 350° for 1 to 1¼ hours, or 15 minutes per pound. One wild duck usually serves 2 to 3 persons.

To roast a stuffed wild duck place it uncovered in a 350° oven, allowing 30 to 40 minutes per pound.

GROUSE

Roast an unstuffed grouse in a 350° oven for 15 to 20 minutes. Serves 1 person.

Roast a stuffed grouse in oven at 425° for 45 minutes. Serves 1 person.

PARTRIDGE

Roast an unstuffed partridge at 325° for 1¼ hours. Serves 1 person.

Roast stuffed partridge at 425° for 45 minutes. Also serves 1 person.

PHEASANT

Roast an unstuffed pheasant at 350° for 1 to 1½ hours. Serves 4 persons.

Roast stuffed bird at 350° for 2 hours, or until tender. Serves 4 persons.

QUAIL

Roast unstuffed quail in a 350° oven for about 1 hour, or until birds are tender. Four quail will make 4 servings.

Roast stuffed quail, breast down, in a 425° oven for 1 hour. Four stuffed quail will serve 4 persons.

WOODCOCK

To cook unstuffed woodcock, *broil* about 6 inches from heat, 8 to 10 minutes on each side, or until tender. Four woodcock will serve 4 persons.

Roast stuffed woodcock in a 350° oven for about 30 minutes. One average-sized woodcock will serve 1 person.

CHICKEN

Just consider what a world this would be if ruled by the best thoughts of men of letters! Ignorance would die at once, war would cease, taxation would be lightened, not only every Frenchman, but every man in the world, would have his hen in the pot.

ALEXANDER SMITH

KINDS OF READY-TO-COOK CHICKEN CLASSIFIED ACCORDING TO AGE AND WEIGHT WITH AMOUNT TO BUY

KINDS	AVERAGE AGE AND WEIGHT	AMOUNT TO BUY PER SERVING
Broilers	8 to 12 weeks old 1½ to 2½ pounds	¼ to ½ bird
Fryers	10 to 16 weeks old 2½ to 3½ pounds	¾ to 1 pound
Roasters (either sex)	Under 8 months old 3½ to 6 pounds	½ to ¾ pound
Capons (desexed males)	7 to 10 months old 4 to 8 pounds (the average is 6 to 8 pounds)	½ to ¾ pound
Rock Cornish Hens	6 to 7 weeks old 1 to 2 pounds	1 bird of the smaller size, ½ bird of the larger size
Stewing Hens or Fowls	Over 1 year old 2½ to 5 pounds	¼ to ¾ pound

Wherever civilized men and women take their places at the table, the word France is synonymous with perfection in matters culinary, for the French are serious eaters and will accept nothing less than the finest in food. As a result, French cookery has influenced the cuisine of every country of the Western world.

POULET EN CALVADOS

(MAKES 6 SERVINGS)

WINE SUGGESTION: *White Burgundy; Pouilly Fuissé (De Luze)*

2 chickens (1½ to 2 pounds each), cut into serving pieces, or 3 to 4 pounds meaty chicken parts
2 teaspoons salt or salt to taste
¼ teaspoon ground black pepper
¼ cup (½ stick) butter
½ cup Calvados
4 egg yolks
1 cup light cream

1. Wash chicken, wipe dry, and rub with salt and black pepper.
2. In a 12-inch skillet, melt butter. Place chicken in a single layer in the butter. Cook uncovered until chicken is tender and brown on both sides, not more than 30 minutes.
3. In a small saucepan, heat Calvados. Pour it over the chicken, ignite, and baste the chicken until the flame dies down. Remove chicken to a warm heat-proof platter and keep warm. Set aside the skillet, reserving the Calvados and pan drippings mixture.
4. In a 1-quart bowl, lightly beat egg yolks with the cream. Pour the mixture into the skillet. Stir and cook, over low heat, until the sauce has thickened. Correct seasonings and strain the sauce over the chicken. Serve very hot.

MENU

Poulet en Calvados
Noodles
Hearts of Artichokes
Fruit Compote

Thomas Jefferson, our first ambassador to France, did much to popularize French cooking in America. While serving in Paris, he devoted his spare time to visiting outstanding restaurants and learning the intricacies of French cuisine. After returning to America as Washington's secretary of state, Jefferson continued to import French delicacies via diplomatic pouch.

POULARDE AUX TRUFFES

(MAKES 4 SERVINGS)

WINE SUGGESTION: *Vouvray*

Steps 1 and 2 may be prepared ahead of time.

2 chickens (1½ to 1¾ pounds each), split in halves lengthwise
6 tablespoons (¾ stick) butter
½ cup brandy
½ cup Cointreau
1½ teaspoons salt
¼ teaspoon ground black pepper
½ pound white mushrooms
Hot water
½ cup heavy cream, whipped
4 truffles (1 small jar or 1 can), chopped

1. Wash chicken and wipe dry.
2. In a 12-inch heavy skillet, heat 5 tablespoons of butter until it foams. Add chicken and cook over moderate heat, browning both sides, about 20 minutes.
3. Combine brandy and Cointreau. Heat ¾ cup of the mixture in a small saucepan, pour it over the chicken, and ignite, shaking the skillet to distribute the liquors. Reserve the remaining ¼ cup of the liquor mixture to use later.
4. Sprinkle chicken with salt and black pepper, cover, and cook over low heat until chicken is tender, about 20 minutes.
5. Remove chicken to a warm heat-proof platter and keep warm.
6. Wash mushrooms, cover with hot water, and let them stand 2 to 3 minutes to keep them white. Drain off water, reserving 3 tablespoons.
7. To the pan drippings in the skillet, add mushroom water and mushrooms, reserving 4 of the largest ones to use later. Cook, uncovered, over moderate heat 3 to 4 minutes or until mushrooms are tender.
8. Gradually fold in whipped cream. Add truffles and the remaining ¼ cup brandy and Cointreau mixture. Stir and cook gently over low heat. Then pour the mixture over the chicken.
9. Sauté the reserved 4 mushrooms in the remaining 1 tablespoon butter and garnish the dish with them. Serve hot.

The things we do with Roquefort cheese! We put it in salads, potatoes, spread it on steaks and hamburgers, melt it on toast, combine it with cream cheese, break off a piece and let it melt on our tongues or add it to sour cream for salad dressings. We do just about everything with it and never have a failure. Happily, I managed to get this recipe from a reluctant restaurateur in southern France.

CHICKEN ROQUEFORT

(MAKES 4 SERVINGS)

WINE SUGGESTION: *Red Bordeaux; Clos de l'Amiral (St.-Julien)*

Steps 1 through 3 may be prepared ahead of time.

1 ready-to-cook chicken (2 to 2½ pounds), quartered
2 tablespoons bottled steak sauce
¼ cup (½ stick) butter, melted
½ teaspoon salt
1 cup sour cream
¼ cup (1 ounce) crumbled Roquefort cheese
½ teaspoon imported paprika
1 scallion (bulb and top), chopped

1. Wash and dry chicken.
2. Combine steak sauce, butter, and salt and brush the mixture over the chicken. Place chicken in a 13 x 9 x 2-inch baking dish.
3. Mix sour cream with cheese and paprika. Spread the mixture over the chicken.
4. Preheat the oven to 325° (slow) for 10 minutes. Place chicken in the oven and bake, uncovered, until chicken is golden brown, about one hour.
5. Sprinkle chopped scallion over the chicken 10 minutes before baking time is over. Serve hot from the dish.

MENU

Chicken Roquefort
Buttered Tiny Whole Potatoes
Asparagus Vinaigrette
Petits Fours

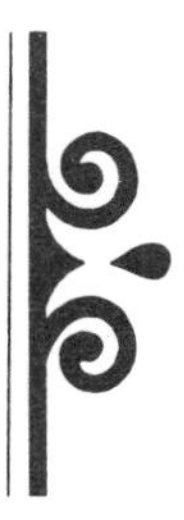

This poulet recipe has been in my family for generations and has upheld its reputation as being easy to prepare and having an incomparable taste and texture. I have altered this dish since the advent of convenience foods, making it a joy rather than a chore.

POULET SAUTE LYONNAISE

(MAKES 4 SERVINGS)

WINE SUGGESTION: *Schloss Vollrads (Rheingau)*

1 ready-to-cook chicken (2 to 2½ pounds), cut into serving pieces
¾ teaspoon salt or salt to taste
¼ teaspoon ground black pepper
2 tablespoons butter
2 tablespoons cooking oil
1 can (10½ ounces) chicken consommé
1 dozen small white onions, peeled
¼ pound (1 stick) butter, melted
¾ cup fine dry bread crumbs
½ cup dry white wine
¼ cup beef consommé (canned or bouillon cube and water)

1. Wash chicken, wipe dry, and sprinkle with salt and black pepper.
2. In a heavy skillet, heat the 2 tablespoons butter until it sizzles; add the oil.
3. Place chicken, in a single layer, in the hot butter and oil. Cook, uncovered, over moderate heat until chicken is brown on both sides, 20 to 25 minutes.
4. In a 2-quart saucepan, bring chicken consommé to boiling point. Add onions and cook, uncovered, 5 minutes. Cover and cook until onions are crisp-tender, about 15 minutes.
5. Drain off consommé, leaving onions in the saucepan. Add the ¼ pound melted butter, rotating the pan to coat the onions. Then sprinkle bread crumbs over the onions and toss them lightly, coating the onions well.
6. Add onions to the skillet 5 minutes before chicken is

done, adding all the loose crumbs. Simmer, uncovered, 5 minutes.

7. Arrange chicken on a warmed serving platter. Surround with onions and keep hot while making the sauce.
8. Add wine to the pan drippings and cook over high heat until the mixture has been reduced to two-thirds the original amount.
9. Add beef consommé, correct seasonings, and bring to boiling point. Pour the sauce over the chicken. Sprinkle with chopped parsley. Serve promptly.

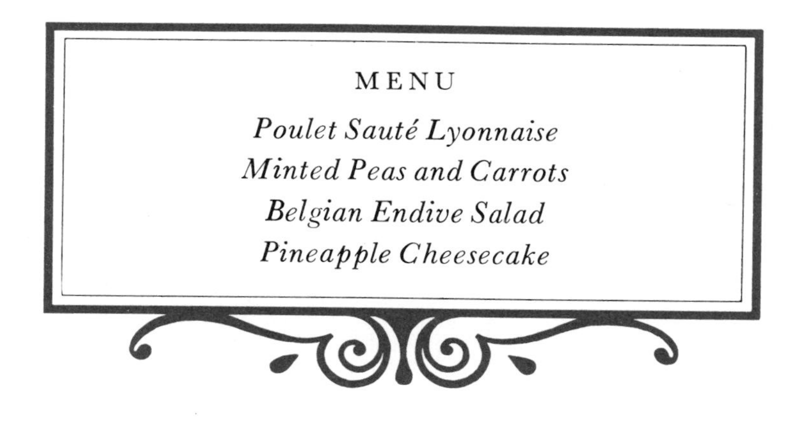

MENU

Poulet Sauté Lyonnaise
Minted Peas and Carrots
Belgian Endive Salad
Pineapple Cheesecake

My Aunt Fannie was, after my mother, the dearest and most lovable woman I knew. The windows of my aunt's kitchen were always steamed from the wondrous things that were bubbling on the stove. On special days, she would make her own noodles, cutting them into various shapes and sizes. Her small brown icebox was crammed with Epicurean morsels. Aunt Fannie could not read; she played it by ear. This is one of her recipes. I had to translate a pinch of this and a dash of that to make sense out of it. It was worth the time and effort.

AUNT FANNIE'S MASTERPIECE

(MAKES 4 SERVINGS)

WINE SUGGESTION: *Red Bordeaux; Château Beycherelle (St.-Julien)*

Steps 1 through 6 may be prepared ahead of time.

1 chicken with giblets (3 pounds), cut into serving pieces
½ cup flour
2½ teaspoons salt
¼ teaspoon ground black pepper
⅓ cup cooking oil
1¾ cups boiling water
1 chicken bouillon cube
¾ cup chicken stock, made from giblets and bouillon cube
3 tablespoons flour
¾ cup light cream

1. Wash chicken, reserve giblets, and set aside.
2. In a brown paper bag or plastic bag, place flour, 2¼ teaspoons of the salt, and black pepper. Add chicken a few pieces at a time and shake the bag, coating the chicken with the flour mixture. Repeat until all the pieces have been coated.
3. In a heavy 12-inch skillet, heat oil. Place the chicken, in a single layer, in the skillet, and cook, uncovered, until chicken is brown on both sides, about 25 minutes.
4. Add ¼ cup of the boiling water and simmer, covered, until chicken is tender, 35 to 45 minutes.
5. Meanwhile, put the giblets, the remaining 1½ cups boiling water, the bouillon cube, and the remaining ¼ teaspoon salt in a saucepan. Cook, covered, until giblets are tender and the liquid has been reduced to ¾ cup.
6. Remove giblets from the stock; cool until they can be handled. Chop and set aside.
7. When chicken is done, remove it to a warmed platter and keep hot.
8. Pour off all but 3 tablespoons of the pan drippings from the skillet. Stir in flour and brown it lightly.
9. Add the ¾ cup chicken stock and cream. Cook, stirring constantly, until the gravy begins to bubble and thicken slightly.

10. Add chopped giblets and adjust seasonings. Serve in a sauceboat to spoon over the chicken.

MENU

Aunt Fannie's Masterpiece
Narrow Egg Noodles with Chopped, Salted Peanuts
Spinach Salad
Pumpkin Pie

The chef was good, service excellent, wine list better than usual, and it was a lovely evening in El Paso. Although the restaurant was very small, the menu was more than adequate. I love these quick one-two-three recipes.

CHICKEN EL PASO

(MAKES 4 SERVINGS)

BEVERAGE SUGGESTION: *A fine beer or Chianti*

Steps 1 through 4 may be prepared ahead of time.

1 ready-to-cook chicken (2 to 2½ pounds), cut into serving pieces, or 2 to 2½ pounds meaty chicken parts
1½ teaspoons salt
¼ teaspoon ground black pepper
¼ cup olive oil
½ cup (1 medium) onion, chopped
1 clove garlic, minced
2 tablespoons ground coriander
1 teaspoon ground cumin seed
1 teaspoon paprika
¾ cup chicken stock or ¾ cup hot water and

1 chicken bouillon cube
2 cups hot cooked rice

1. Wash chicken, wipe dry, and sprinkle with salt and black pepper.
2. In a heavy 12-inch skillet, heat oil. Add chicken and cook until brown on both sides, about 20 minutes.
3. Add onion, garlic, and spices. Cook over low heat, stirring frequently, about 5 minutes, being careful not to burn the onion and spices.
4. Add chicken stock or water and bouillon cube. Cook, covered, 10 minutes or until chicken is tender.
5. Add rice and gently incorporate it into the pan juices. Cover and let stand a few minutes. Serve from the skillet if desired.

MENU

Chicken El Paso
Tomato and Avocado Salad
Pecan Pie

I found this recipe at Petit Norman in Paris. Lapère, the chef who originated this recipe, has garnered numerous honors for his culinary genius.

SUPREMES DE VOLAILLE MAURICE

(MAKES 4 SERVINGS)

WINE SUGGESTION: *White Burgundy; Pinot Chardonnay*

Steps 1 through 5 may be prepared ahead of time.

4 whole, boned chicken breasts with skins attached
1 package (10 ounces) frozen spinach, defrosted
½ cup seasoned dry bread crumbs
¼ pound (1 stick) butter, melted
1 large egg, beaten lightly
¼ teaspoon instant minced onion

1/8 teaspoon garlic powder
Salt
1 teaspoon seasoned salt
1/4 cup sherry
Mushroom Sauce (recipe below)
Parsley

1. Preheat oven to 350° (moderate).
2. Wash chicken breasts, wipe dry, and set aside.
3. Drain defrosted spinach well. Add bread crumbs, half the melted butter, egg, instant minced onion, garlic powder, and salt to taste. Mix well but lightly.
4. Spread chicken breasts on a flat surface, skin side down, and place a heaping tablespoon of the spinach mixture on each.
5. Fold the ends and sides of the chicken breasts over the spinach in envelope fashion. Fasten flaps with skewers or toothpicks. Sprinkle breasts with seasoned salt and place them, in a single layer, in a 10 x 6 x 2-inch baking dish.
6. Bake 35 to 45 minutes, basting with the remaining melted butter mixed with sherry and 1/4 teaspoon salt. Serve promptly with Mushroom Sauce spooned over each serving. Garnish with crisp parsley.

MUSHROOM SAUCE

(MAKES APPROXIMATELY 2 CUPS)

1/3 cup sliced onions
2 tablespoons butter
1 can (10 1/2 ounces) cream of mushroom soup, undiluted
1 cup milk
1/4 teaspoon salt
1/8 teaspoon ground thyme

1. In a 1-quart saucepan, cook onions in butter until soft, 4 to 5 minutes. Add mushroom soup and mix well.
2. Stir in milk, salt, and thyme. Cook, stirring, until sauce is hot. Serve over chicken breasts.

MENU

Suprêmes de Volaille Maurice
Wild Rice
Romaine and Cherry Tomato Salad
Fresh Fruit

Italian chefs have a particular genius for blending flavors into one magnificent dish. The important point in this recipe is not to overcook the tender, delicately flavored lobster tails. As soon as the lobster meat loses its translucency it is done. Drop thawed or frozen lobster tails into a large kettle of boiling water with 1 teaspoon salt for each quart. When water reboils, lower heat and begin to count time. (Six minutes for frozen tails, 4 minutes for thawed.) Drain immediately and drench in cold water.

CHICKEN SALERNO

(MAKES 8 SERVINGS)

WINE SUGGESTION: *White Burgundy; Chambolle-Musigny*

Steps 1 through 6 may be prepared ahead of time.

4 chicken breasts, cut in half lengthwise
1¼ teaspoons salt
¼ teaspoon ground black pepper
4 tablespoons (½ stick) butter
2 tablespoons dry sherry
3 tablespoons prepared, seasoned chicken base
½ pound mushrooms, sliced (caps and stems)
2 tablespoons flour
1½ cups chicken broth (homemade or canned)
1 tablespoon tomato paste
1 bay leaf, crumbled
2 tablespoons chopped chives

1/8 teaspoon ground black pepper
4 uncooked rock lobster tails (5 ounces each)
3 medium-sized fresh tomatoes, quartered

1. Wash and dry chicken breasts and sprinkle with 1 teaspoon salt and the 1/4 teaspoon black pepper.
2. In a 12-inch skillet, heat butter, put chicken breasts in the hot butter, and brown on both sides over moderate heat.
3. Heat oven to 450° (very hot).
4. Remove chicken to a buttered, shallow baking dish. Sprinkle with sherry and prepared chicken base. Bake, covered tightly, until chicken is tender, about 30 minutes.
5. To the butter remaining in the skillet, add mushrooms and cook 5 minutes, stirring frequently. Blend in the flour. Stir in chicken broth and simmer, uncovered, until the mixture has thickened.
6. Add tomato paste, bay leaf, chives, the remaining 1/4 teaspoon salt, and the 1/8 teaspoon black pepper. Simmer, uncovered, 15 minutes, stirring occasionally.
7. Cook lobster tails according to directions preceding this recipe. Remove the meat from the shells, slice thinly, and add to the mushroom sauce.
8. Add tomatoes to the sauce and heat only until hot.
9. Arrange chicken breasts on a warmed platter. Spoon the sauce over them and carefully arrange lobster meat and tomatoes attractively over the top. Serve promptly.

This cloudlike soufflé is for the devoted chicken lover. I was first attracted to this fluffy preparation when it was served in Marseille, France. It was accompanied by noisette potatoes and a nicely chilled asparagus vinaigrette. Perfect for luncheon, a light entrée, or an after-theatre supper.

CHICKEN SOUFFLE

(MAKES 6 SERVINGS)

WINE SUGGESTION: *Inglenook Chablis*

3 tablespoons quick-cooking tapioca
1 cup milk, scalded
3 large eggs, separated
½ cup grated, mild Cheddar cheese
1 cup diced cooked chicken
1 teaspoon salt
⅛ teaspoon ground white pepper
Paprika

1. Preheat oven to 375° (moderate).
2. In a 2-quart saucepan, cook tapioca in the milk until the tapioca is clear, 1 to 2 minutes.
3. Beat egg yolks and gradually add them to the tapioca and milk. Stir in cheese, chicken, salt, and white pepper.
4. Beat egg whites until they stand in soft, stiff peaks, but not dry, and carefully fold them into the chicken mixture.
5. Turn the mixture into a 6-cup soufflé dish, having only the bottom of the dish buttered. Place the dish in a pan a little larger than the soufflé dish. Pour in hot water to a depth of 1 to 1½ inches.
6. Bake 45 minutes, or until a knife inserted in the center comes out clean. Serve promptly, from the dish, at the table.

MENU

Chicken Soufflé
Noisette Potatoes
Chilled Asparagus Vinaigrette
French Pastries

We were four for dinner; suddenly we were six. I ransacked the cupboards and refrigerator searching for something to help out that tiny chicken. I was quite pleased with the successful outcome of this unorthodox combination of ingredients.

CHICKEN CASSEROLE AND THINGS

(MAKES 4 TO 6 SERVINGS)

WINE SUGGESTION: *Red Bordeaux; Château Angludet (Margaux)*

Steps 1 through 3 may be prepared ahead of time.

1 ready-to-cook chicken (2 to 2½ pounds) cut into serving pieces, or 2½ pounds meaty chicken parts
2¾ teaspoons salt
¼ cup cooking oil
1 clove garlic, split
4 pork sausage links
1 cup uncooked rice
⅛ teaspoon crumbled saffron
2 cups boiling water
1 pimento, minced
1 small bay leaf
1 can (4½ ounces) shrimp

1. Wash chicken and rub with 1¾ teaspoons of the salt.
2. In a 12-inch heavy skillet, heat oil. For easy removal, insert a toothpick in each half of the garlic and add

to the hot oil. Cook 2 to 3 minutes. Add chicken and sausage and cook over moderate heat until browned on all sides.

3. Remove chicken, sausage, and garlic from the skillet, discarding the garlic. Drain excess oil from the skillet. Add rice and stir and cook over moderately low heat 4 to 5 minutes or until rice begins to brown and stick to the sides and bottom of the skillet.
4. Dissolve saffron in the boiling water and add to rice. Stir in the remaining 1 teaspoon salt, pimento, and bay leaf. Place chicken and sausage on the rice. Simmer, covered, until rice is tender and has absorbed all the water, about 15 minutes. Do not stir while cooking.
5. Add shrimp and steam 5 minutes or until shrimp is hot.
6. Serve hot from the skillet with a portion of each chicken, sausage, and shrimp, placed on each serving of rice.

MENU

Chicken Casserole and Things

Citrus Salad

French Dressing

Apple Turnovers

After this luscious chicken is stuffed there is nothing to do but wait for it to get tender and brown in the oven. The chestnut purée flavor permeates the chicken. In Florence, Italy, this dish was served with the bacon as a garnish, but it isn't essential. This is also excellent served cold, including the dressing.

CHICKEN TUSCANY

(MAKES 4 TO 6 SERVINGS)

WINE SUGGESTION: *Llords & Elwood Cabernet Rosé*

1 ready-to-cook roasting chicken (4 to 5 pounds)
½ cup wine vinegar
1 clove garlic, minced
1½ teaspoons salt
Tuscany Stuffing (recipe below)
3 slices uncooked bacon
Parsley

1. Wash and wipe chicken dry.
2. Combine vinegar, garlic, and salt, and rub on the skin of the chicken. Let the chicken stand one-half hour.
3. Preheat oven to 375° (moderate).
4. Stuff neck and body cavities of the chicken loosely with the Tuscany Stuffing. Close openings with skewers. Lift each wing, fold the tip under, and press it against the back, akimbo fashion, to give the chicken a base on which to rest in the roasting pan.
5. Place bacon strips across the chicken breast, and wrap the chicken in heavy-duty foil, allowing an air space between the chicken and the foil.
6. Place chicken on a rack in a shallow baking pan. Roast for 2 hours. Then open foil, remove bacon, and continue to roast, with foil opened, until chicken is brown and tender.
7. Spoon dressing into a bowl. Cut chicken into serving pieces and arrange the pieces on a warmed platter. Garnish the dish with parsley.

TUSCANY STUFFING

1 tablespoon butter
Raw chicken giblets, chopped
1 tablespoon chopped parsley
¼ cup chopped onion
½ teaspoon salt
⅛ teaspoon ground black pepper

4 slices firm-textured white bread, diced
½ cup dry white wine
1 cup canned chestnut purée

1. In a 2-quart saucepan, melt butter. Add giblets and cook, stirring frequently, over moderate heat, for 20 minutes.
2. Stir in parsley, onion, salt, and black pepper.
3. Combine bread, wine, and chestnut purée and mix with the giblets. Spoon the mixture lightly into the neck and body cavities of the chicken.

MENU

Chicken Tuscany
Green Beans
Chocolate Mousse

A spatchcock is a chicken that has been split along the back from top to bottom without cutting all the way through. Then it is flattened, broiled or barbecued, placed on a large heated platter, and cut into serving pieces before your guests' eyes. This richly colored dish is one of Jurgensen's vast collection of recipes. Jurgensen's is a small chain of twenty gourmet shops throughout California. Their meats are prime and their vegetables immaculate. Twice a month they put out *Epicurean,* a brochure advertising their specialties. On the back page of each *Epicurean* are several recipes and this is one.

BROILED SPATCHCOCK

(MAKES 4 SERVINGS)

WINE SUGGESTION: *Red Bordeaux; Château Lynch-Boges (Pauillac)*

The Diable Sauce for this dish may be prepared ahead of time.

1 ready-to-cook roasting chicken (3 to 4 pounds)

½ stick butter, melted
1 teaspoon salt
Dijon mustard
Soft coarse bread crumbs
Sauce Diable (recipe below)

1. Preheat oven broiler to 350° (moderate).
2. Wash chicken, split lengthwise down the back, but without cutting it all the way through, leaving it in one piece. Then spread the chicken so that it will lie flat.
3. Brush both sides of the chicken with some of the melted butter. Then sprinkle with salt.
4. Place chicken, skin side up, on a rack in a shallow baking dish. Broil 1 to 1¼ hours, or until chicken is tender, turning to brown both sides.
5. Turn chicken on the rack, skin side up, and spread it thinly with mustard.
6. Mix bread crumbs with the remaining melted butter, and sprinkle them over the chicken. Return to the broiler to brown the crumbs.
7. Bring chicken, on a heated platter, to the table and carve it into serving pieces in the presence of the guests. Pass the sauceboat of Sauce Diable to spoon over the chicken.

SAUCE DIABLE

2 tablespoons (¼ stick) butter
3 shallots or scallions, minced
¼ cup lemon juice or vinegar
2 teaspoons Worcestershire sauce
2 teaspoons Dijon mustard
A good dash of Tabasco
1 can (10½ ounces) beef gravy

1. In a 1-quart saucepan, melt butter. Add shallots or scallions, and cook, stirring, until they are soft, 3 to 4 minutes.
2. Add the remaining ingredients and mix well. Cook,

uncovered, until sauce is hot, 3 to 4 minutes, stirring occasionally.

3. Serve in a sauceboat.

Oxford Chicken does not come from Oxford. It originated in a small roadside restaurant in Maine, not far from the outskirts of Portland.

OXFORD CHICKEN

(MAKES 6 TO 8 SERVINGS)

WINE SUGGESTION: *Red Burgundy; Clos du Roi (Beaune)*

This dish may be prepared ahead of time. Reheat and flambé just before serving.

2 ready-to-cook chickens (2 to 2½ pounds each)
2¼ teaspoons salt
¼ teaspoon ground black pepper
4 sprigs snipped parsley
2 sprigs fresh thyme
2 small sprigs snipped fresh marjoram
2 small bay leaves, crumbled
2 teaspoons grated lemon rind
2 small cloves garlic, minced
2 raw chicken livers, diced
2 tablespoons cooking oil

Sweet vermouth
½ teaspoon crumbled dried rosemary or
1½ teaspoons snipped fresh rosemary
4 tablespoons (¼ cup) brandy

1. Preheat oven to 400° (hot).
2. Wash chickens, wipe dry, leave whole, and set aside.
3. Mix salt and black pepper. Rub ½ teaspoon of the mixture inside the body and neck cavities of each chicken.
4. In a wooden chopping bowl, place parsley, thyme, marjoram, bay leaf, lemon rind, garlic, and chicken livers. Mix well, chop, and put half the mixture in the body cavity of each chicken. Close openings with skewers.
5. Rub the skin of each chicken with 1 tablespoon of the cooking oil. Sprinkle each with ¾ teaspoon of the salt and black pepper mixture.
6. Place chickens on a rack in a shallow baking pan and roast 10 minutes.
7. Pour 2 to 3 tablespoons vermouth over each chicken and sprinkle each with ¼ teaspoon dried rosemary or ¾ teaspoon of the snipped fresh rosemary.
8. Roast chickens 1½ to 2 hours or until tender. Remove and discard herb and chicken-liver mixture or if desired, serve it with the chickens. Remove chickens to a warmed platter.
9. In a very small saucepan, heat brandy, pour it over the chickens, ignite, and bring to the table flaming.

MENU

Oxford Chicken
Rice
Young Beets with Greens
Strawberry Shortcake

This light entrée or late-supper dish is simply beautiful and steeped in aromatic flavors. I was first served this dish at the home of a friend who had just returned from Europe and had invited a few friends for a late supper. The chicken and its sauce keeps well in the upper portion of a double boiler over barely simmering water.

CHICKEN WITH GREEN NOODLES

(MAKES 4 SERVINGS)

WINE SUGGESTION: *Charles Krug Rosé*

The chicken and mushroom sauce may be prepared the same morning or the day before serving. Reheat chicken and sauce and cook noodles just before serving.

2 tablespoons butter
2 tablespoons flour
1 cup hot chicken stock (homemade or canned)
½ teaspoon grated onion
½ teaspoon salt
⅛ teaspoon ground black pepper
½ teaspoon imported paprika
2½ cups (½ pound) diced fresh mushrooms (caps and stems)
1 cup dry sherry
2 cups diced cooked chicken
¼ cup light cream
2 cups green noodles, cooked according to package directions
2 tablespoons butter

1. In a 2-quart saucepan, melt 2 tablespoons butter. Remove saucepan from heat and blend in flour. Stir and cook until the mixture bubbles, but does not brown.
2. Remove saucepan from heat and gradually beat in the hot stock. The sauce will begin to thicken. Then add onion, salt, black pepper, and paprika. Stir and cook until sauce has thickened, 1 to 2 minutes. Set aside and keep warm.
3. Meanwhile, put mushrooms and sherry in a 2-quart

saucepan, bring to boiling point, reduce heat, and simmer 5 minutes.

4. Stir in chicken, adding more sherry, if needed. Simmer 5 minutes. Do not boil. Add this mixture to the sauce and simmer 5 minutes longer.
5. Stir in cream and simmer 5 minutes. Adjust seasonings.
6. Cook noodles, drain them well, and toss them with the remaining 2 tablespoons butter. Serve promptly on individual serving plates with sherried chicken and mushroom sauce spooned over each.

Grand occasions like these can be handled with ease and elegance. The chicken may be kept waiting in a heated oven or in a chafing dish for some time, then spooned into *vol-au-vents* (puff pastry cases), patty shells, or on toast points and served with the chilled wine. This idea occurred to me when I had leftover chicken and was reluctant to serve it "naked."

SUNDAY BRUNCH

(MAKES 10 TO 12 SERVINGS)

WINE SUGGESTION: *White Burgundy; Corton Charlemagne*

May be prepared ahead of time and reheated just before serving.

10 tablespoons (1¼ sticks) butter

8 tablespoons flour
4 chicken bouillon cubes
3 cups boiling water
3 cups light cream
2 cans (8 ounces each) sliced mushrooms, drained
½ cup diced green pepper
4 cups diced cooked chicken
2 cans (6 ounces each) pimento, cut into narrow strips
2 teaspoons salt or salt to taste
½ teaspoon ground black pepper
10 to 12 vol-au-vent *cases, patty shells, or toast points*

1. In a 4-quart saucepot, melt 1 stick of the butter. Remove from heat and blend in flour. Stir and cook, over moderate heat, until the mixture bubbles, but does not brown.
2. Meanwhile, dissolve bouillon cubes in the boiling water and gradually beat it into the butter-flour mixture. Stir and cook until the sauce begins to thicken.
3. Add cream and cook, stirring, until the sauce is medium thick.
4. In a 1-quart saucepan, melt the remaining 2 tablespoons butter. Add mushrooms and green pepper. Cook, stirring, until green pepper is soft, 5 to 6 minutes. Add to the sauce and mix well.
5. Stir in chicken, pimento, salt, and black pepper and cook over low heat or hot water until hot, stirring frequently. Serve hot in *vol-au-vents*.

MENU

Sunday Brunch
French Fried Potatoes
Mixed Green Salad
Hearts of Celery and Assorted Relishes
Coffeecake or Rum Torte

With the permission of Jurgensen's, I am including this exquisite chicken entrée. The addition of cream glazes the crisp skin and enriches the entire dish.

ROAST CAPON

(MAKES 6 SERVINGS)

WINE SUGGESTION: *Red Burgundy; Clos de Vougeot (Moillard-Grivot)*

1 ready-to-cook roasting chicken or capon (6 to 8 pounds)
2 tablespoons cognac
¾ teaspoon salt
1/16 teaspoon ground black pepper
1 chicken liver, coarsely chopped
1 tablespoon flour
1 tablespoon unsalted butter (sweet butter)
1 small onion, studded with 2 whole cloves
2 tablespoons lightly salted butter, melted
1 cup heavy cream, heated

1. Preheat oven to 425° (hot).
2. Wash chicken, wipe dry, and rub body cavity with cognac, ¼ teaspoon of the salt, and black pepper.
3. Combine chopped chicken liver, flour, and unsalted butter and knead the mixture into a ball. Put the ball and the clove-studded onion in the body cavity. Close the opening with skewers.
4. Mix the 2 tablespoons melted butter with the remaining ½ teaspoon salt. Brush the mixture over the skin of the chicken.
5. Place chicken on a rack in a shallow baking pan. Put into the hot oven and bake 15 minutes. Reduce the oven temperature to 350° (moderate).
6. Pour the hot cream over the chicken. Continue roasting and basting with cream every 10 minutes until chicken is tender and the skin is golden and crusty, 2½ to 3 hours.
7. Cut chicken into serving pieces and arrange them on a platter. (Discard liver ball and onion.)

8. Bring the pan drippings to boiling point, strain, and serve in a sauceboat.

MENU

Roast Capon
Buttered Broad Noodles
Brussels Sprouts
Lime Pie

A cold buffet and assorted imported beers make a welcome change. Good indoors, outdoors, summer, or winter. The avocado sauce should be prepared not more than 1 hour before serving. Stack beer bottles into several large buckets, packed with ice.

COLD CHICKEN MEXICALI

(MAKES 8 SERVINGS)

BEVERAGE SUGGESTION: *Assorted beers*

This dish may be prepared a few hours ahead of time.

4 large boned chicken breasts
Chicken stock (homemade or canned)
White wine
2 teaspoons fresh lemon juice
2 teaspoons salt
2 large ripe avocados
2 small cloves garlic
2 teaspoons grated raw onion
Olive oil
Dash of Tabasco

1. Wash chicken breasts, wrap them in cheesecloth, tie with a string, and set aside.

2. In a large saucepot or Dutch oven, pour in equal parts of stock and wine, having sufficient quantity to cover the chicken breasts. Bring to boiling point, add the breasts, reduce heat, and simmer until tender, 35 to 40 minutes.
3. Cool chicken breasts in the broth and then remove them from the cheesecloth.
4. Cut the breasts into long slices and arrange them on a large platter. Refrigerate.
5. In a medium bowl, put lemon juice, salt, and avocado. Mash until smooth.
6. Put garlic through a garlic press, holding it over the mashed avocado so the juice can drip into it. Add onion and enough olive oil to make a fluffy, smooth mixture.
7. Blend in Tabasco to taste. Spoon some of the mixture over the chicken slices. Serve the rest of the mixture in a small bowl.

MENU

Cold Chicken Mexicali
Potato Salad
Assorted Crisp Vegetable Relishes
Cream Puffs or Chocolate Éclairs

Mexico—Land of the Aztecs, pyramids, high-rise hotels, burros, posh restaurants, and colorful mariachi. This culinary masterpiece was created by a Spanish woman who owned the most magnificent inn I had ever seen. It was walled off from the rest of the world and you slept, ate, swam, danced, and relaxed in its sunny splendor.

POLLO CUERNAVACA

(MAKES 4 SERVINGS)

WINE SUGGESTION: *Llords & Elwood Cabernet Rosé*

Steps 1 through 2 may be prepared ahead of time.

1/4 cup (1/2 stick) butter
4 chicken breasts, cut in half
3/4 teaspoon salt
4 green onions (bulbs and tops), sliced
1/2 cup blanched almonds, slivered
1/2 teaspoon crumbled dried tarragon
1/2 cup chopped parsley
1 can (1 pound, 13 ounces) peach halves, drained
3/4 cup (3 ounces) grated Swiss Gruyère cheese

1. In a heavy 10- or 12-inch skillet, melt butter. Rub chicken breasts with salt and place them in the hot butter. Cook, over moderate heat, browning both sides. Remove chicken to a 9 x 9 x 2-inch baking pan.
2. To the skillet in which chicken was browned, add onions, almonds, tarragon, and parsley. Mix well and pour the mixture over the chicken.
3. Preheat oven to 350° (moderate).
4. Bake, covered, 45 minutes. Arrange drained peach halves in the baking pan around the chicken breasts. Sprinkle peaches and chicken with the grated cheese. Bake, uncovered, 15 minutes longer.
5. Arrange chicken breasts on a warmed platter and garnish with the peach halves. Serve hot.

This recipe comes from Le Petit Auberge. This Grand Marnier dish is Parisian and there is scarcely anything more flavorsome than the blending of Grand Marnier, oranges, and peaches.

POULET GRAND MARNIER

(MAKES 4 SERVINGS)

WINE SUGGESTION: *White Burgundy; Meursault Casse Tête*

Steps 1 through 3 may be prepared ahead of time.

1 ready-to-cook chicken (2 to 3 pounds), quartered
1/2 cup flour
1 teaspoon salt or salt to taste
1/8 teaspoon ground black pepper
3 tablespoons cooking oil
1/2 cup peeled orange sections
1/2 cup Grand Marnier
1 1/2 cups sliced canned peaches
3 tablespoons brown sugar
1 tablespoon white vinegar
1 teaspoon ground nutmeg
1 teaspoon basil
1 clove garlic, minced

1. Wash and dry chicken.
2. Mix flour, salt, and black pepper and dredge chicken in the mixture.
3. In a 12-inch skillet, heat oil. Place chicken in the hot oil and cook until brown on both sides, 20 to 25 minutes.
4. Remove chicken from the skillet and pour out the excess oil. Return chicken to the skillet and cook, covered, 20 minutes over very low heat, turning the chicken 3 to 4 times.
5. Meanwhile, combine oranges, Grand Marnier, peaches, brown sugar, vinegar, nutmeg, basil, and garlic in a 1 1/2-quart saucepan. Simmer 10 minutes.
6. Remove chicken to a warm platter and spoon some of the Grand Marnier sauce over it. Serve the remaining sauce in a sauceboat.

MENU

Poulet Grand Marnier
Spinach Purée *Boiled New Potatoes*
Escarole Salad
Boursault or Camembert Cheese
Chilled Tokay Wine

Imported golden Swiss Gruyère cheese is a poem in itself, but when it is molten and bubbling atop thick, white asparagus spears and chicken it is perfection. Yvonne, the wife of the *hôtelier,* invented this excellent combination.

SUPREMES DE VOLAILLE YVONNE

(MAKES 4 SERVINGS)

WINE SUGGESTION: *White Burgundy; La Pièce-sous-le-Bois (Meursault)*

4 boned chicken breasts, flattened
1/2 cup flour
1 teaspoon salt
1/8 teaspoon ground black pepper
2 small eggs, beaten
4 tablespoons (1 ounce) grated Swiss Gruyère cheese
2 tablespoons butter
1 tablespoon cooking oil
12 thick, white asparagus spears, blanched

1. Wash and wipe chicken breasts dry.
2. Combine flour, salt, and black pepper and dredge the chicken breasts in the mixture, coating them well.
3. Mix eggs and 2 tablespoons of the cheese and dip the breasts into the mixture.
4. Meanwhile, in a 12-inch heavy skillet, heat butter and oil. Add the chicken breasts and cook over moderate heat until breasts are golden brown on both sides, 10 to 15 minutes.

5. If the handle of the skillet is heat-proof and if it fits into the broiler oven, drain and discard fat from the skillet, leaving the chicken breasts in the pan. If not, transfer the breasts to a shallow baking dish. Place 3 asparagus spears on each breast and sprinkle them with the remaining 2 tablespoons grated cheese, using more if needed.
6. Broil in a preheated broiler oven until cheese is melted and golden. Serve promptly.

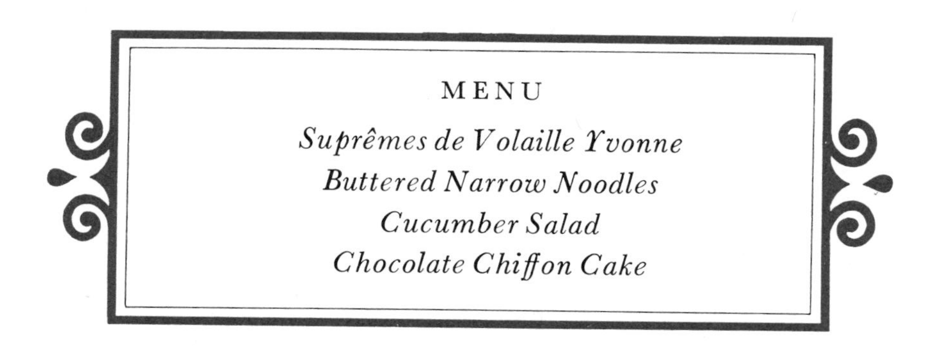

MENU

Suprêmes de Volaille Yvonne
Buttered Narrow Noodles
Cucumber Salad
Chocolate Chiffon Cake

I have heard people say that the food, generally, in Great Britain is inferior. We have dined in many London restaurants and found the food exceptionally good, well prepared, and impeccably served. Bring out your most elegant flameproof casserole, cook this recipe in it, and serve at the table.

CHICKEN WITH OYSTERS

(MAKES 4 SERVINGS)

WINE SUGGESTION: *Charles Krug Chenin Blanc*

Steps 1 through 3 may be prepared ahead of time.

1 ready-to-cook chicken (3 to 3½ pounds), quartered
½ cup flour
Salt
¼ teaspoon ground black pepper

3 tablespoons cooking oil
½ cup hot milk
1 cup heavy cream
1 cup (½ pint) shucked and drained oysters
⅛ teaspoon ground white pepper

1. Wash chicken and drain well.
2. In a brown paper bag or plastic bag, mix flour, 1½ teaspoons salt, and black pepper. Add chicken, a piece at a time and shake the bag to coat the pieces well.
3. In a heavy 12-inch skillet, heat oil. Add chicken and cook, uncovered, until it is golden brown on both sides, 20 to 25 minutes.
4. Preheat oven to 375° (moderate).
5. Remove chicken to a casserole. Pour in hot milk, cover, place in the oven, and cook until tender, about 1 hour.
6. Remove casserole from the oven and add cream, oysters, white pepper, and ⅛ teaspoon salt. Cover and return to the oven. Bake one-half hour longer.
7. Serve very hot with sauce spooned over each serving.

Some of the country's finest restaurants are in Milwaukee, Wisconsin. This outstanding, succulent dish was served at Sammy's Place, one of Milwaukee's restaurants, and brought to our table glistening with the dark sauce and giving off tantalizing aromas.

SUPREMES DE VOLAILLE BERNARDO

(MAKES 4 SERVINGS)

WINE SUGGESTION: *Extra dry Moët & Chandon Champagne*

Steps 1 through 3 may be prepared ahead of time.

4 boneless chicken breasts, skins removed
1¼ teaspoons salt
⅛ teaspoon ground black pepper
½ cup flour
8 tablespoons (1 stick) butter
2 cups dry white wine
4 slices firm-textured bread, ¼ inch thick
4 slices pâté de foie gras, ¼ inch thick
12 truffles
1 cup Brown Sauce (recipe below), or 1 package prepared brown gravy mix

1. Wash chicken breasts, rub with salt and black pepper, and dredge in flour.
2. In a 10- or 12-inch skillet, heat 4 tablespoons (½ stick) butter. Add chicken breasts and brown on both sides over moderate heat, 20 to 25 minutes.
3. Drain fat from the skillet, leaving the chicken breasts in the pan. Add wine, cover, and simmer 12 to 15 minutes or until tender.
4. Remove crusts from bread, leave them in squares or cut them into large rounds. Just before serving, melt the remaining 4 tablespoons (½ stick) butter in a heavy skillet, add bread and brown, over moderate heat, on both sides.
5. Place a slice of the browned bread on each of 4 warmed dinner plates. Cover each with a slice of pâté de foie gras and a chicken breast in the order given.
6. Garnish with truffles and cover with brown sauce. Serve promptly.

BROWN SAUCE

2 tablespoons butter
2 tablespoons flour
1½ cups hot beef consommé (homemade or canned)
Madeira

1. In a 1-quart saucepan, melt butter. Add flour and cook, stirring, until flour has browned.
2. Remove saucepan from the heat and gradually beat in consommé. Return saucepan to the heat and cook, stirring, 1 minute or until medium thick.
3. Add Madeira to taste.

NOTE: If brown gravy mix is used, prepare it according to package directions. Keep hot and add Madeira just before serving.

MENU

Suprêmes de Volaille Bernardo
Green Peas with Baby Onions in Parsley and Butter
Boston Lettuce Salad
Fruit Compote

Anything as delicious as this has no right to be so easy to prepare. The brandy not only enhances the flavor, it colors and crisps the skin to perfection. If desired, the chicken may be marinated for twenty-four hours. This recipe originated in the kitchen of a friend from Bar Harbor, Maine.

BRANDIED CHICKEN

(MAKES 4 TO 6 SERVINGS)

WINE SUGGESTION: *White Burgundy; Chablis Fourchaume Premier Crû*

This dish may be prepared ahead of time and reheated in the oven just before serving.

1 ready-to-cook chicken (3½ pounds), cut into serving pieces, or 3½ pounds meaty chicken parts
1 cup brandy
1 cup dry white wine
1 teaspoon salt or salt to taste
1 teaspoon ground black pepper
¼ teaspoon dried thyme leaves
1 tablespoon minced parsley
½ bay leaf
1 medium onion, thinly sliced
3 tablespoons cooking oil
2 tablespoons (¼ stick) butter
1 medium clove garlic, minced
2 cups sliced mushrooms

1. Wash chicken and place it in a large bowl.
2. Combine brandy, wine, salt, black pepper, thyme, parsley, bay leaf, and onion. Mix well and pour the mixture over the chicken. Cover and marinate in the refrigerator 12 hours or overnight.
3. Preheat oven to 375° (moderate).
4. In a 2-quart casserole, heat oil and butter. Remove chicken from the marinade. With a paper towel wipe dry the pieces and place them in the hot oil and butter. Reserve the marinade.
5. Bake the chicken, uncovered, 20 minutes. Add reserved marinade, garlic, and mushrooms. Bake, covered, until tender, about 1 hour.
6. Serve hot with pan juices spooned over the top. The remaining pan juices may be passed in a sauceboat.

MENU

Brandied Chicken
Baked Sweet Potatoes
Braised Celery
Cantaloupe Balls in Cointreau

The restaurant in which we were served this savory entrée was situated on the side of a mountain. Bright red flowers blazed beneath the golden sunshine as we partook of this spectacular dish. Excellent for buffets.

POULARDE ITALIENNE AU PILAU

(MAKES 6 SERVINGS)

WINE SUGGESTION: *Llords & Elwood Cabernet Sauvignon*

The stuffing for this dish may be prepared the day before, refrigerated in a covered bowl, and spooned into the chicken just before cooking.

1 ready-to-cook roasting chicken (4 to 4½ pounds)
1 teaspoon salt
¼ teaspoon ground black pepper
Pilaf Stuffing (recipe below)
2 tablespoons butter, softened

1. Preheat oven to 325° (slow).
2. Wash and dry chicken.
3. Mix salt with black pepper and rub ½ teaspoon of the mixture inside the neck and body cavities, reserving the remaining salt and pepper mixture to use later.
3. Spoon cooled Pilaf Stuffing loosely into the chicken's neck and body cavities. Close openings with skewers.
4. Lift each wing, fold the tip under, and press it against the back, akimbo style, to give the chicken a base on which to rest in the roasting pan. Tie legs together and fasten them to the tailpiece.
5. Blend the remaining salt and pepper mixture with the softened butter and rub it over the skin of the chicken.
6. Place chicken on a rack in a roasting pan and roast 3 to 4 hours or until chicken is tender and brown.
7. Spoon Pilaf Stuffing onto a warmed platter and keep it warm. Cut chicken into serving pieces and arrange attractively over the stuffing.

PILAF STUFFING

½ cup butter (1 stick)
1⅓ cups quick-cooking rice

½ cup diced celery with leaves
¼ cup onion, chopped
1½ teaspoons salt
⅛ teaspoon pepper
½ teaspoon poultry seasoning
1½ cups chicken broth (fresh or canned)
½ teaspoon poultry seasoning
½ cup cocktail shrimp, cooked and split lengthwise

1. Preheat oven to 350°.
2. Melt ½ cup butter in a large skillet, add rice, celery, and onion.
3. Cook over medium heat for 2 minutes, stirring. Add salt, pepper, poultry seasoning, and broth. Bring to a boil.
4. Reduce heat and simmer for 2 minutes longer.
5. Remove skillet from heat and add shrimp to the skillet.
6. Fluff rice with the tines of a fork.
7. Cool slightly and stuff the neck and body cavity of chicken.

MENU

Poularde Italienne au Pilau
Cranberry Mold
Eggplant Parmesan
Pistachio Ice Cream

A well-prepared Chinese dish should do more than please the taste buds. It should also appeal to the senses with its color, texture, and aroma. If you want to get the most from home-cooked Chinese dishes, keep the flavors and textures distinct. This means that the ingredients should be finely sliced and cooked just enough to blend the flavors, leaving the vegetables tender-crisp.

KOWLOON ROASTED CHICKEN

(MAKES 8 TO 10 SERVINGS)

BEVERAGE SUGGESTION: *Beer*

This dish may be prepared ahead of time.

2 ready-to-cook chickens (4 to 5 pounds each)
2 tablespoons sugar
Peel from 2 tangerines, slivered
2 cloves garlic, minced
2 teaspoons sesame oil
1/4 cup peanut oil
1/2 cup soy sauce
1 1/2 cups hot chicken stock (homemade or canned)
2 tablespoons butter, melted

1. Wash and dry chickens and place them in a large bowl.
2. Combine sugar, tangerine peel, garlic, sesame oil, peanut oil, soy sauce, and chicken stock. Pour the mixture over the chickens.
3. Cover and marinate in the refrigerator overnight or several hours, turning in the marinade occasionally.
4. Remove chicken from the marinade, wipe dry, and rub the skins with melted butter. Place chickens on a rack in a large roasting pan.
5. Cover and roast in a preheated slow oven (325°) until tender, 2 1/2 to 3 hours.
6. Remove chickens from the oven and baste with pan juices.
7. Carve chicken into serving pieces, place them over hot steamed rice, and serve with unthickened pan juices.

MENU

Kowloon Roasted Chicken
Steamed Rice
Bean Sprout Salad
Vanilla Ice Cream

Spain's food is as bright and colorful as its sun. Nothing is lacking in this medley of flavor and variety except the wine and the company.

POLLO SEVILLA

(MAKES 4 SERVINGS)

WINE SUGGESTION: *Beaujolais; Saint Amour (Depagneux)*

Steps 1 and 2 may be prepared ahead of time.

1 ready-to-cook chicken (3 pounds), cut into serving pieces, or 3 pounds meaty chicken parts
2 teaspoons salt or salt to taste
1/4 teaspoon ground black pepper
Olive oil
2 cloves garlic, minced
1 cup cooked and sliced green beans
1 cup cooked green peas
2 cooked artichoke hearts, quartered
1 small bay leaf
1/8 teaspoon crumbled saffron dissolved in 2 teaspoons water
1 cup quick-cooking rice, cooked

1. Wash chicken, wipe dry, and rub with 1 teaspoon of the salt and the black pepper.
2. In a 12-inch skillet, heat enough olive oil to cover the bottom generously. Add chicken, in a single layer, and brown it on both sides, 20 to 25 minutes.

3. Pour excess oil from the skillet, leaving the chicken in the pan. Add garlic, beans, peas, artichoke hearts, bay leaf, and saffron. Sprinkle with the remaining 1 teaspoon salt.
4. Cook, covered, over moderately low heat until chicken is tender, about 25 minutes.
5. Add cooked rice, turn off heat, cover, and let stand until rice is hot. Serve steaming hot on individual serving plates.

MENU

Pollo Sevilla
Sliced Orange and Watercress Salad
Flan or Baba au Rhum

This memorable recipe was garnered from an army chef during World War II. Its existence proves that army food can be delicious indeed.

CHICKEN NERO

(MAKES 4 SERVINGS)

WINE SUGGESTION: *Red Bordeaux; Château Bel-Air-Marquis-d'Aligre (Soussans-Margaux)*

Steps 1 through 5 may be prepared ahead of time.

2 ready-to-cook chickens (1½ pounds each), split lengthwise
½ cup flour
2 teaspoons salt
¼ teaspoon ground black pepper
4 tablespoons (½ stick) butter

3 tablespoons olive oil
1/3 cup chopped onion
1/4 cup Prosciutto ham, cut in strips
1/4 cup dry white wine
1/2 teaspoon ground rosemary or 3 to 4 spikes dried rosemary
1 1/2 cups diced, peeled raw tomatoes or 2 cups (16 ounces) peeled canned tomatoes (home canned or commercial)
2 medium green peppers, seeded and cut into strips 1/2 inch wide

1. Wash chicken and wipe dry.
2. Mix flour with 1 teaspoon of the salt and the black pepper and dredge the chicken in the mixture.
3. In a 12-inch heavy skillet, heat butter and 1 tablespoon of the olive oil. Add chicken and cook until browned on both sides, 12 to 15 minutes.
4. Remove chicken from the skillet and set aside. Add onion to the skillet and cook until browned lightly, 3 to 4 minutes.
5. Return chicken to the skillet, add ham, wine, rosemary, and the remaining 1 teaspoon salt. Cook, uncovered, until wine has been absorbed, about 5 minutes. Add tomatoes and simmer, covered, 20 to 30 minutes.
6. While chicken cooks, heat the remaining 2 tablespoons oil in a separate skillet. Add green pepper strips and fry over moderate heat about 10 minutes, stirring frequently. Add to the chicken and continue cooking until chicken is tender.
7. Adjust seasonings and serve very hot.

MENU

Chicken Nero
Rice
Carrots with Chives
Pineapple Ice or Cranberry Sherbet

French cooking, as we know it today, came with the Italians when the fourteen-year-old Italian princess Catherine de'Medici migrated to France to marry King Henry II, taking her chefs, foods, and maids with her. This example of haute cuisine is Italian in origin and comes from a restaurant in Piedmont.

SUPREMES DE VOLAILLE AU VIN

(MAKES 4 SERVINGS)

WINE SUGGESTION: *Loire; Pouilly-Fumé*

4 boned chicken breasts, skinned
1/3 cup flour
1 1/2 teaspoons salt
1/8 teaspoon ground black pepper
3 tablespoons butter
1/2 cup Marsala or the juice of 1/2 lemon
6 tablespoons grated Parmesan cheese
1/2 cup chicken stock (homemade or canned)

1. Place chicken breasts on a flat, smooth surface and flatten them with a rolling pin.
2. Mix flour, salt, and black pepper. Dredge the chicken breasts in the mixture.
3. In a 12-inch skillet, heat butter. Put the breasts in the hot butter and cook, over moderately low heat, until they are brown on both sides, turning several times. Lower heat and cook 5 to 8 minutes.
4. Add Marsala or lemon juice and let the pan drippings bubble about 1 minute. Sprinkle the breasts with the Parmesan cheese and then sprinkle with the chicken stock. Cover and cook gently for 5 minutes. Serve very hot with the pan drippings spooned over each serving.

MENU

Suprêmes de Volaille au Vin
Creamed New Potatoes and Peas
Boston Lettuce Salad
Black Bottom Pie

I was visiting a friend in Virginia when this *suprêmes* entrée was prepared before my eyes. The cook was a genius with a great sense of humor. When she prepared this dish, she flambéed the chicken with the flourish of a magician and threw her head back and laughed as though she might explode. She insisted that the twenty-five minutes it took to prepare this recipe in a chafing dish was worth it. It is good either way, skillet or chafing dish.

SUPREMES DE VOLAILLE REGENCE

(MAKES 4 SERVINGS)

WINE SUGGESTION: *White Burgundy; Beaujolais Blanc*

This dish may be prepared ahead of time.

4 boned chicken breasts, skins removed
1 teaspoon salt
1/4 teaspoon ground black pepper
6 tablespoons (3/4 stick) butter
1/4 cup brandy
1/4 cup Cointreau
2 1/2 cups (1/2 pound) sliced mushrooms
1 can truffles, chopped
1 cup heavy cream, whipped
Watercress (optional)

1. Wash chicken breasts, wipe dry, and sprinkle with salt and black pepper.
2. In a 12-inch skillet, heat 4 tablespoons (1/2 stick) of the butter until it foams. Add chicken breasts and brown them on both sides over moderate heat.
3. In a 1-cup measure, mix brandy and Cointreau, pour 1/3 cup over chicken and ignite it. When the flame dies down, simmer, covered, for 25 minutes. Remove chicken to a warmed platter and keep hot.
4. In the skillet, melt the remaining 2 tablespoons butter. Add mushrooms and cook until they are tender, about 10 minutes. Stir in truffles.
5. Add whipped cream slowly and gently blend in the remaining brandy and Cointreau.

6. Pour the sauce over the chicken breasts. Garnish with watercress.

The good things in life are in this dish—honey, orange juice, wine, and grapes. This is a very old French recipe and I tried it many years ago. It has been a standby ever since in our house.

POULARDE VERONIQUE

(MAKES 4 SERVINGS)

WINE SUGGESTION: *Château Beaulieu (Sauvignon Blanc)*

Steps 1 through 3 may be prepared ahead of time.

1 ready-to-cook chicken (2½ pounds), quartered, or 2½ pounds meaty chicken parts
½ cup flour
1 teaspoon salt
½ teaspoon ground black pepper
¼ cup cooking oil
½ cup chicken stock (homemade or canned)
⅓ cup orange juice
1½ tablespoons honey
1 tablespoon chopped parsley
½ cup dry white wine
3 tablespoons orange peel, cut in julienne strips

1 cup seedless green grapes
Orange slices

1. Wash chicken and wipe dry.
2. Mix flour with salt and 1/4 teaspoon of the black pepper and dredge the chicken in the mixture.
3. In a 12-inch skillet, heat oil. Add chicken and brown it, over moderate heat, on all sides. Add chicken stock, orange juice, honey, parsley, wine, and the remaining 1/4 teaspoon black pepper. Simmer, covered, 30 minutes, turning the chicken 1 or 2 times to prevent it from sticking to the skillet.
4. Add wine and orange peel. Cook, covered, 10 to 15 minutes over low heat. Remove chicken to a heated platter and keep warm.
5. Add grapes to the pan drippings and simmer 2 minutes, stirring occasionally. Pour the pan juices over the chicken. Garnish with orange slices.

MENU

Poularde Véronique
Brown Rice
Spinach Soufflé
Cranberry Cheesecake

True Spanish flavoring of food is much milder in pepper and Tabasco content than Latin American flavoring, and the Spanish cooks use less garlic than the Portuguese. This recipe is wonderfully flavored without the use of Tabasco or garlic.

POLLO ESPANOL

(MAKES 4 SERVINGS)

WINE SUGGESTION: *Red Bordeaux; Château Prieuré Lichine (Margaux)*

This dish may be prepared ahead of time and reheated before serving.

1 ready-to-cook chicken (2 to 2½ pounds), quartered
2 teaspoons salt or salt to taste
½ teaspoon ground black pepper
3 tablespoons olive oil
1 cup sliced mushrooms (stems and caps)
1 cup diced raw potatoes
2 medium-sized raw tomatoes, sliced
2 tablespoons flour
1 cup chicken stock (homemade or canned)
½ cup dry sherry
1 tablespoon imported paprika
2 tablespoons coarsely chopped parsley

1. Wash and dry chicken and rub with 1 teaspoon of the salt and ¼ teaspoon black pepper.
2. In a 10- or 12-inch skillet, heat olive oil. Add chicken and brown on both sides over moderate heat. Arrange chicken in a 13 x 9 x 2-inch baking dish. Set aside.
3. In the drippings in the skillet, cook mushrooms, potatoes, and tomatoes over moderate heat until potatoes are tender, 15 to 20 minutes. Add flour and mix well.
4. Stir in chicken stock, sherry, paprika, the remaining 1 teaspoon salt, and the remaining ¼ teaspoon black pepper. Simmer, covered, ½ hour. Adjust salt.
5. Meanwhile, heat oven to 375° (moderate).
6. Pour the cooked vegetable mixture over the chicken and bake, covered, 45 minutes.
7. Garnish with chopped parsley and serve hot from the baking dish.

MENU

Pollo Español
Rice Pilaf
Buttered Small Whole Beets
Fresh Fruit

The recipe for this entrée was a gift from Robert Hom, a very dear friend who owns the Chunking Inn in Sherman Oaks, California. Curry lovers can't get enough of this chicken feast.

CHICKEN MINGSU

(MAKES 4 SERVINGS)

BEVERAGE SUGGESTION: *Beers; Asahi, Nippon, Tiger or Chianti*

This dish may be prepared ahead of time and reheated just before serving.

2 boned chicken breasts with skins attached, cut in half lengthwise
2 tablespoons (1/4 stick) butter, melted
1/2 cup fine dry bread crumbs
1/2 teaspoon salt
1 egg, lightly beaten
1/3 cup peanut oil
1 teaspoon cornstarch
1 1/2 teaspoons sugar
1 teaspoon curry powder
1 cup pineapple juice
1 tablespoon soy sauce
1 cup uncooked rice, cooked
1/2 cup chopped blanched almonds

1. Wash chicken breasts and wipe dry. Place each breast between waxed paper and flatten with the broad side of a cleaver or a heavy knife.
2. Combine bread crumbs and melted butter and set aside.
3. Rub chicken breasts with the salt, dip them into the beaten egg, and then into the buttered crumbs. With a spatula or fingers, pat the breasts lightly to make the crumbs adhere. Set aside a few minutes to dry.
4. In a 10- or 12-inch skillet, heat oil. Place chicken breasts in the hot oil and cook, uncovered over moderate heat, until they are golden brown on both sides, about 15 minutes.
5. In a small bowl, mix cornstarch, sugar, curry powder,

pineapple juice, and soy sauce. Pour the mixture over the chicken breasts and simmer, covered, until tender, 20 to 25 minutes.

6. Serve on hot cooked rice, sprinkled with chopped almonds.

These hot, crunchy morsels are perfect for buffets, picnics, or just to nibble on while watching the late, late movie. They are also a hostess's dream to serve at a New Year's Eve party; just double or triple the recipe.

BUFFET CHICKEN CRISPS

(MAKES 8 SERVINGS FOR BUFFET SERVICE)

BEVERAGE SUGGESTION: *Punch, coffee*

This dish may be prepared ahead of time and reheated just before serving.

4 chicken legs (drumsticks)
4 chicken thighs
4 tablespoons (½ stick) butter
1 teaspoon salt

1. Preheat oven to 325° (slow).
2. Wash and dry chicken legs and thighs.
3. In a 9 x 9 x 2-inch baking dish, melt butter. Add salt and mix well.

4. Roll chicken legs and thighs in the salted butter and arrange them, in a single layer, in the same baking dish.
5. Bake chicken 30 minutes, turn and baste with the pan juices and bake 30 minutes longer or until very tender.
6. Serve as a finger food or with fried rice.

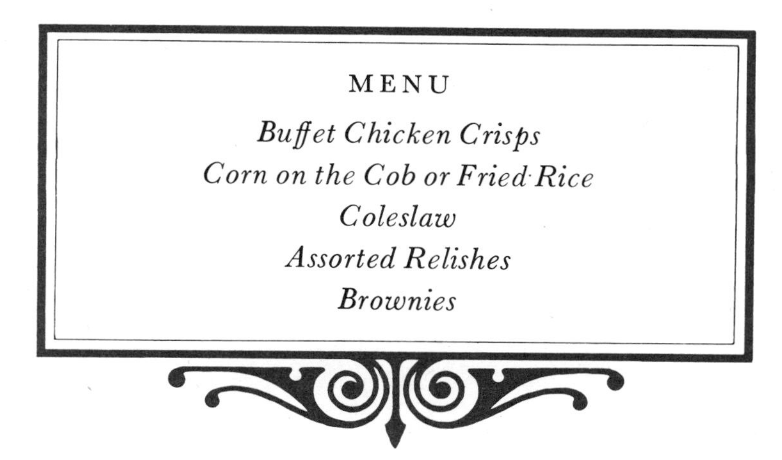

If you have never savored chicken prepared with nutmeg, milk, and almonds, you have missed a gastronomic treat. This is perfect for either daily or special occasion service; it needn't be especially for brunch.

HOLIDAY BRUNCH

(MAKES 6 TO 8 SERVINGS)

WINE SUGGESTION: *Rhine; Niersteiner*

Steps 1 through 3 may be prepared the day before. Refrigerate, covered, until ready to finish preparing the dish.

3 chicken breasts (12 ounces each), whole or split
1 cup water
1 small onion, quartered
2 teaspoons salt or salt to taste
6 whole peppercorns (black peppers)
A few celery tops

½ cup (1 stick) butter
8 tablespoons flour
⅛ teaspoon ground black pepper
Dash nutmeg
1½ cups cream
1½ cups milk
1 cup green seedless grapes, cut in half (fresh or canned)
½ cup toasted, slivered blanched almonds

1. Wash chicken breasts and put them in a 2-quart saucepan with water, onion, 1 teaspoon of the salt, peppercorns, and celery tops. Simmer, covered, ½ hour or until tender.
2. Remove chicken breasts from the broth and cool until they can be handled. Reserve broth. Remove skins and bones from the breasts and dice the meat. There should be 4 cups diced meat.
3. Strain the broth into a 2-cup measure and add water, if necessary, to make 1½ cups liquid, and reserve it.
4. In a 3-quart saucepot, melt butter, remove pan from heat and blend in flour, black pepper, nutmeg, and remaining 1 teaspoon salt.
5. Cook, stirring, until bubbly. Remove saucepan from the heat and gradually beat in the reserved 1½ cups broth, cream, and milk. Stir and cook over moderately low heat or hot water until the sauce thickens and boils gently for 1 minute.
6. Add chicken and cook until hot. Stir in grapes and almonds. Spoon the mixture into a chafing dish or into a warmed serving dish. Garnish with a wreath of chopped parsley.
7. If served for a buffet, spoon the mixture over hot, toasted muffins or biscuits. If served for a sit-down meal, spoon the mixture over hot buttered rice or noodles.

MENU

Holiday Brunch
Asparagus with Brown Butter Sauce
Mandarin Orange and Bibb Lettuce Salad
Jellied Fruit Mold
Assorted Petits Fours

If fresh blueberries are out of season, the frozen or canned do very well. This faintly rum-flavored dish is suitable for both a sit-down dinner or buffet service. The recipe is an old American classic from the secret file in Grandma's head.

BLUEBERRY CHICKEN

(MAKES 4 TO 5 SERVINGS)

WINE SUGGESTION: *Beaujolais; Moulin-à-Vent*

This dish may be prepared ahead of time and reheated before serving.

1 ready-to-cook chicken (3 pounds) or 3 pounds meaty chicken parts
1¾ teaspoons salt
½ teaspoon ground black pepper
4 tablespoons (½ stick) butter
½ cup chopped parsley
1 cup (½ pint box) fresh blueberries or ½ package (10 ounces) frozen blueberries or 1 cup canned blueberries
1½ teaspoons sugar (omit if using canned blueberries)
2 tablespoons white rum
1 tablespoon lemon juice

1. Wash chicken, and wipe dry. If whole chicken is purchased, cut into serving pieces.

2. Rub chicken with salt and black pepper.
3. In a heavy 12-inch skillet, melt butter, add chicken and brown on both sides. Cook, covered, 10 minutes longer.
4. Crush blueberries and add to the chicken. Add sugar (unless canned blueberries are used), rum, and lemon juice.
5. Cover and simmer until chicken is tender, 15 to 20 minutes. Serve very hot.

MENU

Blueberry Chicken
Corn Fritters
Summer Squash
Tossed Green Salad
Watermelon Wedges

This recipe originated in Reims, France. It is one of those all-in-one dishes, and it holds up beautifully for parties and lingering dinners.

POULARDE SAUTE REGINE

(MAKES 6 SERVINGS)

BEVERAGE SUGGESTION: *Assorted beers or Chianti*

This dish may be prepared ahead of time and reheated just before serving.

4 pounds meaty chicken parts (breasts, legs, and thighs)
2¼ teaspoons salt or salt to taste
½ teaspoon ground black pepper
½ cup (1 stick) butter
¾ cup (6 bulbs) finely chopped green onions

1 large carrot, grated
¼ teaspoon ground thyme or thyme to taste
1 bay leaf
1 bottle (12 ounces) light beer
1 cup stewed tomatoes (homemade or canned)
1 tablespoon flour
2 tablespoons water

1. Wash chicken, wipe dry, and rub with 2 teaspoons of the salt and black pepper.
2. In a heavy, deep, 12-inch skillet, melt ½ stick of the butter. Add as many pieces of the chicken at a time as the skillet will accommodate without crowding. Cook, uncovered, over moderate heat until chicken has browned on both sides. Remove chicken from the skillet and keep warm. Repeat, using the remaining butter and chicken, adding more butter if needed.
3. Put all the browned chicken, onion, carrot, thyme, and bay leaf in the skillet. Sprinkle the vegetables with the remaining ¼ teaspoon salt. Add beer and cook, covered, until chicken is tender, 50 to 60 minutes, or 30 minutes if chicken is young.
4. Remove chicken from the sauce and keep warm. Simmer the sauce, uncovered, to about half the original amount, if it has not already reduced by half.
5. Stir in stewed tomatoes. Blend flour with the 2 tablespoons water until smooth. Add to the sauce and cook, stirring, until the mixture has thickened.
6. Serve the chicken on individual serving plates with some of the sauce spooned over each serving.

MENU

Poularde Sauté Régine
Rice
Mushroom Salad
Fresh Plums
Assorted Cookies

When I first saw the combination of cayenne, cream, buttermilk, and garlic, I thought someone was making a bad joke. I finally gathered up my courage and prepared this dish step-by-step. The results astonished me and now Asian Chicken is at the top of my menu list.

ASIAN CHICKEN

(MAKES 6 SERVINGS)

WINE SUGGESTION: *Beaulieu B.V. "Beaumont" Pinot Noir*

This dish may be prepared ahead of time and reheated just before serving.

1 ready-to-cook chicken (3½ pounds) cut into serving pieces, or 3½ pounds meaty chicken parts
6 tablespoons (¾ stick) butter
1½ cups thin onion slices
1 teaspoon ground ginger or 2 slices fresh ginger, 1 inch in diameter
2 cloves garlic, minced
⅛ to ¼ teaspoon ground chili pepper or cayenne
1½ cups buttermilk
1½ cups (2 medium) diced raw tomatoes or canned tomatoes
¼ cup ground or finely chopped blanched almonds
⅛ cup (2 tablespoons) ground or finely chopped cashew nuts
2 teaspoons salt
¼ cup heavy cream
½ pound noodles, cooked and buttered

1. In a heavy 12-inch skillet, melt butter. Add onion and cook, stirring, over moderate heat until onions are soft, 4 to 5 minutes.
2. Stir in ginger, garlic, and chili powder or cayenne. Stir and cook, over low heat 2 to 3 minutes.
3. Add buttermilk and tomatoes. Simmer, uncovered, 10 minutes.
4. Add almonds, cashew nuts, and salt. Mix well and simmer, uncovered, 10 minutes. Arrange chicken in

the sauce and cook, uncovered, 50 to 60 minutes or until chicken is tender.

5. Pour cream over chicken and blend with the sauce. Heat but do not boil.
6. Serve over hot buttered noodles.

This recipe comes from La Napoule Plage, which is on the French Riviera and specializes in seafood and poultry. Originally, this dish was served with a sauce velouté, which made it much too rich. It is much improved by the Mâitre d'Hotel Butter Sauce. Even the restaurateur agreed with me. The Mâitre d'Hotel Sauce may be frozen for future use.

SUPREMES DE VOLAILLE ALPHONSE

(MAKES 2 SERVINGS)

WINE SUGGESTION: *Charles Krug Sauvignon Blanc*

2 boned chicken breasts
2 tablespoons olive oil
Salt and ground black pepper
1 center slice boneless ready-to-eat ham, cut 1/4 inch thick
4 tablespoons butter
4 mushroom caps
2 slices firm-textured white bread, toasted

1 teaspoon chopped parsley
Dash lemon juice
6 sprigs watercress

1. Set oven temperature control to broil. Oil the rack of the broiler pan and set aside.
2. Wash chicken breasts and wipe dry. Brush both sides of the breasts with some olive oil, sprinkle with 1/4 teaspoon salt and a dash of ground black pepper, and place them on the oiled broiler rack. Set aside.
3. Cut ham slice in half, crosswise, and brush both sides of each half with the remaining oil. Arrange the slices on the rack of the broiler pan.
4. Broil 4 to 5 inches from the source of heat until ham is brown on both sides, about 7 minutes. Remove ham from the broiler rack and keep warm.
5. Return chicken to the broiler oven and broil 10 more minutes or until chicken is brown on both sides and the thickest part of the breast is done.
6. While chicken broils, melt 1 tablespoon of the butter in a small skillet or saucepan. Add mushrooms and cook 3 to 4 minutes.
7. Arrange ham slices on the toast, and top each with a chicken breast and 2 mushroom caps.
8. Meanwhile, in a small bowl, soften the remaining 3 tablespoons butter. Add parsley and lemon juice, salt and black pepper to taste. Refrigerate until ready to use. Just before serving the *suprêmes,* top each with a dollop of this butter.

MENU

Suprêmes de Volaille Alphonse
Hot Marinated Snap Beans
Broiled Tomato Halves
Baked Apple with Whipped Cream

Fried Walnut Chicken originates from the province of Yang Chow, China. When you bring this entrée to the table, your guests will think you have a professional chef in the kitchen. Do not omit the walnuts, they are essential.

FRIED WALNUT CHICKEN

(MAKES 4 SERVINGS)

BEVERAGE SUGGESTION: *Assorted beers or Chianti*

Steps 1 through 9 may be prepared ahead of time. Just before serving, heat in a preheated moderate oven (350°).

1 ready-to-cook chicken (2½ to 3 pounds), cut into serving pieces
¼ cup flour
2 tablespoons cornstarch
1/16 teaspoon ground black pepper
1 small egg, beaten
2 tablespoons finely chopped green onion
1 teaspoon grated fresh ginger root
Soy sauce
1 tablespoon gin or brandy
¾ cup shelled English walnuts
Boiling water
1 quart peanut oil
Prepared hot mustard

1. Wash chicken, wipe dry and set aside.
2. In a medium bowl, mix flour, cornstarch, and black pepper.
3. In a small bowl, combine egg, onion, ginger, 2 tablespoons soy sauce, and gin or brandy. Mix well and add to the flour mixture. Beat until the batter is smooth.
4. Add chicken to the batter, mix well, coating all pieces, and let stand in the batter for 15 minutes.
5. Put walnuts in a bowl, add boiling water to cover them, and let stand for 2 minutes.
6. Remove walnuts from water, peel off skins, and spread on a towel to dry.

7. In a deep saucepot or Dutch oven, heat oil to 350°. Add walnuts. Stir and cook until they have browned lightly, 1 to 2 minutes, watching closely to prevent burning. Remove walnuts from the oil and drain them on paper towels. Set aside.
8. Increase the temperature of the oil to 375°. Stir chicken in the batter, and drop the pieces, one at a time, into the hot oil. Fry until chicken is brown, 8 to 10 minutes.
9. Remove chicken from the hot oil and drain a few minutes on paper towels. Arrange chicken on a warmed platter and garnish with the browned walnuts.
10. To serve, place a teaspoon hot prepared mustard in the center of each serving plate and pour soy sauce around it. Dip the chicken in this sauce as it is eaten.
11. Pass Turkish fingertip towels, hot and damp, for wiping the fingers.

MENU

Fried Walnut Chicken
Rice
Bean Sprout Salad
Tart Salad Dressing
Almond Cookies

The first time we were served this light and delicate entrée was in Toulouse, France. We had discovered a small inn and found the food exceptional; we ate there as often as possible. The ginger-champagne-cream combination intrigued us. Since then I have prepared this chicken hundreds of times, mainly because it takes no time at all.

CHICKEN IN CHAMPAGNE SAUCE

(MAKES 4 SERVINGS)

WINE SUGGESTION: *Mumm's Champagne; Cordon Rouge*

Steps 1 through 4 may be prepared ahead of time.

1 ready-to-cook chicken (3 pounds), quartered
1/4 cup flour
2 teaspoons salt or salt to taste
1/4 teaspoon ground black pepper
1/4 teaspoon ground ginger
2 tablespoons cooking oil
2 tablespoons butter
1 medium onion, quartered
1 medium carrot, quartered
1 bay leaf
6-ounce bottle champagne or 1 cup dry white wine
3/4 cup (6 ounces) uncooked wild rice
1 cup heavy cream

1. Wash chicken and set aside.
2. In a brown paper bag or plastic bag, place flour, salt, black pepper, and ginger. Shake to mix well.
3. Add chicken and shake until it is coated with the mixture.
4. In a 12-inch heavy skillet, heat oil and butter. Place chicken, in a single layer, in the skillet and cook over moderate heat, uncovered, until it has browned on both sides, 20 to 25 minutes.
5. Add onion, carrot, bay leaf, and champagne. Simmer, covered, until chicken is tender, about 25 minutes.
6. Meanwhile, cook wild rice according to package directions and spoon onto each of 4 individual serving plates. Place a serving of chicken on each.
7. Discard onion, carrot and bay leaf. Add cream to the pan drippings and mix well. Heat but do not boil. Spoon the sauce over the chicken. Serve hot.

MENU

Chicken in Champagne Sauce
Sautéed Whole Mushrooms
Tiny White Onions
Red Leaf Lettuce Salad
Coffee Ice Cream

DOVES AND SQUABS

To Make Pies That the Birds May Be Alive In Them and Flie Out When It Is Cut Up

Make the coffin of a great pie or pasty, in the bottome thereof make hole as big as your fist, or bigger if you will, let the sides of the coffin bee somewhat higher then ordinary pies, which done put it full of flower and bake it, and being baked, open the hole in the bottome, and take out the flower. Then having a pie of the bigness of the hole in the bottome of the coffin aforesaid, you shal put it into the coffin, withall put into the said coffin round about the aforesaid pie as many small live birds as the empty coffin will hold, besides the pie aforesaid. And this is to be done at such time as you send the pie to the table, and set before the guests: where uncovering or cutting up the lid of the great pie, all the birds will flie out, which is to delight and pleasure shew to the company. And because they shall not bee altogether mocked, you shall cut open the small pie, and in this sort you may make many others, the like you may do with a tart.

EPULARIÒ

The great vineyard of Montrachet, in the Côte de Beaune region of France, produces some of the best white Burgundies in the world. The bouquet of these wines is tremendous—they are flowery, pleasantly dry, with an underlying quality of luscious softness. Montrachet wine goes particularly well with doves.

DOVES IN WINE

(MAKES 6 SERVINGS)

WINE SUGGESTION: *White Burgundy; Clos de Mouches (Beaune)*

This dish may be prepared ahead of time. Reheat before serving.

6 ready-to-cook doves
Salt and ground black pepper
2 tablespoons butter
2 tablespoons cooking oil
1 cup chopped onion
8 strips bacon, diced
1¾ cups dry white wine
1¾ cups chicken broth (homemade or canned)
2 pounds (2 cups) shelled green peas (fresh or frozen)

1. Wash and dry doves thoroughly. Rub inside and out with salt and black pepper. Set aside.
2. In a large flameproof casserole heat butter and oil over low heat. Add onion and cook, stirring often, until it is golden, about 5 minutes. Stir in bacon.
3. Add doves and cook until browned on all sides, turning often. Pour in wine and let the mixture bubble 2 minutes. Then add chicken broth. Season the liquid mixture with salt and black pepper to taste.
4. Cover casserole tightly and simmer doves until tender, about 1¼ hours. Add peas, cover, and simmer 15 minutes longer.
5. Serve at the table from the casserole.

MENU

Doves in Wine
Potato Pancakes
Applesauce
Hearts of Palm
Peach Tart

This recipe was originated by Alfred Meek, who prepared it for the 1956 Culinary Olympics. If doves are not available, purchase very small Cornish game hens. If shallots are not available, use scallions. The *brunoise* is only a simple vegetable mixture flavored with wine and cooked until reduced.

DOVES IN RED WINE

(MAKES 4 SERVINGS)

WINE SUGGESTION: *Red Bordeaux; Haut-Cadet (St.-Emilion)*

Steps 1 through 8 may be prepared ahead of time. Reheat and flambé just before serving.

4 ready-to-cook doves
Salt and ground black pepper
4 strips bacon, cut in halves
5 tablespoons butter
2 medium carrots, scraped and diced
2 small white onions, diced
3 shallots, chopped
1/8 teaspoon ground nutmeg
3/4 pound raw mushroom caps and stems, chopped
1 1/4 cups dry red wine
4 raw dove livers, mashed
Freshly ground black pepper
3 tablespoons brandy
Croutons, sautéed in butter

1. Preheat oven to 350° (moderate).
2. Wash doves and dry thoroughly. Sprinkle, inside and out, with salt and black pepper.
3. Place doves on a rack in a shallow roasting pan. Cover the breast of each with 2 pieces (1 strip) bacon.
4. Place doves in the oven and roast, uncovered, until they are very tender, about 45 minutes. To brown the doves, remove bacon from the breasts 10 minutes before they are done.
5. Transfer doves to a warmed heat-proof serving platter and place them in the oven to keep warm. Be sure

the oven heat is turned off. Reserve pan drippings to use later.

6. Meanwhile, melt 1 tablespoon of the butter in a 2-quart saucepan. Add carrots, onions, and shallots. Stir and cook until onions are soft but not brown. Add the nutmeg and salt to taste. This mixture is known as *brunoise*.

7. Stir in mushrooms and wine. Simmer until the wine is reduced to about one half the original volume. Strain and set aside.

8. In a bowl, blend mashed dove livers with the remaining 4 tablespoons softened butter. Mix with the pan drippings and add the mixture to the *brunoise*. Reheat without boiling, stirring frequently.

9. Adjust salt and add freshly ground black pepper to taste.

10. When ready to serve, sprinkle warmed brandy over the doves and ignite. When the flame dies out, spoon the hot sauce over the doves. Garnish with croutons. Serve promptly.

This dish is from Barcelona. Obviously, this highly sophisticated preparation is not country-type food. What sets it apart is the pecan-apple medley.

DOVES A LA MADRID

(MAKES 4 SERVINGS)

WINE SUGGESTION: *Red Burgundy; Chambertin Lavaux (St. Jacques)*

4 ready-to-cook doves
Salt and ground black pepper
3 tablespoons butter
3 green onions, bulbs and tops, chopped
½ cup finely chopped button mushrooms
¼ cup chopped pecans
¼ cup chopped unpeeled apples
¾ cup fine dry bread crumbs
Dry vermouth
4 slices bacon, cut in half crosswise
4 slices hot buttered toast

1. Preheat oven to 450° (very hot).
2. Wash and dry doves thoroughly and sprinkle inside and out with salt and black pepper. Set aside.
3. In a large heavy skillet or saucepan, melt butter. Add onions and mushrooms and cook, stirring frequently, until onions are soft, about 5 minutes.
4. Stir in pecans, apples, and bread crumbs. Season to taste with salt and black pepper and add only enough vermouth to bind the ingredients. Spoon the mixture into the body cavities of the doves. Close openings with skewers.
5. Arrange doves, side by side, on a rack in a shallow roasting pan. Lay 2 half slices bacon over each breast. Pour 1 cup vermouth into the pan. Roast 20 minutes or until doves are tender, basting often with vermouth.
6. Serve each dove on a slice of hot buttered toast with some of the roasting pan sauce spooned over it.

MENU

Doves à la Madrid
Cold Zucchini and Cucumbers in Sour Cream
Brie, Bel Paese, Camembert Cheese
Fresh Fruit

Every household should have a set of glass bells. So many times hot foods lose their flavor before ever reaching the table, because the precious aromas have dissipated into the air. With the *cloche* in place, all the flavor, juices, and aromas are locked inside the bell.

PIGEONNEAU SOUS CLOCHE

(MAKES 6 SERVINGS)

WINE SUGGESTION: *Red Burgundy; Louis Martini Barbera*

6 ready-to-cook baby pigeons (squab)
Salt and ground black pepper
Butter
18 mushroom caps
Lemon juice to taste
½ cup dry sherry
1 cup heavy cream
1½ tablespoons flour
6 slices lean broiled ham

1. Wash and dry pigeons thoroughly and sprinkle them inside and out with salt and black pepper. Set aside.
2. In a heavy 12-inch skillet, melt 4 tablespoons butter. Add pigeons and cook them over moderate heat until they are golden brown on all sides. Cover skillet and continue cooking until pigeons are tender.
3. Meanwhile, rub enough softened butter over the bottom of a saucepan to just cover it. Add mushroom caps and cook about 5 minutes, or until tender, stirring frequently. Add lemon juice to taste. Set aside in a warm place to keep hot.
4. Remove pigeons from the skillet and keep them hot.
5. Into the unwashed skillet, pour sherry and cream. Then blend flour with 1½ tablespoons softened butter until smooth, add to the sherry and cream, and cook, stirring, 1 to 2 minutes or until thickened. Season to taste with salt and black pepper.
6. On 4 warmed serving plates, put a slice of hot broiled ham, place a pigeon on each, and spoon some of the

sauce over both. Garnish plates with the mushroom caps. Bring each plate to the table covered with a glass bell.

MENU

Pigeonneau Sous Cloche
Potato Puffs
Artichoke Salad in Vinaigrette Dressing
Lemon Sherbet

The first Chinese came to America between 1820 and 1850, settling on the West Coast. When the discovery of gold in California brought a flood of prospectors from the East, the Chinese found a new way to make a living. The prospectors, being single or having left their families behind, required places to eat—so the Chinese opened restaurants. Their food was excellent and they flourished.

CHINESE DOVES

(MAKES 6 SERVINGS)

WINE SUGGESTION: *Red Bordeaux; Château Margaux (Margaux)*

Steps 1 and 2 of this dish may be prepared ahead of time.

6 ready-to-cook doves, quartered
2/3 cup peanut oil
2 cups sliced mushrooms
1 can (11 ounces) water chestnuts, drained and sliced
2 cups Chinese pea pods (fresh or frozen), sliced
3 cups chicken consommé (homemade or canned)
1/2 cup dry sherry

¼ cup cornstarch
¼ cup soy sauce

1. Wash doves and dry thoroughly.
2. In a heavy large skillet, heat oil. Add doves, cover and cook until doves are tender, turning often.
3. Add mushrooms, water chestnuts, pea pods, and 2 cups of the consommé. Cook, covered 5 minutes. Remove doves and vegetables to a warmed heat-proof platter and keep warm.
4. To the pan juices left in the skillet add the remaining 1 cup consommé, sherry, and the cornstarch blended with the soy sauce. Simmer 5 minutes, stirring occasionally.
5. Pour the hot sauce over the doves and vegetables. Serve steaming hot.

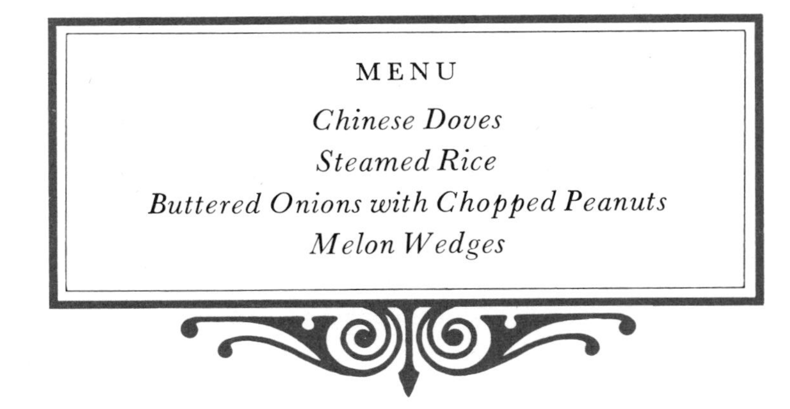

I cannot imagine the Italians cooking without their tomatoes or the Northern Europeans cooking without their white potatoes or the Indians cooking without sweet potatoes, peanuts, chocolate, and their favorite spice and flavoring agent, the chili pepper. These peppers have been adopted for cooking in almost every part of the world. They warm the curries of India, the *rijsttafel* of Indonesia, the *Paprika Schnitzel* of Central Europe, and the dishes of Mexico and South America.

PALOMA DE SUD AMERICA

(MAKES 6 SERVINGS)

WINE SUGGESTION: *Red Bordeaux; Haut-Cadet (St.-Emilion)*

This dish may be prepared the day before serving it.

6 small ready-to-cook doves
4 medium onions, thinly sliced
3 cloves garlic, minced
2 pimentoes, thinly sliced
2 tablespoons chopped parsley
1 rib celery, chopped
4 small bay leaves
½ cup tarragon vinegar
½ cup dry white wine
1 cup olive oil
½ teaspoon ground black pepper
⅛ teaspoon ground chili pepper
1 teaspoon salt

1. Wash and dry doves thoroughly. Split them in half, lengthwise.
2. Put half the sliced onions in the bottom of a large earthenware casserole. Place the doves over the onions.
3. Cover the doves with the remaining onions, the garlic, pimento, parsley, celery, and bay leaves.
4. In a medium bowl, combine vinegar, wine, oil, black pepper, chili pepper, and salt. Pour the mixture into the casserole over the doves, onions, and other ingredients.
5. Cook, covered, over low heat for 45 minutes or until doves are tender.
6. Remove doves to a deep bowl, bring the casserole juices to the boiling point, and cook over high heat until the liquid has reduced by half the original volume. Pour the liquid over the doves. Cover the bowl and refrigerate until the doves are very cold, 10 to 12 hours, or overnight.
7. Serve doves cold with the sauce spooned over them.

MENU

Paloma de Sud América
Chilled Cooked New Potatoes in Jackets
Tomato and Avocado Salad
Pecan Pie

Alsace, France, has very rich fields in which to grow grains, and the soil is probably the richest in all of France. Not only do some of the finest wines come from Alsace but Strasbourg is world famous for its *Pâté de Foie Gras.* Now Strasbourg is also famous for doves with sweetbreads.

DOVES WITH SWEETBREADS

(MAKES 6 SERVINGS)

WINE SUGGESTION: *Red Bordeaux; Château Dauzal (Labarde)*

6 ready-to-cook doves with livers and gizzards
2 teaspoons salt
2 teaspoons ground black pepper
2 cloves garlic, minced
1 pair veal or lamb sweetbreads
Cold water
1 tablespoon vinegar
½ pound (2 sticks) butter
1 medium onion, chopped
1 cup chopped mushrooms
2 cups medium-fine uncooked noodles
1 cup light cream
¾ cup dry sherry

1. Wash and dry doves thoroughly. Set aside.
2. In a cup, mash salt and 1 teaspoon of the black pepper with garlic to a smooth paste. Rub the mixture into the skin of each dove. Set aside.

3. Grind livers and gizzards in a food chopper, using the medium blade. Set aside.
4. Soak sweetbreads in cold water 1 hour, changing the water several times. Drain sweetbreads and put them in a saucepan with 1 cup cold water and the vinegar. Bring water to boiling point, reduce heat, and simmer 10 minutes. (Do not boil.)
5. Remove sweetbreads from the hot water, hold them under running cold water immediately, and with the fingers, slip off the membrane. Cut out and discard the dark veins and thick connective tissue. Then cut sweetbreads into small cubes. Set aside.
6. In a large heavy skillet, melt 1 stick of the butter, add onion, and cook, stirring often, until onion is transparent.
7. To the onion add cubed sweetbreads, ground livers and gizzards, mushrooms, noodles, cream, sherry, and the remaining 1 teaspoon ground black pepper. Mix well.
8. Preheat oven to 375° (moderate).
9. Spoon the onion and sweetbread stuffing into the doves. Close openings with skewers.
10. Melt remaining 1 stick butter in a large casserole, add doves and brown them on all sides over moderate heat.
11. Place casserole in the oven and roast the doves, covered, until they are tender, about 35 minutes, basting frequently with the butter.
12. Remove casserole from the oven and arrange doves on a large warmed platter. Remove skewers. Garnish with cherry tomatoes, if desired. Serve hot.

This lovely tidbit was served at a very elegant picnic for six persons. Everything was brought to the spot, very cold, and then assembled on individual plates in a matter of minutes. The squabs may be braised the day before and refrigerated. The vegetables may be cooked the day before, then covered and refrigerated.

BRAISED SQUAB WITH VEGETABLE SALAD

(MAKES 2 SERVINGS)

WINE SUGGESTION: *Portuguese Mateus Rosé*

This dish may be prepared ahead of time and refrigerated until ready to serve.

2 ready-to-cook squabs
Salt and ground black pepper
Flour
3 tablespoons cooking oil
1 cup hot water
1 cup Vegetable Salad (recipe below)
4 thick slices tomatoes
4 sprigs parsley

1. Wash and thoroughly dry squabs and sprinkle them with salt and black pepper inside and out. Then roll them in flour.
2. In a heavy 9- or 10-inch skillet, heat oil. Add squabs and brown them on all sides over moderate heat.
3. Remove squabs from the skillet. Add 2 tablespoons flour to the pan drippings and cook, stirring, until flour has browned. Stir in hot water.
4. Return squabs to the skillet. Cook, covered, over low heat, until they are tender. Serve hot or cold.
5. To serve hot, cut each squab into 8 pieces and put the pieces in the center of a platter or on 2 individual serving plates. On one side of the squab, place Vegetable Salad; on the opposite side, arrange tomatoes and garnish with parsley. Spoon hot gravy over the squabs.
6. To serve cold, leave squabs whole, transfer them to a cold pan. Pour the sauce over them. (Some of the

sauce will drip to the bottom of the pan.) Refrigerate until the sauce jellies. Just before serving, arrange squabs on a platter or put one on each serving plate. Cut the jellied sauce into small squares and place them around the squabs.

7. Place Vegetable Salad and tomatoes on the platter or plates according to directions given in Step 5. Garnish with parsley sprigs.

VEGETABLE SALAD

1/4 cup cold cooked green peas
1/4 cup cold cooked green beans
1/4 cup cold cooked diced carrots
1/4 cup cold cooked cauliflowerets
1/2 teaspoon vinegar
2 to 3 tablespoons mayonnaise
Salt and ground black pepper to taste

1. The vegetables in this salad may be fresh or frozen. They should be cooked separately, only until crisp-tender, and drained well.
2. In a bowl place all vegetables. Blend vinegar with mayonnaise, using only enough to bind the vegetables. Sprinkle with salt and black pepper to taste. Toss lightly with 2 forks. Chill and serve with braised squabs.

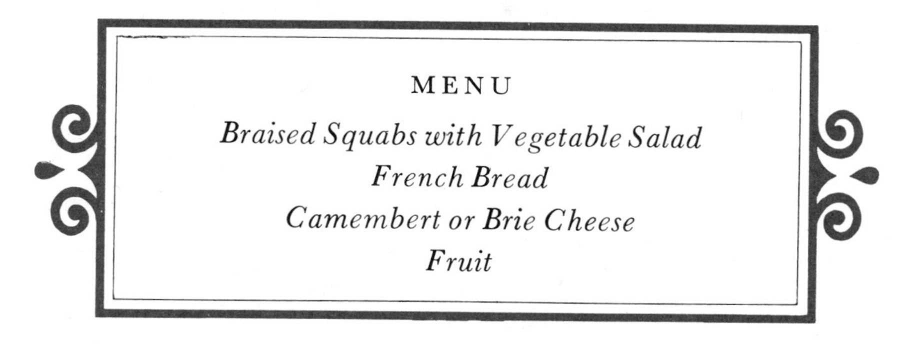

The *bouquet garni* is another French culinary delight. It consists of several herbs, usually including parsley, thyme, and bay leaf, tied in a bunch or put in a small cheesecloth bag and added to stews, soups, and sauces. Thus, it can be easily removed at any stage in the cooking.

SQUABS WITH PORK

(MAKES 4 SERVINGS)

WINE SUGGESTION: *Red Burgundy; Château Greves (Beaune)*

This dish may be prepared ahead of time. Reheat before serving.

4 ready-to-cook squabs
Salt and ground black pepper to taste
½ pound fresh lean pork, diced
Cold water
5 tablespoons butter
16 small white onions, peeled and left whole
2 cups shelled peas (fresh or frozen)
3 sprigs parsley
*2 sprigs fresh thyme**
1 sprig fresh marjoram
½ teaspoon chopped fresh or freeze-dried chives
1 small bay leaf
(the 6 lines above: Tied in a bag (bouquet garni))
⅛ teaspoon sugar
Fresh parsley for garnish

1. Wash and thoroughly dry squabs. Sprinkle inside and out with salt and black pepper. Set aside.
2. In a 1-quart saucepan, place diced pork, cover with cold water, bring to boiling point, and boil 5 minutes. Drain well and pat dry with paper towels.
3. In a heavy 12-inch skillet, melt 1 tablespoon butter, add boiled pork, and cook, stirring frequently, until pork has browned. With a slotted spoon, remove pork and set aside.
4. In the same skillet (do not wash skillet), fry onions

* If fresh thyme and marjoram are not available, replace them with ¼ teaspoon each dried thyme and dried marjoram.

until golden, turning frequently. With a slotted spoon, remove onions and set them aside with the pork.

5. In the same unwashed skillet, melt the remaining 4 tablespoons butter. Add squabs, cover and cook 30 minutes or until they are very tender, turning several times to brown them on all sides.
6. Remove squabs to a warmed platter and keep them hot.
7. To the same unwashed skillet, return onions and pork. Add peas, *bouquet garni,* sugar, and 2 tablespoons water. Cook, covered, over brisk heat 10 to 15 minutes.
8. Return squabs to the skillet and cook only until hot. Do not boil. Adjust salt and remove bouquet garni.
9. Arrange squabs on a serving platter and spoon the sauce over them. Garnish with parsley and serve promptly.

DUCK

When the hunters or the purveyors furnish them in large numbers in the country, and one wants to make an entrée of them, they may be made into salmis, served over an olive ragoût or on mushroom caps in béchamel sauce. We cannot agree that they may be cooked with turnips, as the Almanach des gourmands *advises. This is too vulgar an accompaniment for albrans, wild ducklings, or even wild ducks. It is suitable only for farmyard ducks and ducklings. We follow rather the precept and decision of M. Brillat-Savarin:*

"Preparation of this noble game with such a vegetable would be an unsuitable and even an insulting procedure, a monstrous alliance, degradation and dishonor."

LA MARQUISE DE CRÉQUI

We left Paris and headed into Provence, arriving early in the morning when the red-tiled roofs were still wet with dew. Further south we got our first glimpse of the Côte d'Or region, location of the world's most famous Burgundy vineyards. *Canard Côte d'Or* is also one of the riches from that region.

CANARD COTE D'OR

(MAKES 4 SERVINGS)

WINE SUGGESTION: *Red Burgundy; Corton Clos du Roi (Aloxe-Corton)*

Steps 1 through 4 may be prepared ahead of time.

½ cup (1 stick) butter
½ cup flour

3 cups hot milk
2¼ teaspoons salt or salt to taste
Dash cayenne
1 tablespoon tomato paste
1 cup button mushrooms, cooked, sliced, and drained
2 cups small chunks cooked lobster meat
2 truffles, diced
1 ready-to-cook duck (5 to 6 pounds)
¼ teaspoon ground black pepper
2 tablespoons butter, melted

1. In a large saucepan, melt butter. Remove from heat and stir in flour. Cook, stirring, until the mixture is bubbling but not browned. Remove from heat and gradually beat in hot milk. Stir and cook until the sauce is very thick.
2. Add 1½ teaspoons salt, cayenne, and tomato paste and mix well.
3. Stir in mushrooms, lobster, and truffles. Adjust seasonings. Refrigerate until the mixture is well-chilled.
4. Preheat oven to 325° (slow).
5. Wash and dry duck, reserving giblets for another use. Mix the remaining ¾ teaspoon salt and the black pepper and sprinkle ½ teaspoon inside the neck cavity.
6. Close the neck opening tightly either by sewing it with small tight stitches or lacing it tightly with string and skewers so the sauce will not seep out while cooking.
7. Spoon the thick chilled lobster sauce into the duck cavity, tipping the duck back so the sauce will not run out. Close the cavity opening by sewing it with small, tight stitches.
8. Sprinkle the remaining salt and black pepper mixture over the skin of the duck. Pierce the skin, but not the meat. Fold the wings back in akimbo fashion, and tie the legs in place.
9. Place duck on a rack in a shallow roasting pan. Roast, uncovered, 2 to 2½ hours, piercing the skin several times to release the excess fat.

10. Brush the skin of the duck 2 to 3 times with the melted butter during the last 20 minutes cooking time.
11. Remove duck from the oven when the skin is crisp and golden. Remove stitches and skewers. Spoon the sauce into a warmed bowl. Carve the duck and serve very hot with some of the sauce spooned over each portion.

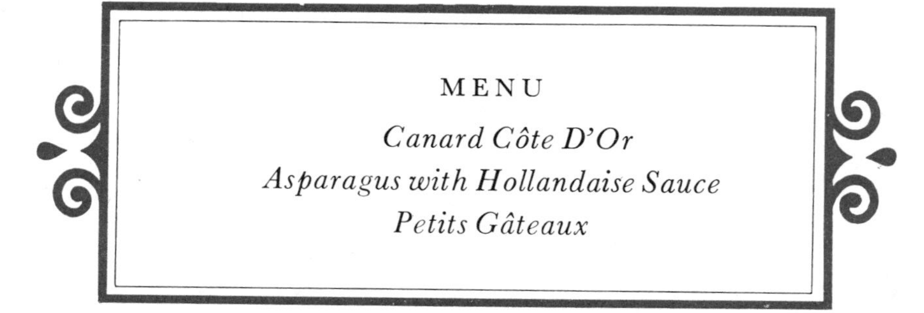
MENU

Canard Côte D'Or
Asparagus with Hollandaise Sauce
Petits Gâteaux

King Louis XIV of France was a notorious glutton. He has been credited, however, with many recipes and gastronomical customs.

One of the famous recipes of the sixteenth century was *Caneton en Ragoût* (duck stew). The duck was roasted whole, then a ragoût with sweetbreads, artichokes, mushrooms, *fines herbes,* salt, and pepper was prepared and poured over the finished duck. *Caneton en Ragoût* is an ancestor of Braised Duck St. Andrew.

BRAISED DUCK ST. ANDREW

(MAKES 4 SERVINGS)

WINE SUGGESTION: *Red Burgundy; Samuele Sebastiani*

Stuffing may be made ahead of time and refrigerated until ready to use.

1 ready-to-cook duck (4 to 5 pounds)
Salt
Ground black pepper
Wild Rice Stuffing (recipe below)

2 small onions, peeled and quartered
1 cup hot water
1 tablespoon flour
1 cup chicken bouillon
Peel from 1 medium lemon, cut in julienne strips
Peel from 1 medium orange, cut in julienne strips
1/4 cup water
1/3 cup port wine
1/8 teaspoon Dijon mustard
1 tablespoon currant jelly
Dash cayenne
Dash ground ginger
1 medium navel orange, peeled and sliced or sectioned

1. Preheat oven to 325° (slow).
2. Wash duck, drain well, and dry. Reserve giblets for use in another recipe.
3. Sprinkle neck and duck cavities lightly with salt and black pepper and fill them loosely with Wild Rice Stuffing. Close cavity openings with skewers and string.
4. Rub the skin of the duck lightly with salt and ground black pepper. Place duck on a rack, breast side up, in a shallow roasting pan. Add onions and the 1 cup water to the pan.
5. Roast duck, uncovered, 35 to 40 minutes per pound, basting every 30 minutes with pan juices. (If duck tends to brown too quickly, cover it loosely with foil.) Remove duck to another pan and keep warm while making the sauce.
6. Skim off and discard excess fat, leaving 2 tablespoons of the drippings in the pan. Blend the flour with the drippings in the pan. Add bouillon and simmer, uncovered, over low heat, 20 minutes, stirring occasionally. Strain gravy and set aside in a warm place.
7. In a small saucepan, put lemon and orange peels and the 1/4 cup water. Cover and boil 5 minutes. Drain off and discard the water and add the lemon and orange peels to the sauce. Stir in wine, mustard, jelly, cayenne, and ginger. Set aside.

8. Place uncarved duck on a platter or, if desired, quarter the duck with duck shears or kitchen shears and arrange the quarters attractively on the platter. (Each quarter is a serving.) Garnish with orange slices or sections.
9. Heat the sauce and spoon some over the duck. Serve the remaining sauce in a sauceboat.

WILD RICE STUFFING

4 tablespoons butter
1/4 cup chopped shallots
1 cup uncooked wild rice
2 1/2 cups chicken consommé
1/2 teaspoon salt

1. In a 2-quart saucepan, melt 2 tablespoons of the butter. Add shallots and cook, stirring, until they are transparent.
2. Stir in rice and cook until rice puffs and begins to change color, stirring constantly.
3. Add consommé, salt, and the remaining 2 tablespoons (1/4 stick) butter. Cook, covered, 20 minutes or until rice is tender. Fill the duck with this stuffing.

MENU

Braised Duck St. Andrew
Green Beans with Almonds
Mixed Green Salad
Rum Chiffon Pie

The story goes that long ago the Chinese used knives and forks but they found that silver sometimes impaired the delicate flavor of foods. Besides, silver spoons with hot food were apt to burn the tongue, so they changed to chopsticks and china spoons. Chopsticks were named *chu,* meaning helper, in the beginning. Because the word had the same pronunciation as *stop* in Chinese, the people didn't like its sound so the name was changed to *k'uai-tzu,* meaning quick ones. The character *k'uai* has the same pronunciation as the first character in the Chinese word for *pleasure.* Indeed, it is with pleasure one ought to pick up one's food.

PINEAPPLE DUCKLING

(MAKES 4 SERVINGS)

BEVERAGE SUGGESTION: *Assorted beers*

1 ready-to-cook duck (4 to 5 pounds), quartered
1½ cups canned beef broth
2 cups water
2 tablespoons cooking oil
1½ cups drained, canned pineapple chunks
2 slices fresh ginger, cut ⅛ inch thick, or ¼ teaspoon ground ginger
1 medium green pepper, cut in pieces the size of pineapple chunks
2 tablespoons cornstarch
¼ teaspoon ground black pepper
2 teaspoons soy sauce
⅓ cup pineapple juice

1. Wash and dry duck. Reserve giblets for another dish.
2. Put quartered duck in a large saucepot or Dutch oven. Add beef broth and water. Bring to boiling point, reduce heat, and simmer, covered, 45 minutes. Remove duck from the stock and drain well. Reserve 1½ cups of stock to use later.
3. In a heavy 12-inch skillet, heat oil. Add duck to the hot oil and cook, over moderate heat, 15 minutes longer. Add reserved stock, pineapple, ginger, and

green pepper. Cook covered over low heat, another 15 minutes.

4. Transfer duck to a warmed platter and keep hot. In a small bowl, blend cornstarch, black pepper, soy sauce, and pineapple juice. Pour the mixture into the skillet. Stir and cook until the sauce has thickened.
5. Return duck to the skillet and cook in the sauce, over low heat, 10 minutes. Serve duck with some of the sauce spooned over each portion. Pass remaining sauce in a sauceboat.

MENU

Pineapple Duckling
Brown and White Rice
Green Beans with Mushrooms
Macaroons

The first thing I did when I got back to the United States from France was to purchase a duck press. Of course, we ate pressed duck at La Tour d'Argent, who doesn't? While our entrée was being prepared before our eyes, we had that striking view of Notre Dame as the sun dropped below the horizon.

PRESSED DUCK #1

(MAKES 4 SERVINGS)

WINE SUGGESTION: *Red Burgundy; Chambertin Laveaux (St. Jacques)*

2 ready-to-cook ducklings (4 pounds each)
1 cup dry red wine, warmed
2 duck livers, mashed
Juice of 1 lemon (about 2 tablespoons)

1/8 teaspoon powdered mustard
Hungarian paprika to taste
Salt and ground black pepper to taste

1. Preheat oven to 500° (very hot).
2. Wash and dry ducks and place them on a rack in a shallow roasting pan. Roast 12 to 15 minutes.
3. Remove ducks from the oven and carefully remove breast meat from each. Put the meat in a chafing dish. Reserve legs and wings for another dish.
4. Combine warmed wine, mashed livers, lemon juice, mustard, paprika, salt, and black pepper. Pour the mixture over the breast meat.
5. Cut up both carcasses and put them through a duck press, pressing out all the juices. Add the juice to the chafing dish. Heat, but do not boil.
6. Serve on warmed plates with some of the hot juices spooned over each serving.

When we sit down to a sumptuously laid table we must thank Charlemagne. He was the first of the "lords of the table" and French cookery owes much to him.

Pope Julius I designated December 25th as the day on which Christmas would be held. Soon after, the custom of midnight suppers on Christmas Eve and

New Year's Eve was inaugurated by Charlemagne. Pressed duck is sumptuous and perfect for any one of these festive dates.

PRESSED DUCK #2

(MAKES 4 SERVINGS)

WINE SUGGESTION: *Red Bordeaux; Château Trotanoy (Pomerol)*

Steps 1 through 8 may be prepared ahead of time.

1 ready-to-cook duck with liver (4 to 5 pounds)
1 tablespoon chopped shallots
Butter
Dash coarse salt
Dash freshly ground black pepper
Dash ground nutmeg
1/4 cup red wine
2 tablespoons brandy

1. Preheat oven to 350° (moderate).
2. Remove liver from duck and reserve it to use later in this dish.
3. Wash duck, dry, and place on a rack, breast side up, in a shallow roasting pan. Roast 20 minutes per pound. Remove duck from the oven and let it stand 5 minutes at room temperature.
4. Remove legs and wings from the duck and use them in another dish. Cut breast in thin slivers.
5. Meanwhile in a small saucepan, cook shallots in 1 teaspoon of the butter and sprinkle them over the bottom of a warmed platter. Then sprinkle shallots with a dash of each, salt, black pepper, and nutmeg.
6. Place slivered duck over the shallots.
7. Rub duck liver through a sieve and set aside.
8. Chop duck carcass, sprinkle with wine, and put it through the duck press. Blend the juice with the sieved duck liver.
9. Scatter a few pieces of the butter over the slivered duck, sprinkle with brandy, and ignite, extinguishing the flame immediately.

10. Set the oven control at broil. Pour the liver-thickened juice over the duck and place it in the broiler oven to glaze, 1 to 2 minutes. Serve promptly.

This is a most delicate dish and perfect for an after-theatre supper. And what better way to use up those duck legs and wings after having prepared pressed duck? I have also used turkey in this dish, with great success.

LEFTOVER DUCK

(MAKES 2 SERVINGS)

WINE SUGGESTION: *Red Bordeaux; Château La Lagune (Loudon)*

This dish may be prepared ahead of time. Reheat before serving.

1 tablespoon butter
1 clove garlic, minced
1 small white onion, peeled and chopped
2 cups diced, cooked duck
1 teaspoon dried thyme
1 tablespoon chopped parsley
1 small bay leaf, crumbled
1 tablespoon flour
1 cup canned chicken consommé
½ cup Madeira
1 cup green olives, pitted

Salt and ground black pepper to taste

1. In a 1½-quart saucepan, melt butter, add garlic, and cook, stirring, until butter begins to brown. Add onion and brown lightly.
2. Stir in diced duck, thyme, parsley, and bay leaf. Cook, stirring frequently, over moderately low heat for 10 minutes.
3. Sprinkle duck meat with flour and mix well. Add consommé, Madeira, olives, and salt and black pepper to taste. Simmer, covered, 20 minutes. Serve over wild or white rice.

MENU

Leftover Duck
Wild or White Rice
Steamed Spinach with Sesame Seed
Pineapple Ice

Turnips are not as popular in this country as they are in Europe, especially in France where we were first served this simple but grand dish. It was in Dijon, where the natives never tire of good, nourishing food.

CANETON A LA CHEVALIER

(MAKES 4 SERVINGS)

WINE SUGGESTION: *Red Burgundy; Beaune "Cent-Vignes" (Chevillot)*

1 ready-to-cook duck (4 to 5 pounds)
Salt
Ground black pepper
4 tablespoons butter
16 small white onions, peeled

¾ pound (about 2 cups) cubed, peeled turnips
1 teaspoon sugar
Flour
2 tablespoons dry white wine
Beef consommé (homemade or canned)
1 clove garlic, crushed
1 sprig parsley } *tied in a bag (bouquet garni)*
1 small bay leaf
¼ teaspoon dried oregano
Snipped parsley

1. Preheat oven to 325° (slow).
2. Wash and dry duck. Remove fat from body cavity and sprinkle the cavity with ½ teaspoon salt and 1/16 teaspoon black pepper.
3. In a heavy, large skillet or Dutch oven melt 2 tablespoons of the butter, add duck, and brown it on all sides.
4. Transfer duck to a rack, breast up, in a shallow roasting pan. Place in the oven and cook 20 minutes per pound.
5. Put onions in a saucepan with boiling water to cover. Cook, uncovered, 5 minutes. Drain well and let stand a few minutes, uncovered, to dry.
6. In a heavy, large skillet, heat the remaining 2 tablespoons butter, add onions, and cook, gently, turning to brown all sides. Remove onions from the skillet and keep them hot.
7. In the same skillet and in the same butter, cook turnips until browned lightly on all sides. Sprinkle with ½ teaspoon salt and the sugar. Cook until sugar has caramelized and the turnips have glazed.
8. Sprinkle turnips with a little flour and cook them 2 minutes longer, stirring carefully.
9. Dribble wine over the turnips and add enough consommé to come up to the top of the turnips, but not enough to cover them.
10. Add onions, garlic, and *bouquet garni*. Simmer, uncovered, until turnips are tender. Remove and discard

the *bouquet garni*. Arrange duck on a heated platter.

11. Skim off and discard excess fat from the pan drippings in the roasting pan. Put turnips in the pan and stir them gently to coat them with the drippings.
12. Arrange turnips and onions on the platter around the duck and spoon some of the sauce over them. Serve promptly, garnished with snipped parsley.

The combination of tomato, orange, and orange rind has a faintly tart and pleasing flavor. Canned tomatoes may be used and also cut into strips. The little Italian plum tomatoes are especially delicious.

WILD DUCK IN MARSALA WINE

(MAKES 4 SERVINGS)

WINE SUGGESTION: *Red Burgundy, Corton Bressandes (Aloxe-Corton)*

This dish may be prepared ahead of time.

2 ready-to-cook wild ducks, quartered
2 to 3 tablespoons cooking oil
1/3 cup Marsala wine
2 tablespoons tomato paste
2 tablespoons flour
1 1/2 cups chicken consommé (homemade or canned)
1 1/2 teaspoons salt or salt to taste
1/8 teaspoon ground black pepper

1 bay leaf
½ tablespoon butter
6 medium mushrooms, sliced
½ cup diced green pepper
Orange segments from 1 medium navel orange
1 teaspoon finely chopped orange rind
3 tomatoes, peeled and cut into strips (raw or canned whole)

1. Wash and dry ducks, discarding the giblets.
2. In a deep, heavy 12-inch skillet, heat oil, using only enough to brown the ducks. Add ducks and brown on all sides.
3. Pour Marsala over the ducks, mixing it with the pan drippings and spooning the mixture over the ducks.
4. Blend tomato paste and flour with a little of the consommé. Add the remaining consommé and pour this mixture over the ducks. Add salt, black pepper, and bay leaf. Simmer, covered, until ducks are tender.
5. In a small skillet, melt butter. Add mushrooms and cook, stirring, 4 to 5 minutes. Stir in green pepper, orange segments, orange rind, and tomatoes. Cook until raw tomatoes are soft or until canned tomatoes are hot.
6. Remove ducks to a warmed platter and keep warm.
7. If juices are too thin, add a little more flour, mixed with an equal amount of water, to the skillet. Mix well and stir in the tomato-orange mixture. Stir and cook about 1 minute. Pour the sauce over the ducks and serve hot.

MENU

Wild Duck in Marsala Wine
Steamed White Rice with Minced Mushrooms
Asparagus Vinaigrette
Pears Poached in Red Wine

Once these ducklings have been quickly browned and then put into the oven, they can be left to themselves. There is no need for basting. This recipe is a great convincer for the non-duck lovers.

CANARD AU VIN

(MAKES 4 TO 6 SERVINGS)

WINE SUGGESTION: *Red Bordeaux, Château Figeac (St.-Emilion)*

This dish may be prepared ahead of time. Reheat before serving.

2 ducklings, 3½ to 4 pounds each, quartered
2 teaspoons salt
2½ teaspoons coarsely ground black pepper
1½ cups flour
8 tablespoons (1 stick) butter
¾ cup chopped green onion tops
2½ cups dry white wine
½ cup blanched almonds, shredded
Madeira Sauce (recipe below)
3 tablespoons chopped parsley

1. Preheat oven to 350° (moderate).
2. Wash and dry duckling thoroughly. Set aside.
3. Mix salt and black pepper with flour. Reserve 3 tablespoons of this mixture for use in the Madeira Sauce. Coat the duckling with the remaining flour mixture.
4. In a heavy 12-inch skillet, melt half the butter. Add duckling, as many pieces at a time as the pan will accommodate without crowding. Brown the pieces on both sides. As the duckling pieces brown, remove them to a large casserole. Repeat, until all the pieces have been browned, adding the remaining butter as needed.
5. Sprinkle onion tops over the duckling, then pour in wine and sprinkle with shredded almonds.
6. Bake, covered, 1 hour or until the duckling is very tender.
7. Remove duckling to a large warmed platter and keep it warm.

8. Strain the pan juices into a 1-quart saucepan. Skim off and discard excess fat which rises to the top of the juices. Reserve the juices to use in the Madeira Sauce. Reserve the shredded almonds, which will be left in the strainer, to use later.
9. Make the Madeira Sauce and pour it over the duck. Sprinkle with chopped parsley and the reserved shredded almonds. Serve hot.

MADEIRA SAUCE

3 tablespoons reserved seasoned flour
Pan juices from the casserole in which duck was cooked
1½ cups hot beef consommé
½ cup Madeira

1. Blend seasoned flour with the pan juices until the mixture is smooth. Beat in hot consommé. Stir and cook over low heat about 1 minute.
2. Just before serving, stir in Madeira. Heat about ½ minute or only until hot.

Our staff of life is bread; the Oriental's staff of life is rice. The Chinese eat boiled or steamed rice piping hot throughout the meal or at the end of the dinner. They will take a mouthful of plain rice, then a separate mouthful of flavored food. While they sometimes spoon the sauce of a flavored dish over their plain rice, they never douse it with soy sauce as do many Americans. There are a variety of ways to use rice—steamed; fried; sizzling; mixed with other foods; served on cold mornings for breakfast, as the Chinese do. Rice can also be used as a base for other foods—sweet desserts flavored with sugar, dishes with ham, salted shrimp, vegetables, meat, and even peanuts.

ONION DUCK

(MAKES 4 SERVINGS)

BEVERAGE SUGGESTION: *Beer*

This dish may be prepared ahead of time.

1 ready-to-cook duck (4 to 5 pounds), quartered
3 tablespoons flour
3 tablespoons cornstarch
¼ cup cooking oil
1 cup sliced green onion tops
4 slices fresh ginger root, ⅛ inch thick, or ½ teaspoon ground ginger
¼ cup soy sauce
¼ cup sherry
⅛ teaspoon ground black pepper
Water

1. Wash and dry duck.
2. In a bowl, blend flour and cornstarch and dredge the duck in the mixture.
3. In a heavy 12-inch skillet, heat oil until it swirls. Add onion and fresh or ground ginger. Cook, stirring frequently, until onions turn a bright green color. Add duck and cook, browning both sides.
4. Drain oil from the duck, leaving a small amount in the skillet.
5. In a cup, mix soy sauce, sherry, and black pepper. Pour the mixture over the duck. Then add sufficient water to barely cover the duck. Bring the water to boiling point, reduce heat, and simmer, covered, until

duck is very tender and most of the water has evaporated (1½ to 2 hours). Adjust seasonings.

6. Arrange duck on a warmed platter. Spoon the onion and ginger pan-drippings over the top. Serve with wild rice.

When King Francis I became ill, his physicians prescribed yogurt in great quantities. This diet was soon imitated by the king's courtiers. Also, at every meal during the month of May, the king ate garlic crushed in sweet butter. He attributed his regained strength to the garlic. This too was taken up by the court members and became a great fad.

Who knows, if the king hadn't been ill, we might never have heard of this magnificent bulbous plant of the lily family.

SAUTEED WILD DUCK

(MAKES 4 SERVINGS)

WINE SUGGESTION: *Red Burgundy; Richebourg (Vosne-Romanée)*

2 ready-to-cook wild ducks
Salt and ground black pepper to taste
½ teaspoon dried marjoram leaves
½ teaspoon dried thyme leaves
1 tablespoon snipped parsley
¼ teaspoon ground allspice
1 small bay leaf

½ cup brandy
1 cup dry red wine
1½ cups (2 large) chopped onions
1 tablespoon butter
6 tablespoons olive oil
1 large clove garlic
½ pound fresh mushrooms, sliced

1. Remove and discard giblets from the ducks.
2. Wash, dry, and split the ducks in half lengthwise and flatten the breasts.
3. Place ducks in a large bowl or crock and sprinkle with salt, black pepper, marjoram, thyme, and parsley. Add allspice, bay leaf, brandy, wine, and onion. Mix well. Cover and marinate, at room temperature, 5 hours, turning the pieces in the marinade occasionally.
4. Just before cooking, remove ducks from the marinade and drain them well.
5. In a heavy 12-inch skillet, heat butter, oil, and garlic. Add a few pieces of duck at a time and cook until browned on all sides.
6. Add mushrooms, cover and simmer 1½ hours or until ducks are tender.
7. Serve ducks hot from the skillet or a Dutch oven or on a warmed platter with the sauce poured over them.

MENU

Sautéed Wild Duck
Wild Rice
Green Beans
Strawberries with Crème Anglaise

There was a time when people attributed miraculous healing properties to cabbage. It was supposed to have prevented hair from falling out, to have made one's sense of smell more acute, and to have been a cure for several diseases. None of these beliefs may be true, but fresh or fermented, cabbage is one of nature's generous contributions to mankind's well-being.

SAUERKRAUT-STUFFED DUCKLING

(MAKES 4 SERVINGS)

WINE SUGGESTION: *Paul Masson Red Burgundy*

This dish may be prepared ahead of time.

1 ready-to-cook duck with giblets (4 to 5 pounds)
1 tablespoon lemon juice
½ teaspoon salt
½ teaspoon ground black pepper
½ teaspoon garlic powder
Sauerkraut Stuffing (recipe below)
1 medium apple, cored and quartered
½ teaspoon ground marjoram
½ teaspoon ground tarragon
2 tablespoons butter, melted
1 cup Madeira
Giblet Sauce (recipe below)

1. Remove giblets from duck and reserve for the sauce. Wash duck and wipe dry.
2. Rub duck inside and out with lemon juice, salt, black pepper, and garlic powder.
3. Preheat oven to 450° (very hot).
4. Stuff the body cavity with Sauerkraut Stuffing. Close the opening with skewers and lace tightly with a string.
5. Stuff the neck cavity with the apple quarters. Fold the skin over the neck opening to the back and fasten it to the back with skewers. Tuck the wings under, in akimbo fashion, so the duck will lie flat.
6. Combine marjoram, tarragon, and butter and rub the mixture over the skin of the duck.

7. With a fork, prick the skin several times in the fatty areas to let the fat seep out as the duck cooks. Place the duck on a rack, breast side up, in a roasting pan. Roast, uncovered, 15 minutes.
8. Reduce oven temperature to 350° (moderate) and cook duck, uncovered, 1 hour. Then baste with Madeira. Roast an additional 1½ hours or until duck is tender, basting 3 more times with Madeira.
9. Remove duck from the oven, spoon the stuffing onto a heatproof platter and keep it warm while carving the duck.
10. Cut duck into quarters or serving-size pieces and arrange them on the Sauerkraut Stuffing. Spoon some of the Giblet Sauce over the duck. Serve the remaining sauce in a sauceboat.

SAUERKRAUT STUFFING

2 tablespoons butter
½ cup (1 medium) coarsely chopped onion
2 cups (2 medium) coarsely chopped apples
2½ cups sauerkraut, drained
2 whole cloves
1½ teaspoons caraway seeds

1. In a 9- or 10-inch skillet, melt butter. Add onion and cook, stirring frequently, until it is golden brown.
2. Add apple, mix well, and cook 1 minute.
3. Stir in sauerkraut and spices. Set aside to use as the stuffing for the duck.

GIBLET SAUCE

Duck giblets (neck, liver, and gizzard)
1½ cups water
½ teaspoon salt or salt to taste
Drippings from the roasting pan
¼ cup heavy cream
Ground black pepper to taste

1. Wash giblets and place them in a 2-quart saucepan with water and salt. Cook, covered, until giblets are tender, about 1 hour. Remove giblets from the stock and cool them until they can be handled. Then chop them very fine.
2. Skim off and discard any fat that is floating over the stock. Strain stock into the roasting pan and mix well with the pan drippings, scraping the browned bits from the bottom and sides of the pan. Heat and strain into another saucepan.
3. Stir in cream and black pepper and adjust salt. Heat but do not boil. Serve over the duck.

NOTE: If a sauce with a stronger flavor is desired, add Madeira to taste.

An important aspect of the production of cognac is that it is, in fact, doubly distilled. The first distillation, which is called the *brouillis,* comes out at about 50 proof. The *brouillis* is then redistilled, producing *la bonne chauffe,* which is the raw cognac, about 135 proof. It is this colorless brandy, or *eau de vie,* which is then put into barrels made from Limousin oak, a species of tree that grows only in the forests of nearby Limoges. As the brandy mellows in the barrels, it also loses some of its alcoholic strength.

CANETON A LA BERGERAC

(MAKES 4 SERVINGS)

WINE SUGGESTION: *Red Bordeaux; Beychevelle (St.-Julien)*

Steps 1 through 7 may be prepared ahead of time.

1 ready-to-cook duck (4 pounds)
3/4 teaspoon salt
1 teaspoon poultry seasoning
1/2 teaspoon paprika
2 tablespoons butter
1 cup canned apricot nectar
1/2 cup cognac
1/2 cup water
1 teaspoon Glacé de Viande (recipe below)
1 clove garlic, crushed
1/4 teaspoon marjoram
1 small onion, sliced
1/2 lemon, thinly sliced
2 teaspoons arrowroot

1. Wash and dry duck and remove and discard all excess fat.
2. Mix 1/2 teaspoon of the salt, poultry seasoning, and paprika and rub the mixture in the duck's cavity and over the skin of the duck.
3. Pierce the tail and other fatty areas of the duck with the tines of a fork.
4. In a large heavy skillet, heat butter. Add duck and cook until browned uniformly, about 20 minutes.
5. Meanwhile, preheat oven to 325° (slow).
6. Place duck on a rack in a roasting pan and roast 1 hour, siphoning off the fat which drips into the pan.
7. While duck roasts, drain and discard butter from the skillet in which duck was browned. Add apricot nectar, cognac, water, Glacé de Viande, garlic, marjoram, and the remaining 1/4 teaspoon salt. Heat and scrape up all browned bits from the bottom of the skillet.

8. Add onion and lemon slices and pour the mixture over the duck. Continue roasting until duck is fork tender, about 45 minutes.
9. Remove duck to a warmed platter and keep hot. Drain pan juices from the roasting pan. Skim off and discard fat.
10. Blend arrowroot with pan juices, adding more apricot nectar, if necessary, to make 2 cups. Simmer until sauce is clear, about 5 minutes, stirring frequently.
11. Pour the hot sauce over the duck, and if desired, garnish the platter with whole apricots or pineapple slices.

GLACE DE VIANDE

In a 1-quart saucepan, simmer 2 cups of greaseless clear stock or canned beef bouillon until it coats a metal spoon, about 10 to 15 minutes. If desired, prepare Glacé de Viande ahead of time, pour in a jar, cover and refrigerate or freeze until ready to use. If frozen, remove from the freezer about 2 hours before using to allow time for thawing.

MENU

Caneton à la Bergerac
Rice
Zucchini
Endive Salad
Cold Lime Soufflé

This is similar to the French *cassoulet,* but a thousand times easier to prepare. Casseroles such as these are best when started well before the dinner hour. The longer they cook, the better the flavor. They are excellent as leftovers too. This dish emanates from Jurgensen's secret files.

DUCK AND LENTIL CASSEROLE

(MAKES 4 SERVINGS)

WINE SUGGESTION: *Red Burgundy; Caillerets (Volnay)*

This dish may be prepared ahead of time.

1 ready-to-cook duck (4 pounds)
Salt
Ground black pepper
½ teaspoon crumbled dried thyme
2 small onions, quartered
2 cups uncooked lentils
2 tablespoons butter
1 cup (1 large) chopped onion
1 pound knockwurst or sweet Italian sausage
¾ cup chopped parsley
1 clove garlic, finely chopped
1 cup dry red wine
Buttered fine, dry bread crumbs

1. Wash and dry duck and remove and discard all excess fat.
2. Mix ¾ teaspoon salt, ¼ teaspoon ground black pepper, and thyme. Rub the mixture in the body cavity and over the skin of the duck. Prick the skin with the tines of a fork to release the excess fat.
3. Put the quartered onions in the duck's body cavity. Close opening with skewers.
4. Preheat oven to 325° (slow).
5. Place duck on a rack in a shallow roasting pan and roast 1½ hours, frequently siphoning off the fat that drips into the pan.
6. While duck is roasting, cook lentils according to package directions, being careful not to overcook them. Drain off and reserve liquid.
7. In a small skillet or 1-quart saucepan, melt butter.

Add the 1 cup chopped onion and cook until soft, stirring frequently. Add to lentils.

8. In an 8- or 9-inch skillet, put sausage and a small amount of water. Cook, covered, 10 minutes. Remove sausage, slice and add to lentils.
9. Cut roast duck into small pieces and add to lentils. Add parsley, garlic, salt and black pepper to taste. Mix lightly but well.
10. Increase oven temperature to 350° (moderate).
11. Turn the mixture into a large buttered casserole. Pour in wine, adding some of the reserved lentil broth, if the mixture is too dry.
12. Cover casserole tightly. Bake 30 minutes. Remove casserole from the oven and sprinkle the top generously with buttered bread crumbs.
13. Bake 10 minutes longer or until crumbs have browned. Serve at the table from the casserole.

MENU

Duck and Lentil Casserole
Buttered Artichoke Hearts
Mixed Green Salad
Strawberries in Kirsch

The word Montmorency on the menu means that the dish will be garnished with cherries and brandy, and most likely, orange juice. This recipe combines all three with dramatic results.

CANARD A LA MONTMORENCY

(MAKES 6 TO 8 SERVINGS)

WINE SUGGESTION: *Red Burgundy; Pommard Rugiens (Pommard)*

This dish may be prepared ahead of time and reheated before serving.

2 ready-to-cook ducks (4 pounds each)
1½ teaspoons salt
½ teaspoon ground black pepper
1 cup dry sherry
1½ tablespoons sugar
1½ tablespoons vinegar
1 tablespoon butter
2 tablespoons flour
1 cup beef or chicken consommé
½ cup orange juice
3 tablespoons grated orange peel
2 tablespoons lemon juice
1 teaspoon grated lemon peel
2 tablespoons brandy
1 can (15 ounces) Bing cherries
¼ cup pan juices, fat removed

1. Preheat oven to 475° (very hot).
2. Wash and dry ducks. Remove giblets and reserve for another use. Remove and discard all excess fat from the duck cavities.
3. Mix salt and black pepper and rub the mixture inside the cavities and over the skins of the ducks.
4. Put ducks, breasts up, on a rack in a large shallow roasting pan. Roast 20 minutes. Reduce oven temperature to 350° (moderate) and roast 1½ hours longer, or until ducks are very tender.
5. Put sherry, sugar, and vinegar in a small saucepan. Simmer, stirring occasionally, until the mixture is dark brown. Set aside.
6. In a 1½-quart saucepan, melt butter, add flour, and mix to a smooth *roux*. Add consommé slowly, stirring constantly. Cook, stirring, until boiling point is reached. Reduce heat and simmer 10 minutes, stirring occasionally.
7. Add orange juice and grated peel, lemon juice and grated peel, and brandy. Drain cherries and add 1

cup of the juice to the sauce mixture. Reserve cherries to use later.

8. Skim off and discard fat from the pan drippings and add ¼ cup of the drippings to the sauce. Simmer, stirring occasionally, 15 minutes. Add well-drained cherries and the browned sugar and vinegar mixture. Simmer while carving the ducks.
9. Carve ducks and spoon a little of the sauce over each serving. Pass the remaining sauce in a sauceboat.

Spain's famous restaurants feature international *haute cuisine* but also serve their important native dishes. *Pato de Castellano* comes from sunny San Sebastian and is a sumptuous dish usually served long after your first aperitif so that the partners at the table have ample time to toast each other.

PATO DE CASTELLANO

(MAKES 6 TO 8 SERVINGS)

WINE SUGGESTION: *Red Bordeaux; Haut-Cadet (St.-Emilion)*

Steps 1 through 6 may be prepared ahead of time.

2 ready-to-cook ducks (4 pounds each), quartered
¼ pound (1 stick) butter
2 cans (10½ ounces each) beef consommé

2 cups water
4 tablespoons tomato paste
4 teaspoons salt
1½ teaspoons ground black pepper
1 teaspoon Spanish paprika
½ cup sliced raw mushrooms
1½ cups uncooked rice
1 cup cooked green peas
2 canned pimentoes, thinly sliced
1 cup (4 ounces) grated Swiss Gruyère cheese
⅛ pound cooked ham, julienned

1. Wash and dry ducks.
2. In a large heavy skillet, melt 2 tablespoons of the butter. Add duck, as many pieces at a time as the skillet will accommodate without crowding, and brown them on both sides. Repeat, browning the remaining duck in additional butter, added as needed.
3. Transfer the browned duck to a large saucepot or Dutch oven. Add 1½ cups each consommé and water, 2 tablespoons of the tomato paste, 2 teaspoons of the salt, 1 teaspoon of the black pepper, and paprika.
4. Cook, covered, over low heat 1½ hours or until duck is tender. Skim off and discard fat from pan liquid. Reserve liquid.
5. In a 2-quart saucepan, melt 1 tablespoon of the butter. Add mushrooms and cook, stirring frequently, until they are soft.
6. Add the remaining butter to the mushrooms and heat until melted. Stir in rice. Cook, stirring, until rice begins to brown.
7. Add the following ingredients: the remaining consommé, ½ cup water, 2 tablespoons tomato paste, 2 teaspoons salt, and ½ teaspoon ground black pepper. Cook, covered, over low heat 20 minutes.
8. Add peas, pimento, cheese, and ham. Cook, covered, 5 minutes longer. Adjust seasonings.
9. Serve duck on a large warmed platter encircled with a border of the rice and mushroom mixture. Spoon a

little of the pan juices over the duck and serve promptly.

During the colonial days, Brazilian plantation owners imported West African slaves to work their huge sugar plantations. These slaves found their new land very much like the one they had left. Consequently, their skills and knowledge were very valuable to Brazil. They adapted quickly to their new home and were taught how to grow crops such as bananas, coconuts, and yams. Ultimately, the African cuisine had a marked effect on Brazil's cooking and today it is considered one of the finest types of cooking in the world. Gourmets often make pilgrimages to Bahia where the modern African influence dominates.

BRAZILIAN DUCK

(MAKES 6 TO 8 SERVINGS)

WINE SUGGESTION: *Red Bordeaux; Château Lafite (Pauillac)*

This dish may be prepared ahead of time. Reheat before serving.

2 ready-to-cook ducks (4 to 5 pounds each)
1/4 cup lemon or lime juice
2 teaspoons salt
1 teaspoon ground black pepper

3 cups orange juice (fresh or frozen)
3 tablespoons grated orange peel (fresh)
2 small bay leaves
¼ cup light rum
4 medium bananas, peeled and cut into 1-inch pieces
2 tablespoons flour
2 tablespoons water
¼ cup ground Brazil nuts
¼ cup Curaçao
1 cup (8-ounce glass) currant jelly, cubed

1. Preheat oven to 425° (hot).
2. Wash and dry ducks. Remove and discard excess fat from the body and neck cavities, and rub lemon or lime juice in the cavities and over the skins of each. Then rub with salt and black pepper.
3. Place ducks on a rack, breasts up, in a large roasting pan. Roast, uncovered, 20 minutes. Siphon off fat that has dripped into the roasting pan.
4. Reduce oven temperature to 350° (moderate).
5. Continue roasting duck, uncovered, 50 minutes. Siphon off fat from roasting pan.
6. Pour orange juice over the ducks and sprinkle them with the grated orange peel. Add bay leaf and rum to the roasting pan. Continue cooking 1 hour, basting often with the orange juice mixture that is in the pan. Add bananas 30 minutes before ducks are done.
7. Remove ducks from the oven, skim off and discard fat from the pan juices. Strain the remaining pan juices.
8. In a 2-quart saucepan, blend flour with the water until smooth. Add the strained pan juices, mix well, and bring the mixture to boiling point, stirring frequently.
9. Stir in Brazil nuts and Curaçao. Simmer, stirring frequently for 5 minutes.
10. Cut ducks into quarters and place the pieces on a large warmed platter. Garnish the platter with the cooked banana slices and cubed jelly. Spoon some of

the gravy over the ducks. Pass the remaining gravy in a sauceboat.

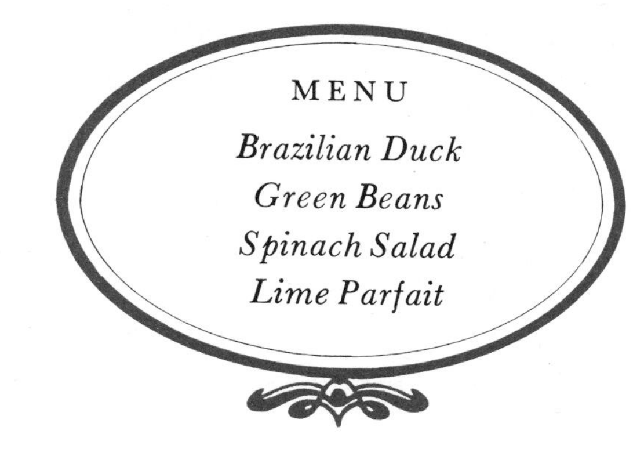

Grand Marnier, flamed over, glazes the skin of the duck so it literally glistens. The flames should flicker as the dish is brought to the table. This recipe is one of many variations of a popular way of cooking duck.

CANETON A L'ORANGE

(MAKES 4 SERVINGS)

WINE SUGGESTION: *Red Burgundy; Clos de Vougeot (Vougeot)*

1 ready-to-cook duck (4 to 5 pounds)
1 teaspoon salt
1/8 teaspoon ground black pepper
1/2 medium-sized unpeeled orange
2 sprigs parsley
Orange sections from 1 large orange
Grand Marnier

1. Preheat oven to 325° (slow).
2. Wash and dry duck. Remove and discard excess fat from the body cavity.
3. Mix salt and black pepper and sprinkle 1/4 teaspoon of the mixture in the body cavity of the duck. Rub the remaining salt and black pepper mixture over the skin of the duck.

4. Put the orange and parsley in the body cavity. Close opening with skewers. Place the duck on a rack, breast up, in a shallow baking pan.
5. Roast duck, uncovered, 2¼ hours. Increase the oven temperature to 375° (moderate) and cook 15 to 20 minutes. Siphon off fat which drips into the roasting pan.
6. Place duck on a warmed platter and garnish with orange sections.
7. In a small saucepan, heat Grand Marnier, pour it over the duck, quickly ignite, and take it to the table flaming.

MENU

Caneton à l'Orange
Small Whole Potatoes with Butter and Parsley
Asparagus with Hollandaise Sauce
Chocolate Torte

There are many excellent restaurants outside Paris. The lovely French countryside makes alfresco dining an experience to remember. Sometimes you are seated beneath brightly colored umbrellas or under arbors laden with bright blossoms. It was at one of these charming outdoor places that we first tasted Canard à la Christophe.

CANARD A LA CHRISTOPHE

(MAKES 8 TO 12 SERVINGS)

WINE SUGGESTION: *Red Burgundy; Chambertin (Moillard-Grivot)*

This dish may be prepared ahead of time. Reheat before serving.

3 ready-to-cook ducks (4 pounds each)
2 teaspoons salt

3 small onions, peeled and quartered
1 large apple, cored and sliced
Cherry and Fig Sauce (recipe below)

1. Preheat oven to 325° (slow).
2. Wash ducks in cold water and dry. Discard giblets and excess fat from the body cavities.
3. Rub salt in the cavities of the ducks and over their skins. Put 1 onion and one-third of the apple slices in the cavity of each duck. Close openings with skewers.
4. Place ducks, breast up, on a rack in a shallow roasting pan. Roast, uncovered, 2½ hours or until ducks are tender, brown, and crisp. Pierce the skins frequently with the tines of a fork.
5. Cut ducks in quarters and place them on a very large warmed platter. Spoon some of the Cherry and Fig Sauce over the ducks. Pass the remaining sauce in a sauceboat.

CHERRY AND FIG SAUCE

2 tablespoons cornstarch
¼ teaspoon salt
¼ teaspoon powdered mustard
1 cup water
¼ cup thawed orange juice concentrate
1 can (1 pound, 13 ounces) whole figs
1 can (1 pound) dark sweet cherries, pitted
2 tablespoons butter
1 tablespoon soy sauce

1. In a 1½ quart saucepan, mix cornstarch, salt, and mustard. Add water and orange juice and mix well.
2. Drain the syrup from figs and cherries, each in a separate bowl. Measure ¼ cup of the fig syrup and 2 tablespoons of the cherry juice and add to the cornstarch mixture.
3. Bring the mixture to boiling point, over moderate heat, stirring constantly. Boil 3 minutes.
4. Add drained figs, cherries, butter, and soy sauce. Heat only until sauce bubbles. Serve with roast duck.

MENU

Canard à la Christophe
Brown Rice
Green and Yellow Snap Beans
Lemon Cheesecake

When I first prepared this dish I had my doubts about cooking with gin, but knowing that the Chinese have been using it for centuries, I tried my luck. I wasn't disappointed.

SOUSED DUCK

(MAKES 4 SERVINGS)

WINE SUGGESTION: *Red Burgundy; Pommard Épenots (Loubet)*

This dish may be prepared ahead of time.

1 ready-to-cook duck (4 to 5 pounds)
1¼ teaspoons salt
1 whole small onion, peeled
1 whole small orange, unpeeled
2 cloves garlic, mashed
4 tablespoons (½ stick) butter, melted, or cooking oil
¾ cup gin
1½ teaspoons powdered ginger

1. Preheat oven to 325° (slow).
2. Wash and dry ducks. Reserve giblets for another use. Sprinkle cavity with ¼ teaspoon of the salt.
3. With the tines of a fork, pierce the onion and the peel of the orange in several places and put both in the cavity of the duck. Close openings with skewers.
4. With the tines of a fork, pierce the skin of the duck to allow fat to seep out. Rub the skin with garlic and melted butter or oil.

5. Place duck on a rack, breast up, in a shallow roasting pan. Roast for 2 hours, siphoning off the fat as it accumulates in the pan.
6. Pour gin over the duck. Blend the remaining 1 teaspoon salt with ginger and sprinkle the mixture over the duck. Roast 1/2 hour longer.
7. Remove and discard onion and orange from the duck's cavity. Cut duck in quarters and place a quarter on each of 4 serving plates. Spoon pan juices over each.

I don't know if ducks have an affinity for nuts, but in cooking they seem made for each other. We discovered this exciting recipe in an excellent restaurant in Brussels. It was served on a heated silver platter and garnished with lightly browned pineapple cubes. If desired, the legs and wings may be used for another occasion.

SUPREMES DE CANETON AUX NOIX

(MAKES 4 SERVINGS)

WINE SUGGESTION: *Red Burgundy; Musigny (Chambolle-Musigny)*

This dish may be prepared ahead of time.

2 ready-to-cook ducklings (3 pounds each)
2 tablespoons cooking oil

2 shallots, chopped
1 cup shelled walnuts, ground
Salt and ground black pepper to taste
Juice of 1 lemon (about 2 tablespoons)

1. Preheat oven to 450° (very hot).
2. Wash and dry ducklings. Reserve giblets to use in another dish.
3. Place ducks, breast up, on a rack in a large roasting pan. Roast, uncovered, 4 minutes to sear ducks.
4. Reduce oven temperature to 325° (slow) and roast ducks 1½ hours or until tender.
5. Meanwhile, in a 1-quart saucepan, heat oil, add shallots, and cook, stirring, over moderate heat for about 1 minute. Add walnuts, salt and black pepper to taste, and lemon juice. Stir and cook, over moderate heat, 1 to 2 minutes.
6. Let ducks stand 5 minutes after removing them from the oven. Then cut only the breast meat into slices and add them to the hot walnuts. Heat until very hot. Serve promptly. Use the meat left on the carcasses in another dish.

MENU

Suprêmes de Caneton aux Noix
Wild Rice
Watercress Salad
Sautéed Button Mushrooms
Melon Balls and Sliced Strawberries in Curaçao

This is a most colorful preparation and perfect for those who love fruit with duck. Do not omit the cognac, otherwise the Curaçao will not ignite. Taken in sequence, this Epicurean delight is uncomplicated and well worth the small effort.

CANARD MOREAU

(MAKES 4 SERVINGS)

WINE SUGGESTION: *Red Burgundy; Les Porrets (Nuits-St. Georges)*

Steps 1 through 4 and the giblet stock may be prepared ahead of time.

1 ready-to-cook duck with giblets (4 to 5 pounds)
3/4 teaspoon salt
1/4 teaspoon ground black pepper
1/3 cup orange juice (fresh or frozen)
1/4 cup pineapple juice
1 teaspoon sugar (optional)
1/3 cup Curaçao
2 tablespoons (1/8 cup) cognac
1/2 cup Giblet Stock (recipe below)
2 tablespoons butter
4 Maraschino cherries
4 thick slices unpeeled navel oranges
4 slices canned pineapple

1. Preheat oven to 325° (slow).
2. Wash and dry duck, reserving giblets to use for making the Giblet Stock.
3. Mix salt and black pepper, sprinkle 1/4 teaspoon of the mixture in the body cavity. Rub the remaining mixture over the duck's skin.
4. Place duck, breast up, on a rack in a shallow roasting pan. Roast 1 3/4 hours. Siphon fat from the roasting pan when necessary.
5. Pour orange juice and pineapple juice over the duck, and if desired, sprinkle with sugar. Roast duck 30 to 40 minutes longer or until tender. Remove duck to a warmed platter and keep warm.
6. Place roasting pan over moderately high heat to reduce the pan drippings. Skim off excess fat. Add Curaçao and cognac, heat, and ignite. Add giblet

stock, bring the sauce to boiling point, then strain the sauce through a cheesecloth. Keep hot.

7. In a large skillet, melt butter. Add cherries, orange slices, and pineapple slices and brown them lightly.
8. Arrange fruit on the platter around the duck. Spoon sauce over the fruit and duck. Serve promptly.

GIBLET STOCK

1 duck liver, diced
1 duck gizzard, diced
½ teaspoon salt
Dash ground black pepper
1 cup cold water

1. Put all ingredients in a 1½-quart saucepan and simmer, covered, until the stock has been reduced by one half the original amount.
2. With a slotted spoon, remove diced liver and diced gizzard from the stock, mince them, and return to the stock. Simmer, covered, 15 minutes. Set aside to use in the sauce.

I was served this small miracle in the dining car of the oldest train I had ever seen. The kitchen was equipped with a charcoal-burning stove. The seats were carved and upholstered in faded green plush and the train boasted an observation car. We were bouncing through the state of Florida, getting the view of the lush countryside, when we heard, "First call for dinner."

CHARCOAL BROILED DUCK BREASTS

(MAKES 4 SERVINGS)

WINE SUGGESTION: *Red Burgundy, Clos de Vougeot (Moillard-Grivot)*

The sauce may be prepared ahead of time, except for the addition of the hot orange juice, sherry, and grated orange peel which should be added just before serving.

2 whole duck breasts, split
Cooking oil
3 tablespoons butter
1 cup canned beef or chicken stock
2 tablespoons arrowroot
Salt to taste
2/3 cup hot orange juice
2 to 3 tablespoons sherry
2 tablespoons grated orange peel

1. Wash and dry duck breasts, rub generously with oil, and let them stand 2 hours.
2. Broil breasts over slow-burning charcoal 10 to 15 minutes, turning to brown both sides.
3. Meanwhile, mix butter, beef or chicken stock, salt, and arrowroot in a 1½-quart saucepan. Simmer until thickened, about 15 minutes.
4. Just before serving, add hot orange juice, sherry, and grated orange peel. Serve, hot, over barbecued duck breasts.

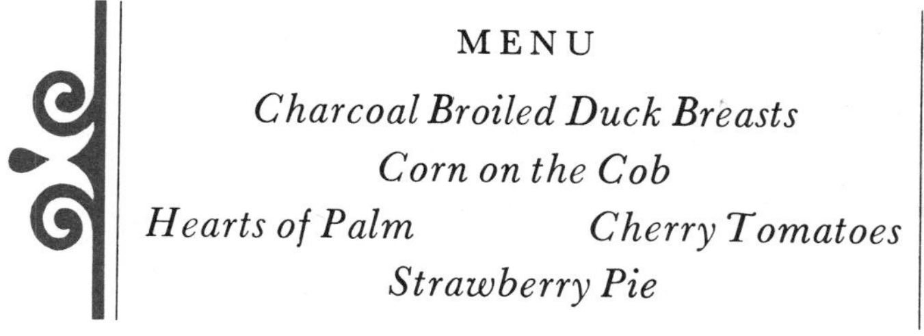

A *mirepoix* is a blend of vegetables (usually including carrots, onions, and celery) and sometimes ham or bacon diced and sautéed with bay leaf and thyme in butter. It is added to sauces and used to season meat, fish, and vegetables while they are braised. The Duc de Mirepoix, a French diplomat of the eighteenth century, was its creator.

DUCKLING SAVANNAH

(MAKES 6 TO 8 SERVINGS)

WINE SUGGESTION: *Red Burgundy; Fixin Clos de la Perrière*

This dish may be prepared ahead of time. Reheat before serving.

2 ready-to-cook ducklings (3½ to 4 pounds each)
Salt to taste
Ground black pepper
3 medium carrots, diced
2 small onions, chopped
3 sprigs fresh thyme or ½ teaspoon dried thyme
3 ribs celery with tops, diced
3 shallots, chopped
1 small bay leaf
2 cloves garlic, finely chopped
2 tablespoons butter
½ cup peach brandy
6 peaches (fresh or canned), peeled and pitted

1. Preheat oven to 400° (hot).
2. Wash and dry ducklings. Remove giblets and discard excess fat from body cavities. Sprinkle ¼ teaspoon salt and a dash of black pepper in the body cavity of each duckling. Rub ½ teaspoon salt and 1/16 teaspoon black pepper over the ducklings' skins.
3. Place ducklings, breast up, on a rack in a large shallow roasting pan. Roast, uncovered, until ducklings are brown, 10 to 15 minutes.
4. While duck is roasting mix carrots, onions, thyme, celery, shallots, bay leaf, and garlic together and sauté the mixture in the butter until soft, or for 10 to 15 minutes. (The French chef refers to this mixture as *mirepoix*.)

5. Remove the ducklings from the roasting pan and place the sautéed *mirepoix* in the bottom of the pan. Put the ducklings back on top.
6. Cover the roasting pan and return it to the oven. Reduce oven temperature to 325° (slow). Roast 1 hour or until ducklings are tender. Remove ducklings to a warmed platter and keep warm.
7. Strain the *mirepoix* and the pan drippings into a saucepan. Skim off and discard fat. Add brandy and bring the mixture to boiling point. Add peaches and heat only until they are hot. Add salt to taste.
8. Remove hot peaches from the sauce and place them on the warmed serving platter around the ducklings.
9. Spoon the sauce over the peaches and the ducklings, after carving. Or, if desired, carve at the table, and pass the sauce in a sauceboat.

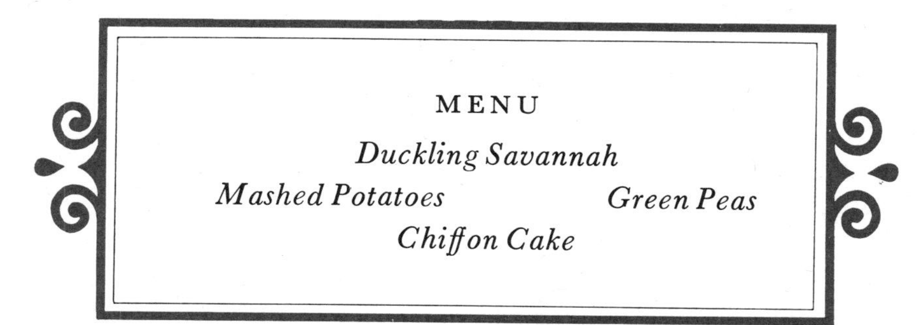

There are several varieties of raisins (grapes which are dried in the sun or by artificial heat). The seedless raisin is produced from seedless grapes such as the Sultana and the Thompson. The seeded raisin has its seeds removed by a special machine. All raisins have a very high sugar content and contain iron and vitamins A and B.

ROAST DUCK WITH RAISIN STUFFING

(MAKES 4 SERVINGS)

WINE SUGGESTION: *Red Bordeaux; Château Haut-Brion (Graves)*

The ingredients for the stuffing may be prepared ahead of time, but do not stuff the duck until just before placing the duck in the oven.

1 ready-to-cook duck (4 to 5 pounds)
1 teaspoon salt
4 cups coarse, soft white-bread crumbs, toasted
3/4 cup minced onion
3/4 cup white raisins
1 teaspoon crumbled dried sage
2 tablespoons butter, melted
3 tablespoons water

1. Wash and dry duck. Sprinkle 1/2 teaspoon of the salt in the body and neck cavities of the duck.
2. In a large bowl, mix bread crumbs, onion, raisins, sage, butter, water, and 1/4 teaspoon of the salt, and spoon into duck cavity. Close cavity openings with skewers. Preheat oven to 400° (hot).
3. Rub the duck's skin with the remaining 1/4 teaspoon salt and place it, breast up, on a rack in a roasting pan. Pierce the skin with the tines of a fork to release fat while duck is roasting. Siphon fat from the roasting pan occasionally.
4. Pour hot water to a depth of about 1/2 inch in the bottom of the roasting pan. Roast duck 20 minutes. Reduce oven temperature to 325° (slow) and roast 2 hours or until duck is tender.
5. Spoon stuffing onto a warmed platter. Quarter the duck and place the pieces on the stuffing. Serve promptly.

MENU

Roast Duck with Raisin Stuffing
Apple Fritters
Chicory Salad
Frosted Pound Cake with Almonds

A friend of ours who owned a small inn nestled in northern Michigan invited us to spend a weekend with him. As luck would have it, we arrived a few days after he had been on a hunting trip. The ducks had been chilled for three full days and were ready to cook. This recipe was dreamed up by our talented friend.

HANNAH'S ROAST WILD DUCK

(MAKES 4 SERVINGS)

WINE SUGGESTION: *Red Burgundy; Château Petrus (Pomerol)*

2 ready-to-cook wild ducks, or 1 domestic duck, 4½ to 5 pounds
1½ teaspoons salt
1 package (9 or 10 ounces) frozen mixed vegetables, partially thawed
1 bay leaf
½ lemon, thinly sliced
1½ cloves garlic, minced
½ cup (1 medium) chopped onion
2 strips bacon
1 cup Madeira
1 tablespoon sour cream
2 tablespoons flour
2 tablespoons water or sour cream
Watercress or parsley

1. Preheat oven to 450° (very hot).
2. Wash and dry ducks and sprinkle ½ teaspoon salt in the body and neck cavities of each. Rub the remaining ½ teaspoon salt over the skins of both ducks.
3. Spread partially thawed vegetables over the bottom of a large roasting pan. Put bay leaf, lemon slices, garlic, onion, and bacon strips on top of the vegetables. Then place ducks, breasts up, over the seasonings and bacon.
4. Roast, uncovered, 40 minutes. Reduce heat to 300° (slow). Pour Madeira over the ducks and roast, covered, 1½ hours or until ducks are tender, basting occasionally.

5. Remove ducks to a warmed platter and keep warm.
6. Place a strainer over a saucepan, pour in the vegetables and pan juices. Let the pan juices drain from the vegetables into the saucepan. Turn the vegetables into a serving bowl and top with the 1 tablespoon sour cream. Keep warm while making the gravy.
7. Skim fat from the pan juices. Blend flour with water or the 2 tablespoons sour cream and add to juices. Stir and cook until the sauce is of desired thickness, 3 to 4 minutes. Serve in a sauceboat.
8. Garnish ducks with watercress or parsley. Carve at the table.

Chinese New Year's Eve dates back to the time of an emperor named Shih Meng who had suddenly become very ill with delirium and imagined all sorts of horrible spirits. One of the emperor's generals suggested that he and another general stand guard at the palace gate to ward off the evil spirits. They did, and the emperor was cured. He was so grateful that he ordered life-sized portraits of the generals painted. These fearful pictures were pasted on the palace gates. To this day, the Chinese mount pictures of the kitchen god and guardians over their hearths and gates every New Year's Eve.

CHINESE NEW YEAR DUCKLING

(MAKES 4 SERVINGS)

BEVERAGE SUGGESTION: *Assorted beers*

This dish may be prepared ahead of time. Reheat before serving.

1 ready-to-cook duckling (4 to 5 pounds), quartered
½ cup flour
1 teaspoon salt
½ teaspoon ground black pepper
½ cup peanut oil
1 cup beef stock (canned)
1½ tablespoons cornstarch
1½ tablespoons soy sauce
¼ cup water
Peaches (fresh or canned)

1. Wash and dry duck. Remove giblets and reserve for another dish. Remove and discard fat from the body cavity.
2. In a bowl, blend flour, salt, and black pepper. Dredge duck in the mixture and set aside for the coating to dry.
3. In a heavy, deep 12-inch skillet or Dutch oven, heat oil. Add duck and brown it on all sides, 20 to 25 minutes.
4. Pour fat from the skillet or Dutch oven, leaving the duck in the pan. Add beef stock. Simmer, covered, 1½ hours. Remove cover 10 minutes before duck is done to crisp the skin.
5. Blend cornstarch with soy sauce and water, add to the sauce in the skillet or Dutch oven, and mix well. Cook, stirring, until sauce is of desired thickness.
6. Serve with fried rice and garnish with peach wedges.

MENU

Chinese New Year Duckling
Fried Rice
Fried Green Pepper Rings
Kumquats
Choice of Ice Cream
Fortune Cookies

Once in a while we will go out on a limb and try a newly opened restaurant, but not until it has been in operation for a few weeks. We like to give the staff time to get the routine working like that well-oiled clock. Timing can make or break the finest meal in the world. In this case, luckily, all was perfect, including this duck dish. It was the beginning of a perfect association with Chez Marcelle and its elegant cuisine.

SWEET RED WINE DUCKLING

(MAKES 6 SERVINGS)

WINE SUGGESTION: *Red Bordeaux; Château Paveil-de-Luze (St.-Julien)*

This dish may be prepared ahead of time. Reheat before serving.

2 ready-to-cook ducklings (4 pounds each), quartered
1½ teaspoons salt
½ cup sweet red wine (Port, Malaga, or Malvasia)
3 tablespoons cooking oil
1 clove garlic, minced
1 tablespoon grated orange peel
1 tablespoon potato starch
1½ cups fresh orange juice
2 tablespoons sweet red wine
2 tablespoons honey
¼ teaspoon ground ginger
⅛ teaspoon ground black pepper
1 cup fresh navel orange sections

1. Preheat oven to 325° (slow).
2. Wash and dry ducks. Pierce the skins with the tines of a fork and rub salt over each piece.
3. Place duck pieces on a rack in a shallow roasting pan. Pour the ½ cup sweet red wine over the ducks and roast 25 minutes per pound, basting with the wine occasionally.
4. Meanwhile, heat oil in a small skillet or saucepan. Add garlic and grated orange peel. Stir and cook about 1 minute.
5. Remove saucepan from the heat, add potato starch,

and stir until it is well blended with the oil and garlic.

6. Gradually stir in orange juice, the 2 tablespoons red wine, and honey. Simmer 1 minute.
7. Add ginger, black pepper, and orange sections. Simmer 5 minutes longer. Serve in a sauceboat.
8. Arrange duck pieces on a warmed large platter. Garnish with watercress and, if desired, arrange additional orange sections on the duck.

The glasses were frosted and the drinks were perfect. The small salad preceding the entrée was superb and the glazed duckling was beyond description. The only flaw in this heavenly atmosphere was the chef, a martinet who ran his tiny place in Bayonne, France, with unbending authority. The most generous gesture he had ever made was to grant me permission to obtain the recipe for this lovely duckling.

GLAZED DUCKLING

(MAKES 4 SERVINGS)

WINE SUGGESTION: *Red Bordeaux; Château Latour-Pomerol*

The Glacé de Viande may be prepared ahead of time and refrigerated or frozen. If frozen, thaw before ready to use.

1 ready-to-cook duck (3¼ to 4 pounds)

¾ teaspoon salt or salt to taste
¼ teaspoon ground black pepper
½ cup water or beef or chicken stock
4 medium navel oranges
2 sugar cubes
3 tablespoons vinegar
½ cup Cointreau
Glacé de Viande (see recipe p. 115)

1. Preheat oven to 325° (slow).
2. Wash and dry duckling. Remove excess fat from cavity and reserve giblets for another dish.
3. Mix salt and black pepper and sprinkle ¼ teaspoon in the duck's body cavity. Rub remaining salt and black pepper over the duck's skin.
4. Place the duck, breast up, on a rack in a roasting pan. Roast from 2¼ to 3 hours, or until duck is tender. Siphon fat from the roasting pan occasionally.
5. Remove duck to another pan and keep hot.
6. Pour fat from the roasting pan, add water or stock to the pan, and bring to boiling point over high heat. Reduce heat and simmer 2 to 3 minutes, scraping up all the browned bits from the bottom and sides of the pan.
7. Add the juice from 2 of the oranges to the roasting pan.
8. Cut the peels from 2 of the oranges in julienne strips, discarding the bitter, white portion. Put the julienne orange peel and ¼ cup water in a small saucepan and simmer 3 minutes. Drain off water and set the peel aside to use later.
9. Heat the sugar cubes in a very small saucepan over low heat until they melt and turn straw color. Add vinegar. The mixture may harden at this point. Bring the mixture to boiling point and boil until the hardened sugar melts. Add to the roasting pan.
10. Stir in the julienned orange peel, Cointreau, and Glacé de Viande. Heat, but do not boil.
11. Quarter the ducklings and arrange them on a warmed

platter. Spoon the hot glaze over them.

12. Slice the remaining 4 oranges and arrange them on the platter around the duck.

In southern Provence there is a restaurant on the waterfront, complete with a small yacht harbor and a filtered swimming pool. If that isn't enough, there is a garden with lovely palm trees. The interior of this delightful oasis is done in the best French décor. This magical duck preparation comes from the chef's bag of tricks.

MARINATED DUCKLING

(MAKES 4 SERVINGS)

WINE SUGGESTION: *Inglenook Pinot Noir*

Steps 1 through 5 of this dish may be prepared ahead of time.

1 ready-to-cook duckling (about 4 pounds), quartered
Marinade (recipe below)
1/3 to 1/2 cup flour
3 to 4 tablespoons cooking oil
12 small, sweet pickled onions
8 large mushroom caps
1 tablespoon potato starch

1. Wash ducklings and put them in a large bowl. Pour in marinade, cover, and refrigerate 48 hours, turning the pieces in the marinade occasionally.

2. When ready to cook, remove ducks from the marinade, wipe dry, and set aside. Strain marinade into a bowl and reserve it for later use.
3. Dredge duckling in flour. Heat oil in a heavy, 12-inch skillet. Arrange the floured duck pieces in the hot oil and brown them on both sides.
4. Add pickled onions, mushrooms, and potato starch blended with a little of the marinade. Add the remaining marinade. Cook, covered, over moderate heat for 1 hour or until duck is tender, spooning the sauce over the duck occasionally.
5. Transfer duck to a large heat-proof platter or shallow baking pan, skin side up. Broil until the skin is very crisp.
6. Arrange duck, onions, and mushrooms on a warmed platter and spoon some of the sauce over the top. Serve hot.

MARINADE

1 cup sauterne
½ cup dry Marsala
1 medium unpeeled navel orange, sliced
1 medium unpeeled lemon, sliced
½ cup water
½ teaspoon celery seed
½ teaspoon dried marjoram
½ teaspoon dried thyme
1 teaspoon salt or salt to taste
⅛ teaspoon ground black pepper
1 tablespoon olive oil

1. In a large bowl, mix all ingredients. Pour the mixture over the duck and marinate 48 hours.

MENU

Marinated Duckling
Buttered Poppy-Seed Noodles
Shredded Cabbage and Radishes
Coronets à la Crème, Josephines

Madrid will never let you down. It is an extremely modern city with artistically landscaped avenues and huge shade trees bordering the walks. The city is punctuated with parks, fountains, and majestic statues. Spanish cuisine is superb, whether it be continental or national. Wherever you go, there are restaurants that defy description.

PATO ESPANOL CON OLIVAS

(MAKES 4 SERVINGS)

WINE SUGGESTION: *Korbel Pinot Noir*

This dish may be prepared ahead of time. Reheat before serving.

1 ready-to-cook duck (4 pounds)
2 tablespoons (¼ stick) butter
2 tablespoons olive oil
¼ pound small white onions, peeled and halved
3 medium carrots, pared and cut lengthwise
3 to 4 tablespoons flour
1 can (13¾ ounces) beef consommé
1 cup sweet sherry
2 cans (8 ounces each) tomato sauce
1 sprig parsley
1 teaspoon salt or salt to taste
¼ teaspoon ground black pepper
3 dozen green olives, pitted

1. Wash and dry duck. Remove excess fat and discard.
2. In a Dutch oven or a large flameproof casserole, heat butter and oil. Add onions and carrots, and brown them over low heat, turning gently. This requires about 20 minutes. Remove vegetables to a warmed dish and cover to keep warm.
3. In the same casserole and in the same fat, brown the duck on all sides, turning often. Remove duck to another pan and set aside in a warm place.
4. Skim off and discard fat from the pan drippings.
5. Blend flour until smooth with ⅓ cup consommé and mix with the sauce in the Dutch oven or casserole.
6. Stir in the remaining consommé, sherry, tomato sauce,

parsley, salt, and black pepper. Mix well.

7. Return duck and vegetables to the casserole. Cook, covered, 1 hour, basting the duck often with the sauce.
8. Remove duck to a warmed platter and keep hot while preparing the sauce.
9. Strain the sauce into a saucepan, add olives, and heat. Serve the sauce in a sauceboat to spoon over the duck.

MENU

Pato Español con Olivas
Parsley Potatoes
Green Bean Salad, Vinaigrette
Caramel Almond Cream (Custard)

GOOSE

Those consecrated geese in orders
That to the capital were warders
And being then upon patrol
With noise alone beat off the Gaul

SAMUEL BUTLER

Goose has been a source of food from medieval times. But it wasn't until the reign of Louis XIV that the preparation of this delectable bird became somewhat sophisticated. During his reign the national dish was the *pot-à-oie*. It was usually stuffed with a variety of meats, particularly with other feathered game and aromatic herbs. The upper classes ate only the stuffing, leaving the goose for the servants and the poor.

OIE DU SOIR

(MAKES 10 TO 12 SERVINGS)

WINE SUGGESTION: *Red Bordeaux; Château Magdelaine (St.-Emilion)*

1 ready-to-cook goose (8 to 10 pounds)
Salt and ground black pepper to taste
3 medium navel oranges
Water
2 large sugar cubes
2 teaspoons vinegar
1 tablespoon canned beef broth
½ teaspoon quick-cooking tapioca

Juice of ½ lemon
4 tablespoons (½ stick) butter

1. Preheat oven to 325° (slow).
2. Wash and dry goose. Remove and discard fat from the body cavity. Sprinkle salt and black pepper in the neck and body cavities.
3. Pull the neck skin to the back, fold the ends of the skin neatly and pin it to the back skin with a skewer. Turn goose breast-side up. Lift each wing and fold the tip under and press it against the back, akimbo style. Close opening of the body cavity with skewers. Rub salt and black pepper lightly over the skin of the goose.
4. Put goose, breast up, on a rack in a shallow roasting pan. Roast until goose is tender. To test for doneness, pierce the second joint. It is done if the juice which runs out is clear and the leg joint moves easily. Time required for roasting an 8-pound goose is 3½ to 3¾ hours. Siphon off the fat that drips into the roasting pan.
5. While goose is roasting, peel 2 of the oranges and cut them into segments to use for garnishing the platter. Sliver the peel from one of the oranges and cook it in boiling water to cover for 5 minutes. Drain off water and reserve the peel to use in the sauce.
6. Rub sugar cubes over the peel of the remaining orange to absorb some of the oil from the peel. Then put sugar cubes in a small saucepan with vinegar. Cook over low heat until sugar melts to a thick syrup consistency. Set aside to use in the sauce. Peel and dice the remaining orange and reserve to use in the sauce.
7. When goose is done, transfer it to a large warmed pan or platter, and let it stand 20 minutes so it will be easier to carve.
8. Skim off and discard all fat from the juices in the roasting pan, and strain through a cheesecloth into a 1-quart saucepan. Add the sugar syrup, beef broth, and tapioca. Simmer until sauce is the consistency of a thin syrup and the tapioca is clear.

9. Remove sauce from the heat, add the boiled slivered orange peel, diced orange, lemon juice, and butter. Heat until butter melts. Adjust salt and keep warm.
10. Shortly before serving, carve goose and arrange the slices on a large warmed platter. Spoon some of the sauce over the meat. Pass the remaining sauce in a sauceboat.
11. Garnish the platter with the reserved orange segments.

Roast goose is to England's Christmas what turkey is to America's Christmas. It was good Queen Bess's favorite back in the sixteenth century. Today, the Church of England celebrates the feast day of St. Michael and All Angels on September 29th every year, and again the goose hangs high.

GOOSE PICCADILLY

(MAKES 8 SERVINGS)

WINE SUGGESTION: *Red Bordeaux; Château Léoville-Poyferré (St.-Julien)*

This dish may be prepared ahead of time. Reheat before serving.

1 ready-to-cook goose (about 8 pounds)
½ cup fresh lemon juice
¼ cup honey
1/16 teaspoon ground allspice
¾ teaspoon salt
8 very small, cored, unpeeled apples

16 blanched almonds
8 teaspoons sugar
Fresh mint

1. Wash goose and dry. Remove giblets and reserve for another dish. Remove and discard fat from the body cavity.
2. Brush goose inside and out with lemon juice. Let goose stand 30 minutes. Then rub goose inside and out with honey. Combine allspice and salt and sprinkle the mixture in the body cavity and over the skin.
3. Pull the skin of the neck cavity to the back and fasten it to the back skin with a skewer.
4. Core apples starting at the stem end, being careful not to break through to the bud end of the apple.
5. Put 2 almonds and 1 teaspoon of the sugar in the hole of each apple and stuff them in the body cavity of the goose. Close opening with skewers.
6. Put goose, breast up, on a rack in a shallow roasting pan. Insert a meat thermometer in the thickest part of the breast or in the center of the inner thigh muscle, being sure that the bulb does not touch a bone. Roast until the thermometer registers 180° to 185°, about 3½ hours, and occasionally siphon off fat from pan as it accumulates. Remove goose from oven and let stand 20 minutes to make carving easier.
7. Remove skewers from neck and body cavities and spoon apples into a separate dish.
8. Transfer goose to a large warmed platter. Garnish with fresh mint. Carve at the table and serve an almond-stuffed apple with each portion.

MENU

Goose Piccadilly
Creamed Onions
Chopped Spinach
Mince or Apple Pie

The origin of brown sauce (called here Sauce Maison) is French. It is one of the two classic basic sauces, the other being white sauce. Brown sauce is traditionally made of rich meat stock to which is added a *roux,* or thickening agent (usually flour and butter browned together), plus a *mirepoix,* or braised vegetables.

OIE AU SAUCE MAISON

(MAKES 10 TO 12 SERVINGS)

WINE SUGGESTION: *Red Bordeaux; Château Latour (Pauillac)*

Prepare the ingredients for the stuffing and make the sauce ahead of time, if desired. Do not stuff goose until just before roasting.

1 ready-to-cook goose (12 pounds), with giblets
¼ teaspoon garlic salt
1 cup cold water
Salt and ground black pepper
4 tablespoons (½ stick) butter
2½ cups (5 medium) finely chopped Spanish onions
6 ribs celery with tops, finely chopped
1 medium green pepper, finely chopped
1½ cups chopped mushrooms
4 medium white potatoes, cooked, peeled, and riced
12 pitted black olives, chopped
½ cup chopped parsley
1 clove garlic, peeled and split
Sauce Maison (recipe below)

1. Remove giblets from the body cavity of the goose. Put the gizzard and neck in a 1-quart saucepan with garlic salt and water. Bring water to boiling point, reduce heat, and simmer, covered, 1 hour or until tender, adding more water if necessary. Cool giblets, chop fine and set aside to use later. Reserve uncooked liver for use in the sauce.
2. Wash and dry goose, remove fat from body cavity and sprinkle cavities with salt and black pepper.
3. In a heavy 10- or 12-inch skillet, melt butter. Add onion, celery, green pepper, and mushrooms. Cook,

stirring frequently, until onions and celery are soft and begin to turn yellow.

4. Add chopped cooked giblets, riced potatoes, olives, parsley, 1 teaspoon salt, and 1/4 teaspoon ground black pepper or salt and black pepper to taste. Mix well.
5. Preheat oven to 400° (hot).
6. Spoon the stuffing loosely into the body and neck cavities. Close openings with skewers.
7. With a fork, prick the skin to release the fat as the goose roasts. Rub the skin with the split garlic clove, 3/4 teaspoon salt and 1/16 teaspoon black pepper. Insert a meat thermometer in the thickest part of the breast or thigh, being sure that the bulb does not touch a bone.
8. Place goose, breast up, on the rack of a large shallow roasting pan. Place in the 400-degree oven and sear 20 minutes. Reduce heat to 325° (slow). Roast 3½ to 4 hours longer or until thermometer registers 180° to 185°. As goose roasts, prick skin occasionally to release fat. Siphon off fat from the roasting pan when necessary.
9. Remove goose from oven and let it stand 20 minutes for easier carving.
10. Spoon stuffing into a large warmed serving bowl. Keep it warm while carving goose.
11. Carve goose and arrange the slices on a large heated platter. Spoon a little Sauce Maison over the meat. Pass the remaining sauce in a sauceboat.

SAUCE MAISON

5 tablespoons butter
4 tablespoons flour
2½ cups hot beef consommé
1 tablespoon cooking oil
1 uncooked goose liver, finely chopped
1 cup (1 large) chopped onion
1 cup sliced mushrooms
1 clove garlic, minced

Coarse salt and ground black pepper to taste
¼ cup Madeira or Madeira to taste

1. In a 2-quart saucepan, melt 4 tablespoons of the butter. When butter foams, blend in flour. Continue to cook, stirring, until the flour and butter mixture is brown.
2. Gradually stir in consommé until sauce is medium thick. Set aside. This is a quick brown sauce.
3. In an 8- or 9-inch skillet, heat the remaining 1 tablespoon butter and the oil. Add liver, onion, mushrooms, and garlic. Cook, stirring frequently, until liver and mushrooms are soft.
4. Season with salt and black pepper to taste. Add the mixture to the brown sauce and mix well. Just before serving, heat and stir in Madeira to taste. Serve with roast goose.

MENU

Oie au Sauce Maison
Spiced Apples or Spiced Peaches
Green Beans Fiesta *
Pumpkin Flan

Grimod de la Reynière, that perfect lord of the table, came to a worthy end—one which we might all wish for ourselves. It was near the end of a most noteworthy dinner which he had shared with a few friends. He dozed off and never woke up. It was midnight on Christmas Eve, 1837.

* Green beans fiesta are cooked only until crisp-tender, drained well, and sautéed briefly in a small amount of butter with a little chopped onion and julienne strips of pimento. They are very good.

He did leave us some of his Epicurean rules—"For a rich man the finest role in the world is that of host." "A gastronome-host who did not know how to carve or serve would be like the owner of a fine library who did not know how to read." "A real gourmand is never late." "The number thirteen is dangerous at the dinner table only when there is just enough to eat for twelve."

GOLDEN GOOSE

(MAKES 10 TO 12 SERVINGS)

WINE SUGGESTION: *Llords & Elwood Velvet Hill Pinot Noir*

Ingredients for stuffing may be prepared ahead of time. Do not stuff goose until just before cooking.

1 can (1 pound) whole marrons (chestnuts)
1 uncooked goose liver
3 chicken livers
3 truffles
1 cup Madeira
6 ounces uncooked pork sausage
Salt and ground black pepper to taste
1 ready-to-cook goose (12 pounds)
Additional Madeira (optional)
10 to 12 peach halves (fresh or canned) (optional)
Fresh lemon juice (optional)
2 tablespoons finely chopped almonds (optional)

1. In a large bowl, place chestnuts and the liquid in which they were canned, livers, truffles, and the 1 cup Madeira. Mix well and refrigerate overnight, stirring occasionally.
2. In a 2-quart saucepan, heat chestnuts, livers, and truffles in the chestnut liquid and Madeira in which they were soaked, 5 to 6 minutes or only until they are hot.
3. Remove the chestnuts, livers, and truffles. Put the chestnuts in a bowl and set aside. Chop the livers and truffles and add them to the chestnuts. Then add sausage and mix well. Blend in the chestnut liquid and Madeira mixture in which the chestnuts, livers, and

truffles were heated. Add salt and black pepper to taste.

4. Wash and pat goose dry, using a paper towel. Remove and discard the excess fat in the body cavity. Sprinkle the cavity with a mixture of ¾ teaspoon salt and ⅛ teaspoon ground black pepper.
5. Preheat oven to 325° (slow).
6. Spoon stuffing loosely into the body cavity of the goose. Close opening with skewers and truss. Prick the skin in several places, rub with salt and black pepper.
7. Place goose, breast up, on a rack in a shallow roasting pan. Roast 4½ hours or until the goose tests done, basting every 30 minutes with Madeira and siphoning off or spooning off excess fat as it drips into the roasting pan.
8. Remove goose to a warmed platter and let it stand 20 minutes for easier carving. Remove stuffing to a warmed serving bowl. Set aside in a warm place while carving the goose.
9. Carve goose and arrange the slices on a warmed platter. If desired, garnish the platter with peaches, sprinkled with a little lemon juice and chopped almonds.

The Scandinavians use dried and fresh fruit with all sorts of foods—hot and cold soups, salads, bastings, and stuffings. This Danish recipe has all the flavor, aroma, and elegance that one could desire. Any favorite cabbage dish is perfect with goose.

DANISH ROAST GOOSE

(MAKES 8 TO 10 SERVINGS)

WINE SUGGESTION: *Red Burgundy; Bonnes-Mares (Morey-St.-Denis)*

Ingredients for stuffing may be prepared ahead of time. Do not stuff geese until just before roasting. Cooking apples may be Winesap, McIntosh, or Rome Beauty.

2 ready-to-cook geese (6 pounds each)
Salt and ground black pepper
1 clove garlic, peeled and split
½ pound dried apricots, soaked in cold water to cover overnight
Dry white wine (Chablis)
½ pound uncooked sausage
6 medium cooking apples, pared and chopped
6 medium onions, peeled and finely chopped
1 bay leaf
½ teaspoon dried thyme
½ teaspoon dried marjoram
1 tablespoon chopped parsley
Dry white wine (Pouilly-Fuissé)
About 1 cup soft bread crumbs
2 tablespoons (¼ stick) butter, melted
¼ teaspoon ground ginger
2 juniper berries, crushed, or 3 tablespoons gin
3 tablespoons brandy
1 tablespoon currant jelly
About 4½ tablespoons flour

1. Remove giblets from geese and reserve them for another dish. Remove and discard fat from body cavities. Sprinkle cavities lightly with salt and black pepper and put ½ clove garlic in each. Set aside.
2. Drain water from apricots, cover with Chablis. Cook,

covered, until apricots are tender, 15 to 20 minutes. Remove apricots from wine and reserve them and the juice in separate containers for later use.

3. In a large, heavy skillet, brown sausage, remove it from the skillet, and set aside to use later.

4. To the sausage fat in the same skillet, add apples and onions. Cook, only until hot, stirring frequently. Add bay leaf, thyme, marjoram, parsley, and enough Pouilly-Fuissé to barely cover the mixture. Cook, covered, until apples and onions are tender. Press the mixture through a sieve.

5. Into this mixture stir the cooked sausage, apricots, and enough soft bread crumbs to make a dry stuffing. Add salt and black pepper to taste. Cool.

6. Preheat oven to 325° (slow).

7. Spoon the cooled stuffing into the body and neck cavities of the geese. Close openings with skewers. Rub the skin with melted butter and sprinkle the skin with salt, black pepper, and ginger.

8. Place geese, breast down, on a rack in a large roasting pan. Cover and roast 1 hour, siphoning off fat from pan as it accumulates.

9. Turn geese breast up and insert a meat thermometer in the thickest part of one of the thighs. Cover and continue roasting one hour longer, or until the thermometer registers 180°–185°. Uncover the pan for the last 15 minutes to brown and crisp the skin.

10. Remove geese to one large warmed platter or two smaller ones. Keep hot.

11. Skim off and discard fat from the roasting pan juices. Measure the roasting pan juices and add to them the reserved Chablis in which apricots were cooked and, if necessary, additional dry white wine to make 3 cups. Pour the mixture into the roasting pan.

12. Add juniper berries or gin, brandy, currant jelly, and the flour blended until smooth with ½ cup of the pan juices. Cook, stirring, until the sauce is about as thick as cream soup. Adjust salt and black pepper. Serve in a sauceboat.

MENU

Danish Roast Goose
Braised Red Cabbage
Grapefruit Sections on Mixed Salad Greens
Cherry Tarts

Normandy, France, is famous for enormous crops of apples and for Calvados, the finest apple brandy in the world. This famous brandy is very much like our applejack, but much drier. The apples used to make Calvados are small, tart red apples grown only in Normandy and similar to the apples called for in this recipe.

OIE NORMANDIE

(MAKES 6 TO 8 SERVINGS)

WINE SUGGESTION: *Red Burgundy; Beaulieu B.V. Burgundy*

The goose may be washed, dried, and seasoned, and the stuffing ingredients may be prepared the day before. Do not stuff goose until ready to cook it.

1 ready-to-cook goose (8 pounds)
2 teaspoons salt
1 teaspoon ground black pepper
2 teaspoons caraway seed
3 cups unpeeled, sliced McIntosh apples
2 tablespoons water
1½ cups soft bread crumbs
½ cup (1 medium) finely chopped onion
Dash cayenne
1 cup ice water

1. Wash and dry goose. Reserve giblets for another dish.
2. Sprinkle the cavities and the skin of the goose with a

mixture of salt, black pepper, and caraway seed. Refrigerate until ready to cook.

3. Preheat oven to 350° (moderate).
4. Put apples and water in a 1½-quart saucepan. Cook, covered, over low heat until apples are very soft, about 20 minutes.
5. Remove apples from heat, mash with fork, and mix well with bread crumbs, onion, and cayenne.
6. Spoon the stuffing loosely into the body and neck cavities of the goose. Close openings with skewers.
7. Place goose, breast up, on a rack in a large roasting pan. Roast, uncovered, 2 hours, siphoning off fat from pan as it accumulates. Then carefully pour 1 cup ice water over the skin of the goose. (This crisps the skin.) Cook 1 hour longer, basting a few times with the liquid in the roaster. The skin should be brown and crisp. When goose is done remove all fat pan drippings.
8. Remove goose from the oven and let it stand 20 minutes for easier carving. Remove stuffing to a warmed serving dish and keep warm while carving the goose.
9. Carve goose and arrange slices on a large warmed platter. If desired, garnish with small clusters of frosted grapes.

FROSTED GRAPES

Small clusters seedless grapes
1 egg white, beaten until frothy
Superfine granulated sugar

1. Dip small clusters of grapes in frothy egg white. Then dip the grapes into superfine granulated sugar.
2. Place grapes on waxed paper to dry.

MENU

Oie Normandie
Sautéed Spinach
Chicory Salad
Fresh Fruit and Cheese

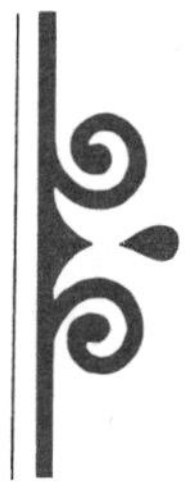

In the small town of St. Étienne, France, we discov ered a charming restaurant. The French menu wa hand-printed in blue ink. There were only three or four choices of entrées; one fish, another beef, and the remainder poultry. We have never regretted choosing this richly flavored goose concoction. Oie St. Étienne is the creation of Chef Lapierre of Le Bistro in Dijon, France.

OIE ST. ETIENNE

(MAKES 10 TO 12 SERVINGS)

WINE SUGGESTION: *Red Burgundy; Louis Martini Barbera*

The stuffing may be prepared the day before; and the geese may be washed, dried, and seasoned. However, do not stuff until ready to roast.

2 ready-to-cook geese (6 pounds each), with livers
4 teaspoons salt
1 teaspoon freshly ground black pepper
2 teaspoons paprika
3 tablespoons caraway seed
10 slices white bread
1 cup milk
4 tablespoons (½ stick) butter
1 cup chopped onion
6 chicken livers
3 tablespoons chopped parsley
1 cup chopped mushrooms
2 eggs
½ cup dry sherry
½ teaspoon ground white pepper
2 cups water

1. Wash and dry geese. Remove and discard fat from body cavities. Reserve livers to use later.
2. Combine 2 teaspoons of the salt, the black pepper, paprika, and caraway seed. Rub the geese inside and out with the mixture. Refrigerate overnight.
3. Preheat oven to 325° (slow).
4. Soak bread in milk for 5 minutes. Then squeeze gently to remove excess milk. Set aside.

5. In a 9- or 10-inch skillet, melt butter. Add onions, livers, parsley, and mushrooms. Cook, stirring, over moderate heat for 10 minutes. Cool and chop fine.
6. To this cooked mixture, add the soaked bread, eggs, sherry, white pepper, and the remaining 2 teaspoons salt. Mix well. Stuff the mixture loosely in the body and neck cavities of the geese. Close openings to cavities with skewers.
7. Place geese on a rack, breast up, in a large shallow roasting pan. Insert meat thermometer in the thickest part of the breast or thigh of one of the geese, being careful that the bulb does not touch a bone.
8. Roast 2½ hours or until the skin is crisp and the geese are tender. Reduce heat to 300° (slow) and continue roasting until the meat thermometer registers 180°–185° F.
9. Remove geese from the oven and transfer them to two warmed platters. Let geese stand 20 minutes for easier carving.
10. Skim off fat and discard it from the pan juices. Add water to the roasting pan and bring it to boiling point over surface heat, scraping up the browned bits on the bottom and sides of the pan.
11. Carve geese and serve with gravy.

MENU

Oie St. Étienne
Buttered Baked Crookneck Squash
Salad Greens
Applesauce Caramel Mold

Miraculous things are done with chestnuts in France. They are cooked and served over vegetables; stuffed into a favorite fowl; or mashed, sweetened, and concocted into a perfect dream of a dessert. This stuffing may be reduced by half and used in other types of fowl, such as a roasting chicken or a small turkey.

OIE ST. MALO

(MAKES 8 TO 10 SERVINGS)

WINE SUGGESTION: *Red Burgundy; Chevret (Volnay)*

The stuffing may be prepared the day before. Do not stuff goose until ready to roast.

1 ready-to-cook goose (9 pounds)
Salt and ground black pepper
3 tangerines
1/4 cup (1/2 stick) butter
1/2 cup diced celery with tops
1 package (8 ounces) prepared bread stuffing (2 1/2 to 3 cups)
1 cup chopped cooked chestnuts (see below) (1/2 pound in shells)
3 cups cooked rice
1/2 teaspoon poultry seasoning or to taste
1/2 cup chicken broth or water

1. Wash and dry goose and remove excess fat from body cavity. Reserve giblets for another dish. Sprinkle goose inside and out with salt and black pepper. Set aside.
2. Peel tangerines, remove the white membrane and seeds, cut sections in half, and set aside to use in the stuffing.
3. In a 2-quart saucepan, melt butter, add celery, and cook, stirring frequently, until celery is soft, about 10 minutes.
4. Add bread stuffing, chestnuts, rice, poultry seasoning, broth, and tangerines. Mix well, but lightly, using a fork. Taste for seasonings and add salt and additional poultry seasoning, if desired.

5. Preheat oven to 325° (slow).
6. Stuff the mixture lightly into the body and neck cavities of the goose. Close openings with skewers.
7. Place goose, breast up, on a rack in a roasting pan. Insert a meat thermometer in the thickest part of one of the thighs or in the stuffing, being careful that the bulb does not touch a bone.
8. Roast until the thermometer registers 180°–185°, if it is inserted in one of the thighs, or 165°, if it is inserted in the stuffing. Remove goose from the oven and let it stand 20 minutes for easier carving.
9. Spoon stuffing into a warmed serving dish and keep warm while carving the goose. Carve goose and place the slices on a warmed platter. If desired, garnish with additional tangerine sections.

To prepare chestnuts for stuffing, make a gash on the flat side of each chestnut by cutting through the shell with the tip of a small, sharp knife. Cover the chestnuts with boiling water and let them simmer 20 minutes, or until the tip of a knife can be inserted in the shell easily. Since chestnuts are easier to peel while hot, remove them from the hot water, one at a time, and take off the shells and brown inner skins that cover the nutmeats, leaving all unshelled chestnuts in the hot water. (Wear rubber gloves and the hot chestnuts will be easy to handle.)

MENU

Oie St. Malo
Baby Peas and Onions
Spinach and Anchovy Salad
Cranberry Cheesecake

GROUSE

The ruddy ripe tomata
In china bowl of ice,
And grouse worth a sonata
Undoubtedly are nice

JOSEPH ASHBY-STERRY

There are several types of olive oil. Virgin olive oil is recommended as being highest in quality. French olive oil is delicate in flavor. The products of Italy, Spain, and Greece are more decidedly olive-tasting. Olive oil is essential in authentic Mediterranean cookery, but it is not recommended as a substitute for butter or a milder vegetable oil.

BROILED GROUSE

(MAKES 4 SERVINGS)

WINE SUGGESTION: *White Burgundy; Pouilly-Fuissé*

4 grouse (1 to 1½ pounds)
1 large onion, halved
3 stalks celery
½ teaspoon salt
Dash pepper
½ cup olive oil

1. Clean grouse and split them down the back.
2. Put the birds in a deep pot and cover with water.
3. Add onion, celery, salt, and pepper. Cover pot and simmer for 30 minutes.

4. Remove birds from pot and drain. Brush with olive oil, then place skin side down on a broiler rack.
5. Broil 15 minutes or until brown, turning once and basting frequently with oil, until well done and tender.

MENU

Broiled Grouse
Baked Potatoes
Tomato and Zucchini Casserole
Apple Crisp

In this dish the delicate flavor of the grouse is enhanced by the piquancy of the tomato sauce, and the two combine to create a decorative appearance and a nourishing dinner.

GROUSE IN TOMATO SAUCE

(MAKES 4 SERVINGS)

WINE SUGGESTION: *Red Burgundy; Corton-Bressandes (Beaune)*

4 ready-to-cook grouse (1 to 1½ pounds each)
Salt and ground black pepper to taste
2 to 3 tablespoons butter
1 cup diced celery
½ cup diced carrots
4 slices of a medium-size onion
4 sprigs parsley
4 small bay leaves
Cold water to cover ingredients
Tomato Sauce (recipe below)

1. Remove breasts from the grouse and sprinkle them with salt and black pepper. Set aside.
2. In a 2-quart saucepot, place the remaining pieces of

grouse, celery, carrots, onion, parsley, bay leaves, 1/2 teaspoon salt, and cold water. Bring water to boiling point, reduce heat and simmer until stock is reduced to 3/4 cup. Strain the stock and reserve it for use in the Tomato Sauce.

3. In a 12-inch skillet, melt 2 tablespoons butter. Place the grouse breasts, in a single layer, in the skillet. Cook, uncovered, over moderate heat, until the breasts have browned on both sides, adding the remaining butter if needed.
4. Arrange the breasts on a warmed serving platter and surround with Tomato Sauce.

TOMATO SAUCE

3 tablespoons butter
4 1/2 tablespoons flour
3/4 cup reserved grouse stock
3/4 cup canned tomatoes
Salt to taste
1 1/2 cups sliced canned mushrooms with liquid
1 tablespoon lemon juice
Dash cayenne
1 teaspoon chopped parsley

1. In a 1-quart saucepan, melt butter. Remove the saucepan from the heat and stir in flour. Cook, stirring, over moderately low heat about 1 minute.
2. Add grouse stock and tomatoes. Mix well. Cook, stirring, until the sauce is of medium thickness, 3 to 4 minutes.
3. Stir in the remaining 5 ingredients. Heat only until the sauce is hot. Pour the sauce on the platter around the sautéed grouse breasts. Serve promptly.

MENU

Grouse in Tomato Sauce
Buttered Rice
Petits Pois in Vermouth
Apple Crisp

Sauerkraut is finely shredded cabbage allowed to ferment in brine made of its own juice and salt. Juniper berries, caraway seeds, or black pepper may be added. It is available in cans, in plastic bags from the frozen foods counter, or in bulk by the pound.

KRAUTED GROUSE

(MAKES 2 SERVINGS)

WINE SUGGESTION: *Red Burgundy; Clos de Vougeot*

2 ready-to-cook grouse (1 to 1½ pounds each)
2 tablespoons butter or bacon drippings, melted
1 pound sauerkraut

1. Split grouse in halves, lengthwise.
2. In a 10- or 12-inch skillet, brown the grouse in the melted butter, turning to brown on both sides.
3. Remove the meat from the grouse bones and set it aside.
4. On the bottom of the unwashed skillet in which the grouse was browned, spread half of the sauerkraut, lay the grouse meat over the top, and cover it with the remaining half of the sauerkraut.
5. Simmer, covered, until the meat is tender, about 2 hours. If needed, add a little hot water to prevent the bottom layer of sauerkraut from scorching.

MENU

Krauted Grouse
Boiled Potatoes with Caraway Seed Butter
Green Peas and Celery with Pimento
Apple Dumplings

The fruit of the almond tree can be either sweet or bitter, but sweet almonds are always used when a recipe calls simply for almonds. Blanched almonds are dried, sweet almonds whose skin has been removed by immersion in boiling water. Burnt almonds are roasted sweet almonds.

GROUSE AMANDINE

(MAKES 4 SERVINGS)

WINE SUGGESTION: *Moselle; Maximin-Grünhaus*

4 grouse (1 pound each)
Salt and pepper to taste
4 slices bacon
6 tablespoons butter, melted
¼ cup blanched almonds, slivered
1 teaspoon lemon juice
4 slices buttered white toast

1. Preheat oven to 350° (moderate).
2. Sprinkle grouse inside and out with salt and pepper.
3. Cover the breasts with bacon and fasten with string or wooden picks.
4. Place grouse, breast side up, in a baking pan.
5. Roast in oven for 15 to 20 minutes, or until meat is tender when pierced with the point of a knife. Baste often with ¼ cup of melted butter.
6. Five minutes before grouse are done, remove strings or picks and the bacon, reserving bacon.
7. Combine remaining butter, almonds, and lemon juice in a saucepan and keep hot.
8. Pour butter-almond mixture over grouse.
9. Serve on buttered toast with bacon.

MENU

Turtle Broth
Grouse Amandine
Small Potato Pancakes
Green Beans
Sliced Fresh Fruit in Kirsch

GUINEA FOWL

The cries of most of the barnyard flock are easily imitated: "Gobble-gobble, cluck-cluck, and cock-a-doodle-do" we know very well. But there's one fowl often found on the farm, whose natural cry is not so easily imitated—and therein lies one of the reasons why many farms maintain a small flock of guineas. For the shrill shriek and harsh cry—"ptrack-ptrack," or "buckwheat, buckwheat"—is sufficiently inimitable to serve a certain purpose. Few are the hawks or other poultry yard marauders who will brave the pugnacious disposition of these guards of the poultry flock. They set up a terrible cry when any stranger—man or animal—comes around, and are regarded as good burglar alarms.

LOUIS P. DE GOUY

This is a recipe that again makes use of the juniper berry. It is an adaptation of the original recipe, which we enjoyed during a trip to New England in a small and charming country inn in Massachusetts.

GUINEA FOWL PIEDMONTESE

(MAKES 3 TO 4 SERVINGS)

WINE SUGGESTION: *Red Bordeaux; Château Belgrave (St. Laurent)*

The stuffing for this dish may be prepared ahead of time. Do not stuff the guinea fowl until ready to roast it.

1 ready-to-cook guinea fowl (2½ to 3 pounds) with liver

Salt and ground black pepper to taste
Bread Stuffing (recipe below)
2 tablespoons butter
1 tablespoon olive oil
1 strip bacon
1 small carrot, sliced
1 or 2 small onions, chopped
1/4 cup chicken broth (homemade or canned)
1/4 cup dry sherry

1. Wash and dry guinea fowl. Reserve liver for use in stuffing. Sprinkle the guinea fowl inside and out with salt and black pepper.
2. Spoon stuffing loosely into the body cavity. Close opening with skewers and tie legs to the tail.
3. Preheat oven to 300° (slow).
4. Brown the guinea fowl, on all sides, in the butter and olive oil.
5. Place the guinea fowl, breast up, on a rack in a small roasting pan. Lay a strip of bacon across the breast.
6. Scatter carrots and onions over the bird and pour broth and sherry over all.
7. Roast bird, uncovered, 50 minutes. Increase temperature to 400° (hot) and continue roasting, uncovered, 10 minutes or until tender, basting with additional broth and sherry.
8. Remove the bird to a warmed platter and keep hot. Press the vegetables and the roasting pan liquid through a sieve. Heat and pour over the bird.

BREAD STUFFING

2 to 3 slices firm-textured bread, 2 to 3 days old
2 tablespoons finely chopped ham
1 uncooked guinea fowl liver, chopped
8 juniper berries, crushed
1/4 teaspoon ground sage
1/8 teaspoon dried oregano
1/2 teaspoon salt

1/16 teaspoon ground black pepper
1 tablespoon butter, melted
Chicken broth (homemade or canned)

1. In a large bowl, crumble bread. Add all the remaining ingredients, except butter and broth. Mix well.
2. Add butter and only enough chicken broth to moisten the stuffing. Pack loosely in the body cavity of guinea fowl.

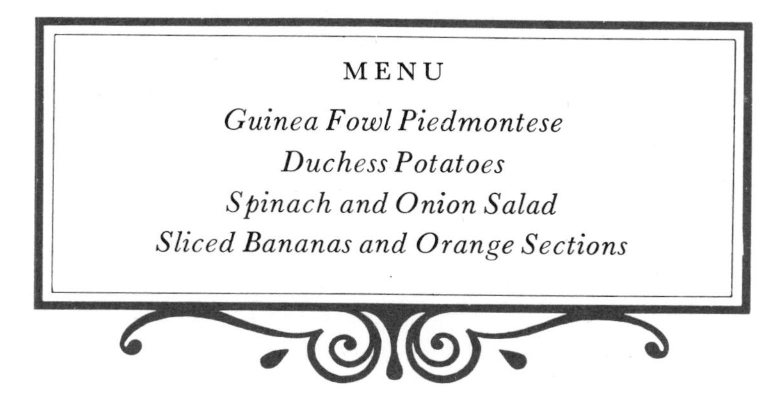

These delicately seasoned *suprêmes* are brought to the table looking like the most expensive, the rarest, and the most difficult of dishes to prepare. However, it takes very little time to assemble. Should there be no guinea hens available, chicken breasts may be substituted. This dish is a complete meal in itself, save for a salad and heated brioches.

ROAST BREASTS OF GUINEA HEN

(MAKES 6 SERVINGS)

WINE SUGGESTION: *Vouvray*

This dish may be prepared ahead of time. Reheat before serving.

6 breasts of guinea hen
5 tablespoons butter
Salt
1 tablespoon cooking oil

Sauce (recipe below)
¾ cup sliced raw mushrooms
3 cups baked rice (recipe below)
6 medium hearts of artichokes, cooked

1. Preheat oven to 275° (very slow).
2. Wash and dry guinea hen breasts. Melt 2 tablespoons of the butter and brush it over the breasts. Then sprinkle with salt.
3. In a large heavy skillet, heat 2 tablespoons of the remaining butter and the oil. Add the guinea-hen breasts and brown them, over moderate heat, on both sides. Arrange them in a single layer, meaty side down, in a 13 x 9 x 2-inch baking dish.
4. Pour the sauce over the breasts, cover, and roast 2 hours. Remove breasts to a warmed dish and keep them hot.
5. Strain the juices from the roasting pan into a saucepan and set aside.
6. Sauté mushrooms in the remaining 1 tablespoon butter and add them to the pan juices. Cook over very low heat only until hot. Add salt to taste.
7. Turn rice onto the center of a large warmed platter. Place breasts around the rice and the artichokes on each side of the breasts. Reheat the strained pan juices and mushrooms. Spoon the mixture over the breasts. They will be nicely glazed. Serve hot.

BAKED RICE

(MAKES 6 SERVINGS)

1 cup long-grain rice
Cold water
2 tablespoons butter, margarine, or cooking oil
1 teaspoon salt
2 cups boiling water

1. Put rice in a strainer and run cold water over it to wash out the excess starch. Drain well.
2. In a heavy 1-quart saucepan, heat butter, margarine, or oil. Add well-drained rice and salt. Stir and cook

over moderate heat until rice is dry and begins to stick to the bottom and sides of the pan.

3. Turn rice into 2 cups boiling water in a 2-quart casserole or baking pan which has a tight-fitting cover. Bake, covered, in a preheated moderate oven (350°) 25 to 30 minutes or until rice has absorbed all the water and is tender. If desired, add 1 cup sliced mushrooms or 1 cup green peas to the rice at the time the boiling water is added.

SAUCE

3 tablespoons butter
2 tablespoons flour
½ teaspoon seasoned salt
1 teaspoon ground white pepper
1 teaspoon Maggi seasoning
1 tablespoon finely chopped parsley
1 tablespoon finely chopped bulb and top of green onion
1 tablespoon grated Parmesan cheese
2 tablespoons Marsala
1 clove garlic
3 cups chicken broth (homemade or canned)
Salt to taste

1. In a 2-quart saucepan, melt butter. Add flour and mix well. Cook over very low heat, stirring, 5 to 8 minutes.
2. Add the remaining 10 ingredients and beat until the mixture is smooth.
3. Pour the hot sauce over the browned guinea breasts.

MENU

Roast Breasts of Guinea Hen
Mandarin Orange and Bibb Lettuce Salad
Cherry Strudel

Several species of the juniper tree exist. They grow in both Europe and the United States. The dark blue juniper berry gives gin its characteristic flavor and it is used, discreetly, to flavor game, beef stew, and other dishes.

GUINEA HEN BLACKHAWK

(MAKES 4 SERVINGS)

WINE SUGGESTION: *Red Burgundy; Latricières-Chambertin*

This dish may be prepared ahead of time. Reheat just before serving.

2 ready-to-cook guinea hens (1½ to 2 pounds)
Salt
12 juniper berries
Butter
1 tablespoon cooking oil
1 tablespoon tomato purée
1 cup dry white wine
Quick Brown Sauce (recipe below)

1. Wash and dry guinea hens, and sprinkle them inside and out with salt.
2. In the body cavity of each hen, put 6 juniper berries and 1 teaspoon butter. Close openings with skewers and tie legs to the tails.
3. Preheat oven to 325° (slow).
4. In a flameproof casserole, heat 2 tablespoons butter and cooking oil. Add guinea hens and brown them on all sides.
5. Meanwhile, combine tomato purée and wine in a saucepan, heat, and pour the mixture over the browned guinea hens.
6. Place the guinea hens in the oven and roast 1 hour or until they are tender, basting occasionally with additional butter to keep them moist.
7. Remove guinea hens to a heated dish and keep warm.
8. Mix the Quick Brown Sauce with the pan juices in the casserole and heat.
9. Split guinea hens lengthwise, arrange them on a

warmed platter, and drizzle some of the sauce over them. Serve the remaining sauce in a sauceboat.

QUICK BROWN SAUCE

2 tablespoons butter
2 tablespoons flour
1½ cups hot beef consommé (canned)
Madeira

1. In a 1-quart saucepan, melt butter. Add flour, mix well, and cook, stirring, until flour and butter have browned.
2. Remove saucepan from the heat and gradually beat in the hot consommé.
3. Add Madeira to taste, just before mixing the sauce with the pan juices in the casserole.

Our first experience with this entrée was in Bordeaux, France. The restaurant was part shop and part upstairs dining room, both charming. There was every sort of *pâté de foie gras,* cheese, fruit, game, and such mouth-watering delicacies as shrimp, sausages, ham, mushrooms, and asparagus as thick as a wrist. The only difficulty was making the choice between woodcock or guinea hen. The guinea hen was superb.

SUPREMES DE POULE DE GUINEE

(MAKES 4 SERVINGS)

WINE SUGGESTION: *Red Burgundy; Chambertin, Lavaux St. Jacques*

2 ready-to-cook guinea hens (1¾ to 2¼ pounds each)
1 tablespoon butter
1 tablespoon cooking oil
½ cup dry white wine
1½ cups sour cream
⅛ teaspoon lemon juice
Cayenne to taste
Quick Brown Sauce (see recipe p. 173)
2 tablespoons dry sherry
4 slices French bread sautéed in butter
1 can (8 ounces) pâté de foie gras

1. Wash and dry guinea hens and remove the breasts in slices. Reserve the remaining guinea meat for another dish.
2. In a large heavy skillet, heat butter and oil. Add the sliced breast meat and cook until brown on both sides and tender, adding more butter and oil if needed.
3. Remove the breast meat to a baking pan, cover, and place in a slow oven to keep warm.
4. To the pan juices in the same skillet, add white wine, sour cream, lemon juice, cayenne, and Quick Brown Sauce. See page 173. Mix well. Stir in sherry and strain through a sieve.
5. Arrange the *suprêmes* (browned breast meat) on the slices of sautéed French bread, spread with *pâté de foie gras* and serve with the hot sauce spooned over the top.

MENU

Suprêmes de Poule de Guinée
Rice
Mixed Green Salad
Chilled Fresh Fruit Compote

Then came the breasts of guinea hen Colbert, one of the finest dishes we ever ate. This small bird originated in Africa, but is now domesticated in America and in Europe and is related to the chicken, partridge, and turkey. Although its meat is darker and gamier than chicken, it can be prepared like chicken or like a game bird.

BREAST OF GUINEA HEN COLBERT

(MAKES 6 SERVINGS)

WINE SUGGESTION: *Red Burgundy; Sebastiani Barbera*

Sauce Colbert may be prepared ahead of time and reheated before serving.

6 breasts of guinea hen
6 tablespoons (3/4 stick) butter, melted
Juice of 1/2 medium lemon
Salt
Freshly ground black pepper
Powdered mustard
Fine dry bread crumbs
6 slices buttered toast
Sauce Colbert (recipe below)

1. Set oven control to broil.
2. Ask your poultry butcher to bone the guinea hen breasts, leaving the wings attached.
3. Blend melted butter with lemon juice and dip each breast into the mixture. Then sprinkle them with salt, black pepper, and mustard.
4. Roll breasts in bread crumbs and arrange them on a rack in a shallow roasting pan.
5. Place the breasts in an electric oven, with heat control set to broil 8 inches from the source of heat. Broil 10 minutes or until breasts are tender and browned on both sides. Or, broil in a gas oven, 4 inches from the source of heat at 400° for 10 minutes.
6. Place broiled breasts on buttered toast and spoon Sauce Colbert over them. Serve hot.

SAUCE COLBERT

1/4 pound (1 stick) butter, melted
Dash cayenne
1/2 teaspoon chopped fresh chervil *
1/2 teaspoon chopped fresh chives
1/2 teaspoon chopped fresh tarragon
1 1/2 teaspoons chopped fresh parsley
1/2 teaspoon powdered mustard
2 chicken bouillon cubes
3 tablespoons hot water
1 tablespoon Madeira

1. In a small saucepan, combine butter, cayenne, all the herbs, and mustard.
2. Dissolve bouillon cubes in the hot water, add to the butter mixture, mix well, and simmer over very low heat for 5 minutes.
3. Stir in Madeira just before serving. Heat but do not boil. Serve over broiled guinea hen breasts.

MENU

Breasts of Guinea Hen Colbert
Nut Pilaf
Cucumber Salad
Fresh Plums *Assorted Cookies*

Napoleon had nothing to do with Napoleon brandy. The public demanded that kind of nonsense, and the directors of the distilleries have had to comply. In the past, people thought brandy of such small account

* If fresh herbs are not available, replace them with 1/4 teaspoon each dried chervil, chives, and tarragon.

that they would pour it freely into their chafing dishes, to the great improvement of their senses.

The not too well known but noble liquid armagnac comes from the vineyards south of Bordeaux, in Gascony. There are many who prefer a good armagnac to all but the very finest cognac.

POULE A L'ARMAGNAC

(MAKES 4 SERVINGS)

WINE SUGGESTION: *Beaujolais; Morgon*

Steps 1 through 7 may be prepared ahead of time.

1 ready-to-cook guinea fowl (4 pounds)
Salt and ground black pepper
3 tablespoons butter
1 tablespoon cooking oil
12 very small white onions
1 cup sliced raw mushrooms
2/3 cup dry white wine
1/4 cup armagnac
2 pairs veal sweetbreads
Cold water
1 quart boiling water
1 tablespoon lemon juice or vinegar
2 sprigs parsley
1 tablespoon chopped onion
3 peppercorns (whole black peppers)
1/3 cup flour seasoned with 1/2 teaspoon salt and 1/8 teaspoon ground black pepper
Butter
Sauce Soubise (recipe below)
Toast points

1. Preheat oven to 350° (moderate).
2. Wash and dry guinea fowl, leave whole, and sprinkle inside and out with salt and ground black pepper.
3. In a large flameproof casserole, heat 1 tablespoon butter and the oil. Add guinea fowl and brown it on all sides, adding additional butter and oil if needed.

4. Add onions and mushrooms, and pour wine and armagnac over them and the guinea fowl. Place in the oven and cook, covered, 1 hour or until tender.
5. Meanwhile, soak sweetbreads in cold water 1 hour, changing the water several times.
6. In a 2½-quart saucepan, put boiling water, lemon juice, or vinegar (acid helps keep sweetbreads white and firm), parsley, chopped onion, peppercorns, and sweetbreads. Cover and simmer 20 minutes. (Do not boil.)
7. Remove sweetbreads from hot water. Hold them under running cold water immediately and slip off membranes with fingers. Cut out the dark veins and thick connective tissue. Then cut sweetbreads in half lengthwise. Refrigerate unless they are to be cooked immediately.
8. Sprinkle sweetbreads lightly with salt and black pepper and roll in flour. Cook in a heavy skillet in hot butter, using 2 tablespoons or more if needed, until lightly browned on both sides. Set aside and keep hot while carving the guinea fowl.
9. Remove guinea fowl to a warmed platter and cut it into quarters, reserving the pan juices to use in Sauce Soubise.
10. Place a quarter of guinea fowl and a serving of mushrooms and onions on each of 4 warmed serving plates. Arrange sweetbreads on toast points next to the guinea fowl. Spoon some of the Sauce Soubise over the guinea fowl. Pass the remaining sauce in a sauceboat.

SAUCE SOUBISE

½ pound small white onions, peeled and minced
2 tablespoons butter
½ cup chicken broth (homemade or canned)
½ cup pan juices or enough to cover onions
1 cup Béchamel Sauce (Basic White Sauce)

1. Sauté onions in butter until they are soft and clear.
2. Add chicken broth and pan juices. Cook, stirring occasionally, until onions are almost puréed.

3. Stir in Béchamel Sauce. Heat only until sauce is hot, stirring frequently.

MENU

Poule à l'Armagnac
Brown Rice
Endive and Watercress Salad
Tortoni

South Americans use sweet potatoes and plantains (green bananas) extensively, especially in the hot jungle lowlands where both these important foods are grown in profusion. Even a housewife living in Bogotá, Colombia, where it is high and cool, will know any number of ways to prepare the green bananas. Plantains are available in New York and other cities in Spanish groceries.

Chicken does very well in this recipe if guinea hen is not available.

SOUTH AMERICAN GUINEA HEN

(MAKES 4 TO 6 SERVINGS)

WINE SUGGESTION: *Red Bordeaux; Château Léoville Las Cases (St.-Julien)*

Steps 1 through 6 may be prepared ahead of time.

2 ready-to-cook guinea hens (3 pounds each)
4 tablespoons (1/2 stick) butter
1 small onion, chopped
1 small clove garlic, finely chopped
1 tablespoon flour
3/4 cup dry white wine
1 cup water

2 teaspoons salt or salt to taste
½ teaspoon ground black pepper
1 bay leaf
3 tomatoes, chopped
3 medium sweet potatoes, pared and cubed
5 medium green-tipped bananas, sliced 1 inch thick

1. Wash and dry guinea hens. Heat 3 tablespoons of the butter in a large, heavy flameproof casserole. Add guinea hens, onion, and garlic. Cook until guinea hens are brown on all sides, turning often and sprinkling with flour as they cook.
2. Add wine, water, salt, black pepper, bay leaf, and tomatoes. Mix well, but gently. Cook, covered, over low heat 20 minutes.
3. Add sweet potatoes and cook, covered, 35 minutes or until guinea hens are tender. Adjust seasonings.
4. In a heavy 12-inch skillet, melt the remaining 2 tablespoons butter. Add bananas and sauté them slowly until they can be easily pierced with a fork.
5. Serve whole or quartered guinea hens in the center of a large warmed platter circled with the sweet potatoes and bananas.
6. From the pan juices in the casserole, skim off and discard the fat. Serve the remaining pan juices as gravy, in a sauceboat, to spoon over the guinea hens.

Coconuts are frequently used in South American cooking. This large, round fruit of a tropical palm tree has a delicious, white meat and a sweetish, liquid called coconut milk. It is a refreshing drink and is frequently used in cooking.

GUINEA FOWL IN COCONUT MILK

(MAKES 4 TO 6 SERVINGS)

WINE SUGGESTION: *Red Bordeaux; Château Rausan-Ségla (Margaux)*

This dish may be prepared ahead of time. Reheat before serving.

2 guinea fowls (3 pounds each)
4 tablespoons (½ stick) butter
1½ tablespoons fresh lemon juice
1½ cups sliced raw mushrooms
¾ cup boiling water
¼ cup coconut milk (recipe below)
1½ teaspoons salt or salt to taste
¼ teaspoon ground black pepper
¼ teaspoon ground mace
2½ teaspoons arrowroot
1 cup light cream

1. Preheat oven to 450° (very hot).
2. Wash and dry guinea fowls and cut them into serving pieces.
3. In a heavy 12-inch skillet, heat butter and lemon juice. Add guinea fowl, as many pieces at a time as the skillet will accommodate without crowding, and cook until browned on both sides.
4. Place the browned pieces of guinea fowl in a large casserole, overlapping one another. Add mushrooms, water, coconut milk, salt, black pepper, and mace.
5. Reduce oven heat to 350° (moderate) and put the casserole in the oven. Roast, covered, 1 hour. Adjust seasonings.
6. Blend arrowroot with cream and add to the casserole. Roast 15 minutes longer.
7. Serve at the table from the casserole or if desired, arrange the guinea fowls on a warmed platter.

COCONUT MILK

In a small saucepan, heat ½ cup milk and add ¼ cup grated fresh or dried coconut. Cover and let the mixture stand 1 hour. Strain and use only the liquid.

MENU

Guinea Fowl in Coconut Milk
Steamed Wild Rice
Tomato and Avocado Salad
Blueberry Cheesecake

PARTRIDGE

Grimod de la Reynière (author of the Almanach des gourmands*) has said that partridges merit such profound respect they should be eaten kneeling.*

ALEXANDRE DUMAS

Garlic is a plant whose bulb or head is greatly prized as a seasoning. This bulb consists of smaller cloves which are broken off individually. Strong and distinctive in taste and aroma, it is excellent rubbed on meat, minced or crushed in casseroles and sauces. It is obtainable as garlic salt (ground garlic plus salt), the stronger garlic powder or minced garlic, and in the form of garlic juice.

PERDRIX AU CHOUX

(MAKES 4 SERVINGS)

WINE SUGGESTION: *White Burgundy; Pouilly-Fuissé*

This dish may be prepared ahead of time. Reheat before serving.

2 ready-to-cook partridges
Salt and ground black pepper
3 tablespoons butter
2-pound head of cabbage
Boiling water
½ pound breast of pork, sliced
Bacon
1 medium carrot, scraped and left whole
1 medium onion, studded with 1 whole clove

3 sprigs parsley or 1/2 teaspoon dried parsley
1 sprig fresh marjoram or 1/4 teaspoon dried marjoram } *bouquet garni*
1 bay leaf
1/4 pound chipolata sausage
1/2 pound uncooked garlic sausage
About 4 cups chicken broth (homemade or canned)

1. Wash and dry partridges and sprinkle them inside and out with salt and black pepper.
2. In a heavy skillet, melt butter. Add partridges and brown them on all sides over moderate heat. Set aside.
3. Remove and discard outer leaves from cabbage head. Separate the remaining leaves and parboil them in boiling water to cover 4 to 5 minutes. Remove cabbage leaves from the water and drain them.
4. Meanwhile, put pork in the same water in which cabbage was parboiled. Bring water to boiling point, reduce heat, and simmer 15 minutes. Remove pork from water and drain.
5. Line a large flameproof casserole with bacon and one-third of the cabbage leaves. On the cabbage leaves, put partridges, carrot, onion, and *bouquet garni.* Cover with half the remaining cabbage leaves.
6. Cover cabbage leaves with sliced pork, chipolatas, and garlic sausage. Cover with the remaining cabbage leaves.
7. Pour enough chicken broth in the casserole to cover all the ingredients. Bring broth to boiling point over surface heat, and then reduce heat to simmer.
8. Cover casserole with a piece of buttered brown paper cut to fit it. Cover brown paper with casserole lid. Simmer 30 minutes.
9. When partridges are almost done, remove sausage and chipolatas and keep them warm. Adjust salt and simmer the remaining ingredients in the casserole 15 minutes longer. Then remove pork and keep it warm. Continue simmering 15 minutes more or until partridges are tender.

10. Remove cabbage leaves from the casserole, drain them well, place them in the center of a warmed platter. Split partridges in half lengthwise and place them, cut side down, on the cabbage. Surround with chipolatas, sliced sausage, and sliced pork.
11. Remove and discard *bouquet garni,* carrot, and onion from the cooking liquid. Pass the remaining cooking liquid in a sauceboat to spoon over the partridges.

MENU

Perdrix au Choux
Barley Pilaf
Cucumber and Watercress Salad
Mangoes   *Macaroons*

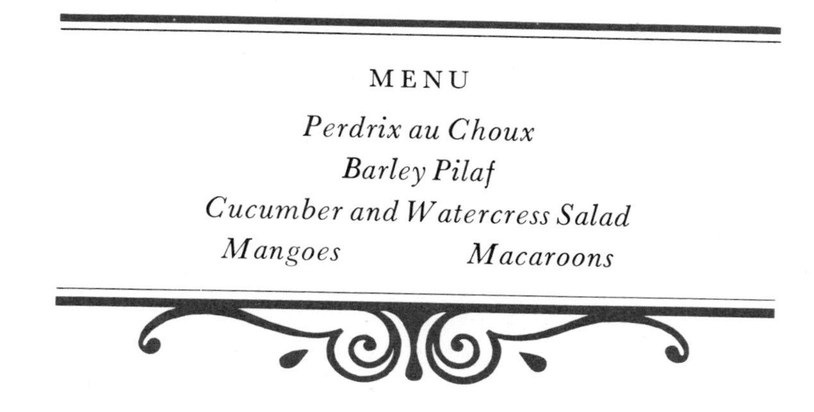

The artichoke is a thistlelike garden plant with a flowering edible head which is generally steamed or boiled and then served hot or cold with melted butter, mayonnaise, or hollandaise sauce. Artichokes can be served either as a vegetable or as an appetizer.

PERDRIX AUX ARTICHAUTS

(MAKES 2 SERVINGS)

WINE SUGGESTION: *Red Graves (Bordeaux)*

This dish may be prepared ahead of time. Reheat before serving.

2 ready-to-cook partridges
Salt and ground black pepper
3 tablespoons butter
3 tablespoons cooking oil
3 medium tomatoes, peeled
1 large sweet onion, sliced

1 clove garlic, sliced
1 dozen artichoke hearts (frozen or canned)
1 bay leaf
1½ cups beef broth (homemade or canned)

1. Preheat oven to 400° (hot).
2. Wash and dry partridges and sprinkle inside and out with salt and black pepper.
3. In a heavy skillet, heat 2 tablespoons of the butter and 2 tablespoons of the oil. Add partridges and brown them on all sides. Remove birds to a flameproof casserole and set aside.
4. In the same skillet (do not wash), heat the remaining 1 tablespoon butter and 1 tablespoon oil. Add tomatoes, onion, and garlic. Cook until onions are golden and limp, and spread the vegetables over the partridges. Add artichokes, bay leaf, and beef broth.
5. Cover casserole, place in the oven, and cook 1 hour. Remove and discard bay leaf.
6. Split the partridges lengthwise and serve skin side up with the vegetables and the sauce.

MENU

Perdrix aux Artichauts
Lyonnaise Potatoes
Cherry Tomatoes
Fresh Peaches and Blueberries with
Sour Cream and Brown Sugar

If you have a choice, take a gray partridge over a red one. The meat is more tender and the flavor is better. Hunters say partridge should be eaten as soon as it is shot. Obviously, this is not always possible, but it should be eaten within two or three days.

PARTRIDGE CHASSEUR

(MAKES 3 TO 6 SERVINGS)

WINE SUGGESTION: *White Burgundy; Corton-Charlemagne (Aloxe-Corton)*

This dish may be prepared ahead of time. Reheat before serving.

3 ready-to-cook partridges, disjointed
Salt and ground black pepper
2 tablespoons butter
¼ cup brandy
4 teaspoons chopped fresh chives or freeze-dried chives
1 tablespoon chopped parsley
⅛ teaspoon ground thyme
⅛ teaspoon ground marjoram
2 tablespoons flour
1 cup beef consommé (homemade or canned)
½ cup dry white wine
2 cups sliced fresh mushrooms

1. Wash and dry partridges and sprinkle them with salt and black pepper.
2. In a heavy 12-inch skillet, melt butter until it foams. Add partridges and brown them on all sides, about 15 minutes.
3. Pour brandy over the birds, ignite, and when the flame dies down, add all the herbs. Cook the birds 2 to 3 minutes more. Then sprinkle the birds with flour and mix with the pan juices.
4. Add consommé, wine, and mushrooms. Simmer, covered, 25 to 30 minutes or until the birds are tender. Adjust seasonings.
5. Arrange partridges on a warmed platter and pour the pan sauce over them. Garnish with croutons.

MENU

Partridge Chasseur
O'Brien Potatoes
Sautéed Brussels Sprouts
Chocolate Meringues

PHEASANT

The pheasant is an enigma, the solution of which is revealed only to the adept. Only they can savor it in all its goodness.

Each substance has its apogee of succulence. Some reach it before maturity—for example, capers, asparagus, gray partridge, and squab. For others it is reached at the moment they attain the full perfection of their destiny, like mutton, beef, roe deer, and red partridges. Others, finally, when they begin to decompose—the medlar, the woodcock, and above all the pheasant.

This bird, eaten within three days of his death, is undistinguished. It is neither so delicate as a fatted chicken nor so flavorful as a quail.

But taken at its point of perfection, its flesh is tender, sublime, and wonderfully savory, for it partakes of the virtues of both poultry and venison.

That so desirable point is reached when the pheasant begins to decompose. Then its aroma develops and mingles with an oil that requires a little fermentation for its distillation, just as coffee requires roasting for its full development.

To the ordinary person, this moment is discovered through a faint odor and a change in the color of the bird's belly. But those truly inspired divine it by a sort of instinct that manifests itself in various ways, similar, for example, to that which tells a cook glancing at a bird on the spit whether it must be removed immediately or left for a few more turns.

ANTHELME BRILLAT-SAVARIN

Calvados and pheasant make a perfect combination and the simplicity of this recipe is unbelievable. If pheasant is not available substitute guinea fowl or chicken.

FAISAN NANCY

(MAKES 2 TO 4 SERVINGS)

WINE SUGGESTION: *Domestic White Burgundy; Korbel Cabernet Sauvignon*

Steps 1 through 7 may be prepared ahead of time.

2 small ready-to-cook pheasants
Salt and ground black pepper
4 tablespoons (½ stick) butter
2 tablespoons cooking oil
6 medium apples, peeled and minced
¾ cup heavy cream
1 cup apple cider
¾ cup Calvados

1. Preheat oven to 450° (very hot).
2. Wash and dry pheasants thoroughly. Sprinkle them inside and out with salt and black pepper. Set aside.
3. In a heavy 10- or 12-inch skillet, heat 2 tablespoons of the butter and the oil, add pheasants, and brown them on all sides over moderate heat.
4. Meanwhile, melt the remaining 2 tablespoons butter in another heavy skillet or in a saucepot, add apples, and sauté them, turning frequently.
5. Place half of the sautéed apples in the bottom of a casserole, place pheasants on top of the apples, and cover them with the remaining sautéed apples. Then pour cream over the top.
6. Roast, uncovered, 20 minutes.
7. Remove casserole from the oven and pour in the apple cider. Return casserole to the oven and roast, uncovered, 30 to 35 minutes longer or until pheasants are tender.
8. Heat Calvados, pour it over the top of the casserole, and ignite. Let the dish stand long enough for the Calvados and the juice from the casserole to blend.

9. Remove pheasants from the casserole, cut them into serving pieces, and arrange them on a warmed platter. Spoon apples around them. Serve piping hot.

I love to prepare a recipe that can go into the oven and to the table in its own baking dish. This exquisite entrée originated in Dijon, in Burgundy. It has been honored since the gallant days of the Burgundian dukes.

PHEASANT IN THICK CREAM

(MAKES 2 SERVINGS)

WINE SUGGESTION: *White Burgundy; Meursault Casse Tête*

This dish may be prepared ahead of time. Reheat before serving.

1 small ready-to-cook pheasant
Salt and ground black pepper to taste
Butter
1 small onion, cut in half
½ cup heavy cream
Lemon juice to taste

1. Preheat oven to 350° (moderate).
2. Wash and dry pheasant thoroughly. Sprinkle it inside and out with salt and black pepper.
3. Put ½ teaspoon of the butter in the body cavity of the pheasant. Close opening with a skewer.

4. In an elegant medium-sized casserole (your prettiest one) melt 2 tablespoons butter. Add onion halves, and place pheasant, breast side down, in the melted butter.
5. Cover casserole and roast pheasant 30 minutes. Turn pheasant breast side up, and pour the cream over it. Continue roasting, uncovered, 20 to 30 minutes or until tender.
6. Remove and discard onion, adjust seasoning, and add lemon juice to taste, 1 to 2 drops at a time, until the sauce is correctly seasoned.

MENU

Pheasant in Thick Cream
Baked Hubbard Squash
Hot Marinated Green Beans
Fresh Strawberries in Orange Liqueur

In Bougival, France, there is a fascinating little spot with a quaint dining room and walls hung with copper pans. There is also a huge rotisserie turning in front of wood coals. The food is not big-city fancy but is prepared with love and great care. Pheasant Marguerite has never failed.

PHEASANT MARGUERITE

(MAKES 2 SERVINGS)

WINE SUGGESTION: *Red Bordeaux; Château Rausan-Ségla (Margaux)*

This dish may be prepared ahead of time. Reheat before serving.

1 small ready-to-cook pheasant, disjointed
Salt and ground black pepper to taste
3 to 4 tablespoons flour
4 small white onions, peeled and left whole
1/4 teaspoon dried marjoram

¼ teaspoon dried thyme
1 tablespoon chopped parsley
Butter
5 ribs of celery with leaves
½ cup beef consommé
½ cup dry red wine

1. Preheat oven to 400° (hot).
2. Wash and dry pheasant thoroughly and sprinkle inside and out with salt and black pepper.
3. Put flour in a paper bag, add pheasant pieces and shake the bag to coat them with flour. Place pheasant in a Dutch oven or small roasting pan.
4. Arrange onions around the pheasant and sprinkle with marjoram, thyme, and parsley. Dot pheasant generously with pieces of butter the size of grapes.
5. Lay celery ribs across the pheasant and onions. Pour consommé and wine over all.
6. Roast, covered, ½ hour, basting once with the pan liquids.
7. Reduce oven temperature to 300° (slow). Continue roasting, covered, 1½ hours, basting every ½ hour with the pan liquids. Add more wine if needed.
8. Remove cover and increase oven temperature to 375° (moderate) to brown pheasant quickly. Adjust seasonings.
9. Remove pheasant to a warmed platter and place onions and celery around it.
10. Add a little more wine to the roasting pan and scrape up all the browned bits from the bottom and sides of the pan. Place over moderate heat only until hot. Spoon the gravy over the pheasant and vegetables.

MENU

Pheasant Marguerite
Wild Rice
Buttered Broccoli
Chocolate Éclairs

This is as easy as boiling an egg. There are hundreds of cold chicken dishes but not too many hostesses serve cold pheasant. It is perfect for buffet service, and, since it must be prepared in advance so it can chill properly, it leaves the hostess free when guests arrive.

COLD BUFFET PHEASANT

(MAKES 6 TO 8 SERVINGS)

WINE SUGGESTION: *Red Burgundy; Chevret (Volnay)*

This dish should be prepared the day before serving.

2 ready-to-cook pheasants
Salt and ground black pepper
1 cup dry white wine, heated
1 cup hot chicken broth (homemade or canned)

1. Preheat oven to 400° (hot).
2. Wash and dry pheasants thoroughly. Sprinkle them inside and out with salt and black pepper.
3. Put pheasants, breasts up, in a large casserole. Place them in the oven and roast, uncovered, 10 minutes.
4. Reduce oven temperature to 350° (moderate) and continue roasting for 1 hour or until pheasants are tender, basting frequently with a mixture of hot wine and chicken broth.
5. Remove pheasants from the oven and let them cool completely in the juices. Then refrigerate in the juices so the juices will jell.
6. When ready to serve, remove pheasants from the jellied pan liquid and cut them into small pieces. Arrange the pieces on a large chilled platter.
7. Slice and cube the jelly. Scatter the cubes around and over the pheasants.

MENU

Cold Buffet Pheasant
Asparagus Vinaigrette
French Bread and Butter
Cheese and Fruit

These lovely birds abound during the fall months, especially in the middle west. It's a hunter's paradise and everyone competes in an annual pheasant-cooking contest held at Crystal Falls, Michigan. This dish won first prize. Much of this recipe may be prepared in advance and refrigerated and it does not have to be rushed to the table.

ELOISE'S STUFFED PHEASANTS

(MAKES 6 SERVINGS)

WINE SUGGESTION: *Red Burgundy; Rugiens (Pommard)*

Ingredients for stuffing, bacon-wrapped livers, and the fruit garnish may be prepared for cooking ahead of time.

2 ready-to-cook pheasants (1½ pounds each)
Salt and ground black pepper
¼ pound pork sausage
¼ cup finely minced raw onion
½ cup finely chopped celery
2 cups soft bread crumbs
1½ teaspoons finely chopped parsley
¼ teaspoon dried sage
1 egg, beaten
2 tablespoons butter, melted
Salt pork
Bacon-wrapped Pheasant Livers and Sausage (recipe below)
Pineapple and Orange Garnish (recipe below)
Watercress
Gravy (recipe below)

1. Wash and dry pheasants thoroughly. Reserve livers to use later. Sprinkle body and neck cavities of pheasants with salt and black pepper. Set aside.
2. In a small skillet or saucepan, crumble sausage and brown it over low heat. With a slotted spoon, transfer sausage to a large bowl, leaving sausage drippings in the skillet.
3. In the sausage drippings, cook onion and celery until soft, adding a little butter if needed. Add the mixture to the cooked sausage.

4. Stir in bread crumbs, 1/8 teaspoon salt, sage, and parsley. Then add beaten egg and mix well.
5. Spoon the mixture loosely into the body and neck cavities of the pheasants. Close cavity openings with skewers. Tie legs to the tails.
6. Brush skin of pheasants with melted butter and sprinkle with salt and black pepper.
7. Place pheasants, breast up, on a rack in a roasting pan. Cover breasts, thighs, and wings with slices of salt pork to prevent the pheasant meat from becoming too dry.
8. Roast, uncovered, 2 hours or until pheasants can be pierced easily with the point of a knife.
9. Remove salt pork from pheasants 10 to 15 minutes before they are done to allow them to brown.
10. Remove pheasants from the oven and turn off heat. Spoon the stuffing into a warmed serving bowl, cover, and put in the oven to keep warm.
11. Place browned bacon-wrapped pheasant livers and sausage in the center of a warmed platter. Cut pheasants into serving pieces and arrange them around the livers and sausage. Then place the warmed pineapple and orange garnish around the pheasants. Tuck watercress around the edge of the platter to form a green border. Serve hot.
12. Pass hot gravy in a sauceboat to spoon over the pheasants and stuffing.

BACON-WRAPPED PHEASANT LIVERS AND SAUSAGE

2 pheasant livers, each cut into thirds
Salt
2 to 3 strips bacon
6 small link sausages

1. Sprinkle pheasant livers with salt.
2. Cut bacon strips in halves or thirds, depending upon the length of the bacon strips. Wrap a strip of bacon around each piece of liver. Hold ends in place with toothpicks.

3. Rub butter over the bottom of a heavy skillet, add bacon-wrapped livers and cook until browned on all sides over moderate heat. Serve hot with roast pheasant.
4. Brown sausages and serve hot with pheasant.

PINEAPPLE AND ORANGE GARNISH

6 slices canned pineapple
6 slices unpeeled navel oranges, cut 1/4 inch thick
6 maraschino cherries
Curaçao

1. Arrange pineapple slices in a shallow baking dish.
2. Place an orange slice and a maraschino cherry on each, and sprinkle with Curaçao.
3. Bake in the oven with the pheasant the last 15 minutes of the roasting time. Place on the platter around the pheasant.

GRAVY

Roasting pan drippings
Water, if needed
1 small onion, quartered
1 small bay leaf
1 small clove garlic, minced
4 peppercorns (whole black peppers)
1/8 teaspooon ground thyme
Salt to taste

1. Skim off and discard fat from the roasting pan. Place the pan over moderately low heat and scrape up all the browned bits from the bottom and sides of the pan.
2. Add water, 1 1/2 to 2 tablespoons, if needed, onion, bay leaf, garlic, peppercorns, and thyme. Bring the mixture to boiling point and add salt to taste.
3. Strain gravy into a sauceboat and pass it at the table to serve over the pheasant and stuffing.

MENU

Eloise's Stuffed Pheasant
Boston Lettuce Salad
Lemon Chiffon Pie

Celery is eaten either raw as an hors d'oeuvre or in salads, or (especially in Europe) cooked and braised. Good celery is always crisp and the leaves, delicious in soups and stews, should not appear wilted or yellowish.

ROAST PHEASANT MARCHAND

(MAKES 6 SERVINGS)

WINE SUGGESTION: *Red Burgundy; Château Montrose (St.-Estèphe)*

The ingredients for the stuffing in this recipe may be prepared ahead of time and refrigerated. Stuff pheasants just before putting them in the oven.

2 ready-to-cook pheasants (2 to 3 pounds each)
Salt and ground black pepper
3 cups soft bread crumbs
6 tablespoons (¾ stick) butter, melted
2 cups diced celery
2 tablespoons grated orange peel
⅛ teaspoon dried chervil
⅛ teaspoon dried marjoram
⅛ teaspoon dried rosemary
⅔ cup diced orange sections
1 egg, beaten
½ cup brandy
1 cup dry red wine

1. Wash and dry pheasants thoroughly. Sprinkle salt and black pepper in the body and neck cavities.

2. Preheat oven to 350° (moderate).
3. In a heavy 2-quart saucepan, sauté bread crumbs in 2 tablespoons of the melted butter. Add celery, grated orange peel, chervil, marjoram, rosemary, and salt and black pepper to taste. Mix well, but lightly.
4. Stir in diced orange sections, egg, brandy, and the remaining 4 tablespoons melted butter. Spoon the mixture loosely into the body and neck cavities of the pheasants. Close openings with skewers and tie legs to the tails.
5. Sprinkle skins of pheasants with salt and black pepper and pour wine over them. Place them on a rack in a roasting pan.
6. Put pheasants in the oven and roast, uncovered, 20 minutes per pound, basting occasionally with the wine. Add more wine if needed.
7. Remove pheasants from the oven and spoon the stuffing into a warmed serving bowl. Cut pheasants into serving pieces, place them on a warmed platter, and spoon the pan drippings over them. Serve promptly.

This is a magnificent feast for either a cold or hot buffet. A small turkey or two small chickens may be substituted if pheasants are not available.

PHEASANT PROVENCAL

(MAKES 4 TO 6 SERVINGS)

WINE SUGGESTION: *Red Burgundy; Gevrey-Chambertin (Moillard-Grivot)*

This dish may be prepared ahead of time. Reheat before serving if serving hot.

2 ready-to-cook pheasants, cut into serving pieces
1 teaspoon salt
1/4 teaspoon ground black pepper
1/2 cup flour
1/4 cup cooking oil
1 medium green pepper, cut into lengthwise strips
4 small white onions, chopped
1 small clove garlic, chopped
1 1/2 cups canned tomatoes, cut in pieces
1/2 cup beef consommé (homemade or canned)
1/2 cup Marsala
1 cup sliced raw mushrooms
1/4 teaspoon dried oregano

1. Wash and dry pheasants thoroughly. Rub with salt and black pepper and dredge with flour.
2. In a deep, large heavy skillet or Dutch oven, heat oil. Add pheasants and brown them on all sides over moderate heat.
3. Mix green pepper, onions, garlic, and tomatoes. Add to the pheasants. Then pour in consommé and Marsala. Simmer, covered, 1 hour.
4. Add mushrooms and simmer, covered, 1/2 hour, adding oregano 10 minutes before cooking time is up.

MENU

Pheasant Provençal
Boiled Tiny Potatoes with Chopped Fresh Dill
Braised Red Cabbage
Cheese: Port du Salut, Tilsit, Blue
Madeira Wine

Green pepper is a mild and decorative variety of pepper used many ways—sliced or as a salad ingredient, as a vegetable when stuffed, and as a flavoring in various cooked sauces. Here it combines with mushrooms, onion, and rice to make a hearty, flavorsome meal—perfect for brisk fall weather.

FAISAN AU VIN

(MAKES 2 SERVINGS)

WINE SUGGESTION: *Red Bordeaux; Château Latour*

This dish may be prepared ahead of time. Reheat before serving.

1 ready-to-cook pheasant
Salt and ground black pepper
2 tablespoons shortening
1 medium onion, sliced
½ medium green pepper, thinly sliced
⅔ cup white port wine, sauterne, or sweet sherry
1 can (10½ ounces) cream of mushroom soup, undiluted
1 can (4 ounces) sliced mushrooms
2 teaspoons prepared horseradish
½ cup wild rice

1. Wash pheasant and dry it thoroughly. Cut into serving pieces and sprinkle with salt and black pepper.
2. In a deep, heavy skillet or Dutch oven, melt shortening. Add pheasant and brown on all sides. Transfer pheasant to a casserole.
3. In the same skillet or Dutch oven, sauté onion and green pepper in the pan drippings. Add wine, mushroom soup, mushrooms, and horseradish. Mix well, but gently. Heat and pour over the pheasant. Adjust salt.
4. Roast, covered, 1 hour or until pheasant is tender.
5. Meanwhile, cook ½ cup wild rice according to package directions and turn it onto a warmed platter. Arrange pheasant over the rice and serve hot.

MENU

Faisan au Vin
Sautéed Summer Squash
Mixed Green Salad with Sliced Black Olives
Buttered Toasted Saltines with
Cream Cheese and Bar-le-Duc

The pecan, with its elongated shape and smooth, brown texture, invites further discovery. Its versatility and its sweet, delicious flavor make it the most popular and economically important nut in America.

The pecan was discovered by the American Indians. It grew wild and in great abundance. The Indians not only ate the nutmeat but also used it to season hominy and corn cakes, to concoct a beverage, and to thicken venison broth. Its name comes from the Indian word for *bone shell* based on the hard-shelled pecan with which we are acquainted.

PHEASANT WITH PECANS

(MAKES 4 TO 6 SERVINGS)

WINE SUGGESTION: *Red Burgundy; Clos du Roi (Beaune)*

2 ready-to-cook pheasants
Salt and ground black pepper
8 tablespoons (1 stick) butter
1 cup fine dry bread crumbs
1/4 cup pecan halves
1 1/2 tablespoons cornstarch
1 1/2 cups beef or chicken broth (homemade or canned)
1/4 cup dry sherry
1 tablespoon heavy cream (optional)
2 raw egg yolks (optional)

1. Wash and dry pheasants thoroughly. Sprinkle salt and black pepper in the neck and body cavities. Set aside.
2. Preheat oven to 350° (moderate).
3. Melt 4 tablespoons (½ stick) of the butter in a skillet, add bread crumbs and pecans, and mix well. Spoon the mixture into the body and neck cavities of the pheasants. Close openings to the cavities with skewers.
4. Blend cornstarch with ¾ teaspoon salt and ⅛ teaspoon black pepper, and rub the mixture over the skin of the pheasants.
5. In a large heavy skillet, melt the remaining 4 tablespoons (½ stick) butter. Add pheasants and brown them on all sides over moderate heat. Place pheasants on a rack in a roasting pan.
6. In a saucepan, heat beef or chicken broth and sherry. Pour the mixture over the pheasants. Roast, covered, 1 hour, basting with the pan liquid 3 to 4 times.
7. Remove cover from the roasting pan and roast ½ hour longer. Transfer pheasants to a large heated platter and keep warm.
8. If desired, blend cream with egg yolks, add to the pan juices. Stir and cook, over low heat, until the gravy has thickened. Do not boil. Serve at the table in a sauceboat to spoon over the pheasants and stuffing.

MENU

Pheasant with Pecans
Boiled New Potatoes
Tomatoes and Zucchini Vinaigrette
Pistachio Ice Cream or Orange Ice

If it weren't for the Renaissance we would never have known the great classic sauces nor would we have known how to cook fish, or glorify poultry. It was during the Renaissance that cooks began to use wines and spirits extensively in preparing meat, game, and fish. This recipe's use of brandy is principally responsible for its distinctive taste.

TIPSY PHEASANT

(MAKES 6 TO 8 SERVINGS)

WINE SUGGESTION: *Domestic White Burgundy; Martin Ray Pinot Chardonnay*

This dish may be prepared ahead of time. Reheat before serving.

4 ready-to-cook pheasants, quartered
Salt and ground black pepper
Butter
4 tablespoons cooking oil
1 cup brandy
1 cup chicken broth (homemade or canned)
1 large onion, chopped
1 clove garlic, crushed
1 quart heavy cream or beaten cottage cheese
1 jar (10 ounces) horseradish
½ pound button mushrooms (fresh or frozen)

1. Preheat oven to 350° (moderate).
2. Rub salt and black pepper over all sides of the pheasant.
3. In each of 2 heavy, 12-inch skillets, heat 4 tablespoons butter and 2 tablespoons cooking oil. Put as many pieces of the pheasant in the hot butter and oil as the skillets will accommodate. Cook until pheasant is brown on both sides, adding additional butter and oil if needed.
4. Arrange pheasants, in a single layer, in a 17¼ x 11½ x 2¼-inch roasting pan.
5. In a 1-quart saucepan, heat brandy, pour over pheasants, and ignite. When the flame dies out, add chicken broth, onion, and garlic. Place pheasant in the oven and roast, uncovered, ½ hour, basting 3 times with brandy.

6. Remove pheasants from the oven and pour cream or cottage cheese and all the horseradish over them. Continue roasting 1½ hours longer. Adjust salt.
7. Meanwhile, cook mushrooms in 2 tablespoons butter and spoon them over the pheasants. Serve with buttered noodles.

This is one of the most versatile dishes I have found. It may be served for luncheon, dinner, as a casserole dish, or as a buffet supper for summer, winter, or fall. The delicate flavor of the cream of celery soup is lovely.

FAISAN ORIENTAL

(MAKES 4 SERVINGS)

BEVERAGE SUGGESTION: *Assorted beers*

This dish may be prepared for baking ahead of time. Bake just before serving.

1 ready-to-cook pheasant, quartered
1 teaspoon salt
Water to cover
2 slices onion
6 whole allspice
Leaves from 1 rib of celery
1 can (10½ ounces) cream of celery soup, undiluted

¼ cup pheasant stock
1 can (4 ounces) sliced mushrooms, drained
½ teaspoon parsley flakes
1 teaspoon curry powder
2 tablespoons chopped pimento
Paprika

1. Preheat oven to 350° (moderate).
2. In a Dutch oven or large saucepot, place pheasant, salt, and enough water to cover pheasant. Add onion, allspice, and celery. Cover, bring water to boiling point, reduce heat, and simmer until pheasant is tender (from 1 to 1½ hours).
3. Cool pheasant in the broth. Then remove meat from the bones and cut it into cubes. Set aside.
4. In a large bowl, combine celery soup, pheasant stock, mushrooms, parsley flakes, curry powder, pimento, and salt and black pepper to taste. Mix well. Stir in the cubed pheasant meat.
5. Turn the mixture into a buttered 1-quart casserole. Bake, covered, 40 to 45 minutes. Serve hot over steamed rice and garnish with paprika.

MENU

Faisan Oriental
Steamed Rice
Brussels Sprouts and Water Chestnuts
Mélange of Fruits

This is a most unusual method for preparing pheasant and it is a perfect dinner after you have spent the afternoon in the pool or on the tennis court. And nothing could be simpler for serving a crowd.

SUMMERTIME PHEASANT

(MAKES 3 TO 4 SERVINGS)

BEVERAGE SUGGESTION: *A selection of fine beers*

The pheasant may be cooked and the batter for frying may be made ahead of time and refrigerated. Fry just before serving.

1 ready-to-cook pheasant, cut into serving pieces
1 teaspoon salt
Water to cover
1½ cups flour
½ teaspoon salt
1½ cups beer
Peanut oil for frying

1. In a Dutch oven or large saucepot, place pheasant, the 1 teaspoon salt, and water to cover. Bring the water to boiling point, reduce heat, and simmer, covered, until pheasant is tender. Cool pheasant in the stock.
2. Meanwhile, combine flour and the ½ teaspoon salt in a large bowl. Beat in beer. Continue beating until the batter is smooth. Refrigerate at least 1 hour.
3. Pour oil into a heavy deep skillet to a depth of 1 inch. Heat until the oil swirls.
4. Dip pheasant pieces into the batter and drop them in the hot oil. Fry until pheasant is crisp and brown. Drain on paper towels. Serve very hot.

MENU

Summertime Pheasant
Rice with Parsley Garnish
Coleslaw
Diced Fresh Fruit with Sherbet

If I had to decide between French or Italian cooking, I would be at a total loss. This light and flavorsome pheasant dish was served in Venice, Italy.

VENETIAN PHEASANT

(MAKES 4 SERVINGS)

WINE SUGGESTION: *Beaujolais; Morgon*

The pheasant may be crumbed, placed in a buttered baking pan, and refrigerated until ready to cook.

1 ready-to-cook pheasant (2½ pounds)
Salt and ground black pepper
1 cup seasoned stuffing mix
⅔ cup grated Parmesan cheese
¼ cup finely chopped parsley
½ cup (1 stick) butter, melted

1. Preheat oven to 375° (moderate).
2. Wash and dry pheasant and cut it into serving pieces. Sprinkle with salt and black pepper.
3. In a bowl, combine stuffing mix, Parmesan cheese, and parsley. Dip the pheasant pieces in the melted butter and then roll them in the crumbed stuffing mixture. Place the pieces in a shallow buttered baking pan far enough apart so the pieces do not touch.
4. Sprinkle pheasant with all the remaining crumb mixture and remaining melted butter.
5. Bake, uncovered, 1 hour or until the crumbs are brown and the pheasant is tender. Serve very hot.

MENU

Venetian Pheasant
Buttered Noodles
Green Beans with Toasted Almonds
Sliced Tomatoes
Tortoni

Plum sauce may be prepared days in advance and refrigerated. Any leftover sauce may be frozen and used as needed for chicken, duck, or any fowl.

PHEASANT, PURPLE PLUM

(MAKES 6 TO 8 SERVINGS)

WINE SUGGESTION: *New York State Champagne, extra dry*

This dish may be prepared ahead of time.

2 ready-to-cook pheasants
Salt and ground black pepper
1 medium onion, cut in half
2 ribs celery, cut in pieces
2 medium unpeeled apples, sliced
4 slices bacon
Plum Sauce (recipe below)

1. Wash and dry pheasants thoroughly. Sprinkle with salt and black pepper inside and out.
2. Put ½ onion, 1 rib of sliced celery, and 1 sliced apple in the cavity of each pheasant. Close openings to cavities with small skewers and tie legs to the tails.
3. Place pheasants on a rack in a roasting pan and lay 2 strips of bacon over the breast of each. Roast, covered, 2 hours, basting with the plum sauce the last 30 minutes of the baking period.
4. Cut pheasants into serving pieces and arrange them on a warmed platter. Spoon some of the plum sauce over them. Serve the remaining plum sauce in a sauceboat.

PLUM SAUCE

1 can (1 pound) purple plums
¼ cup (½ stick) butter
¼ cup chopped onion
3 tablespoons lemon juice
1 cup light brown sugar
2 tablespoons chili sauce
1 teaspoon Worcestershire sauce
½ teaspoon ground ginger

1. Drain plums and reserve the liquid to use later.
2. Remove and discard pits and purée the plums in a blender or put them through a sieve.
3. In a 2-quart saucepan, melt butter. Add onion and cook until golden, stirring frequently.
4. Stir in lemon juice, brown sugar, chili sauce, Worcestershire sauce, ginger, plum purée, and the reserved plum liquid. Simmer, uncovered, 30 minutes, stirring frequently. Serve over pheasants.

MENU

Pheasant, Purple Plum
Fried Rice
Baby Peas and Onions
Mushroom Salad
Watermelon Wedges or Pineapple Sherbet

QUAIL

It was Autumn, and incessant
Piped the quails from shocks and sheaves,
And, like living coals, the apples
Burned among the withering leaves.

HENRY WADSWORTH LONGFELLOW

The water chestnut is the edible fruit, contained in a hard, nutlike husk, of an Asian plant that grows in water. Its meat is white and delicately sweet with a crisp texture. Water chestnuts, used whole, sliced or diced, are one of the staples of Oriental cookery.

QUAIL, CHINESE STYLE

(MAKES 4 SERVINGS)

BEVERAGE SUGGESTION: *Assorted beers*

This dish may be prepared ahead of time. Reheat before serving.

4 ready-to-cook quail, split down the back
Salt and ground black pepper
¼ cup peanut oil
2 cups water chestnuts, chopped
2 cups sliced mushrooms
2 cups bamboo shoots, chopped
3 slices fresh ginger root, minced, or ½ teaspoon ground ginger
1 cup canned beef stock
1 teaspoon gin
2 tablespoons cornstarch

2 teaspoons soy sauce
1 tablespoon water
Shredded lettuce
1 cup diced cooked ham

1. Sprinkle quail inside and out with salt and black pepper.
2. In a heavy, 12-inch skillet, heat oil. Place quail in the hot oil, and cook, over moderate heat, until brown.
3. Add water chestnuts, mushrooms, bamboo shoots, and ginger. Mix well.
4. Mix beef stock and gin and pour the mixture over the quail. Cook, covered, over low heat 15 minutes.
5. In a cup, blend cornstarch with soy sauce and water until smooth. Add to the pan juices and mix well. Continue stirring until the pan juices thicken.
6. Arrange shredded lettuce on serving plate. Place quail on bed of lettuce and spoon some of the pan juices over them. Garnish with diced cooked ham.

MENU

Quail, Chinese Style
Fried Noodles
Fresh Fruit *Almond Cookies*

Quail is considered an aristocrat of game birds and is prepared in many exotic fashions, especially by the French, who often stuff it with *pâté de foie gras* or serve it with truffles.

QUAIL WITH LICHEE NUTS

(MAKES 4 SERVINGS)

WINE SUGGESTION: *Red Bordeaux; Pavie (St.-Emilion)*

4 ready-to-cook quail

Salt and ground black pepper
2 egg yolks
3 tablespoons red port wine
¼ cup light cream
3 tablespoons pâté de foie
8 small mushrooms, minced
¼ cup fine dry bread crumbs
2 tablespoons butter
1 tablespoon cooking oil
1 can lichee nuts with syrup

1. Sprinkle quail inside and out with salt and black pepper and set aside.
2. In a large bowl, mix egg yolks, wine, cream, and *pâté de foie*. Add mushrooms and bread crumbs. Spoon the mixture loosely in the body cavities of the quail. Close cavities with short skewers.
3. Heat oven to 350° (moderate).
4. In a heavy, 12-inch skillet, heat butter and oil. Add quail and cook, over moderate heat, until browned on all sides.
5. Put quail on a rack in a roasting pan and roast, uncovered, until tender, 30 to 40 minutes.
6. Remove quail to a heated platter and keep warm.
7. To the pan juices in the roasting pan, add lichee nuts and syrup, and an additional 2 to 3 tablespoons red port wine. Heat, adjust salt, and serve over the quail. Serve remaining sauce in a sauceboat.

MENU

Quail with Lichee Nuts
Wild Rice
Petit Pois with Onions
Orange Sherbet with Cointreau

This authentic recipe for Quail Stew dates from the reign of Louis XIV: "Split your quail in half. Let them brown in a casserole with some bacon and a little flour to bind the sauce well. Moisten with some broth; add salt, pepper, fines herbes, minced mushrooms and artichoke hearts. When they are thoroughly cooked, add a small glass of liquor and the juice of an orange or a dash of lemon." The following recipe is an adaptation.

BRANDIED QUAIL

(MAKES 2 SERVINGS)

WINE SUGGESTION: *Beaujolais; Moulin-à-Vent*

Steps 1 through 5 of this recipe may be prepared ahead of time.

2 ready-to-cook quail
Brandy
Flour
4 tablespoons (1/2 stick) butter
1 cup sliced fresh mushrooms
1/2 cup chicken consommé (homemade or canned)
1/2 cup beaujolais
1/4 teaspoon celery salt
Freshly ground black pepper to taste
Juice from medium orange, strained

1. Split quail down the back lengthwise.
2. Saturate a cloth with brandy and rub it over the quail. Then dust the quail with flour.
3. In a heavy, 9-inch skillet, heat 2 tablespoons of the butter. Add quail and cook, covered, 5 minutes. Turn quail and cook, covered, 5 more minutes.
4. In a saucepan, melt the remaining 2 tablespoons butter. Add mushrooms and cook, stirring frequently, until tender, and add them to the quail.
5. Pour consommé and wine over the quail and sprinkle with celery salt and black pepper. Simmer, covered, 10 minutes or until quail are tender.
6. Just before serving, add orange juice and heat. Serve hot.

MENU

Brandied Quail
Barley Pilaf
Artichoke Hearts with Braised Carrots
Strawberry Charlotte made with Almond Cream

The grape used in this recipe is the smooth-skinned, juicy seedless variety. It is small, sweet, and pale green in color and is called the Thompson grape after the man who developed it.

SAUTEED QUAIL VERONIQUE

(MAKES 6 SERVINGS)

WINE SUGGESTION: *Red Bordeaux; Mouton-Rothschild (Pauillac)*

6 ready-to-cook quail
Salt and ground black pepper
Canned grape leaves *
6 slices bacon
6 tablespoons (¾ stick) butter
60 green seedless grapes
¼ cup beef consommé
6 slices firm-textured white bread sautéed in butter

1. Heat oven to 450° (very hot).
2. Sprinkle body cavities of quail with salt. Wrap each quail in a grape leaf and then wrap a strip of bacon around each grape leaf. Hold the bacon in place with a toothpick or small skewer or tie it in place with twine.
3. In a flameproof casserole, melt 4 tablespoons of the butter. Add quail and brown them on all sides.

* Grape leaves are available in foreign food markets and in fancy food stores.

4. Melt the remaining 2 tablespoons butter and sprinkle it over the quail. Then sprinkle with salt and black pepper.
5. Roast, uncovered, 5 minutes. Reduce oven temperature to 300° (slow) and continue roasting 20 to 25 minutes.
6. Add all the grapes and pour consommé over all. Cover casserole, return to the oven, and let the pan juices bubble 10 minutes.
7. Remove bacon and grape leaves from the quail and keep the quail hot.
8. Cut bread the same size as the quail and sauté it on both sides in additional butter, and place a quail on each slice. Pass the pan juices in a sauceboat to spoon over the quail. Serve promptly.

MENU

Sautéed Quail Véronique
Noodles and Mushrooms
Purée of String Beans
Watercress Salad
Chocolate Bavarian Cream

Washington, D.C., was not the best place to be during World War II. Each meal was an ordeal, with the long lines of people waiting to get a table. When you finally got a table, the food was splashed on a plate and shoved towards you. Once, just once, did we get a fine meal at a little-known restaurant in Maryland. We found it quite by accident. There was no beef on the menu but there was plenty of fowl, including this quail recipe.

QUAIL BALTIMORE

(MAKES 6 SERVINGS)

WINE SUGGESTION: *Red Burgundy; Clos-des-Chênes (Volnay)*

6 ready-to-cook quail
1½ teaspoons salt
Freshly ground black pepper
¾ cup (1½ sticks) butter
⅓ cup hot water
2 cans (4 ounces each) whole button mushroom caps, drained
Noodles, cooked according to package directions
Watercress

1. Preheat oven to 325° (slow).
2. Split quail lengthwise down the back and sprinkle them with salt and black pepper.
3. Melt ½ cup (1 stick) of the butter in a heavy 12-inch skillet. Add quail and cook them, uncovered, until they have browned on both sides.
4. Add hot water, cover, place in the oven, and cook 25 to 30 minutes or until quail are tender.
5. Cook mushroom caps in the remaining ¼ cup (½ stick) butter 3 to 4 minutes. Toss with well-drained cooked noodles.
6. Place a serving of noodles and mushrooms, topped with a quail, on each of 6 warmed serving plates. Garnish with watercress.

MENU

Quail Baltimore
Sautéed Summer Squash
Chicory Salad
Apple Tart

Marie-Antoine Carême (1784–1833) is regarded as the founder of La Grande Cuisine. One of twenty-five children of a poverty-stricken family, he was abandoned on the streets of Paris by his father, who could not afford to feed him. By chance, he asked for work in a humble cookshop and rose to become a chef to royalty and one of the great gastronomic creators of all time. Carême would cook a quail and then re-create it, feathers and all.

QUAIL MONTPELLIER

(MAKES 8 SERVINGS)

WINE SUGGESTION: *Red Burgundy; Les Charmes Chambertin (Gevrey-Chambertin)*

8 ready-to-cook quail
Salt and ground black pepper
Cooking oil
Fresh lemon juice
4 teaspoons blueberries (fresh, frozen, or canned)
4 teaspoons sugar
8 pats butter
8 small bay leaves

1. Preheat oven to 425° (hot).
2. Sprinkle quail inside and out with salt and black pepper.
3. Blend equal parts of cooking oil and lemon juice and rub the mixture over the quail, inside and out.
4. In the cavity of each quail, put ½ teaspoon blueberries and ½ teaspoon sugar. Close cavity openings with skewers and tie legs to the tails with twine.
5. Place each quail, topped with a pat of butter and a bay leaf, on a square of foil large enough to cover loosely and completely, leaving a double fold of foil over the top to keep in the juices.
6. Put birds, breast side up, in a large baking pan and roast for 1 hour.
7. Remove foil from the quail and put them on a large warmed platter. Pour some of the juices over them. Serve hot.

MENU

Quail Montpellier
Scalloped Potatoes and Sour Cream
Broiled Tomato Halves
Melon Balls

Truffles, a choice table delicacy, are underground fungi. The most famous are from Périgord, France, and are black or dark brown. Truffles vary in size from that of a marble to that of a grapefruit and their skin has a rough texture. They are used sparingly as a garnish, in *pâté de foie gras,* omelets, salads, and sauces. Truffles are very expensive because they are rare and because they have to be rooted out from their subterranean growing places by specially trained pigs or hounds.

QUAIL A LA MARGOT

(MAKES 2 SERVINGS)

WINE SUGGESTION: *Red Bordeaux; Château Lafleur* (*Pomerol*)

The quail may be roasted and the sauce made ahead of time. Cook the wild rice just before serving.

2 ready-to-cook quail
Salt and ground black pepper
2 slices bacon
¾ cup chicken broth (*homemade or canned*)
1 tablespoon dry Marsala
2 tablespoons butter
2 tablespoons hot chicken broth (*homemade or canned*)
1 truffle, thinly sliced
½ cup wild rice, cooked according to package directions

Truffle Sauce (recipe below)

1. Preheat oven to 350° (moderate).
2. Sprinkle quail inside and out with salt and black pepper.
3. Wrap a slice of bacon around each quail and hold the ends in place with toothpicks or small skewers. Place quail in a casserole.
4. In a small saucepan, heat chicken broth with Marsala and pour the mixture over the quail. Roast, uncovered, 20 to 30 minutes or until the quail are tender, basting with the broth and Marsala mixture 3 or 4 times. Turn off the oven heat.
5. Remove quail from the oven and discard bacon. Place quail in the center of a round, heated oven-proof serving dish and put them in the oven to keep warm.
6. Add butter, chicken broth, and truffle to the cooked wild rice. With 2 forks, toss the mixture lightly, but well.
7. Form the wild rice in a ring around the quail. Spoon Truffle Sauce over the quail. Serve hot.

TRUFFLE SAUCE

1 tablespoon flour
½ cup cold chicken broth (homemade or canned)
2 tablespoons butter
1 truffle, sliced
Roasting-pan juices, strained
Salt and ground black pepper to taste

1. In a 1-quart saucepan, blend flour with chicken broth until smooth. Stir and cook until the broth begins to thicken. Add 1 tablespoon of the butter.
2. Melt the remaining 1 tablespoon butter in a small saucepan, add sliced truffle and cook 1 to 2 minutes. Add to the sauce.
3. Stir in the strained roasting-pan juices, and salt and black pepper to taste. Serve over roast quail.

MENU

Quail à la Margot
Chopped Spinach
Crèpes Suzette

Cinnamon is an aromatic, sweetly pungent spice made from the bark of any of several trees native to Southeast Asia, Brazil, and the West Indies. The bark is stripped from shoots of these trees and dried, whereupon it curls into long quills. The quills are sold as cinnamon sticks or ground into cinnamon powder.

QUAIL A LA SAO PAULO

(MAKES 4 SERVINGS)

WINE SUGGESTION: *Brut champagne, Île de France*

This dish may be prepared ahead of time. Reheat and pour the gravy over the quail just before serving.

4 ready-to-cook quail
Salt and coarsely ground black pepper
¼ teaspoon ground rosemary
2 cups drained pineapple bits
1 teaspoon ground cinnamon
½ teaspoon ground nutmeg or ground cloves
Basting Sauce (recipe below)
1 tablespoon flour
1 tablespoon butter
½ cup chicken broth (homemade or canned)
¼ cup dry sherry
Black currant jelly

1. Preheat oven to 450° (very hot).
2. Rub quail inside and out with salt, black pepper, and rosemary. Set quail aside.

3. In a bowl, toss pineapple bits with cinnamon and nutmeg or cloves. Spoon the mixture into the body cavities of the quail. Close openings to body cavities with skewers and tie legs to tails with twine.
4. Brush quail with the hot Basting Sauce and place them in a shallow baking pan. Sear them, uncovered, in the very hot oven 5 to 6 minutes.
5. Baste again with the Basting Sauce. Cover the baking pan, reduce oven heat to 300° (slow), and roast 1 hour longer. Remove quail to a warmed platter and keep hot.
6. Blend flour with butter until smooth to form a *roux,* and add it to the roasting pan juices. Stir in chicken broth and sherry. Place the roasting pan over high heat, and cook, stirring, until the mixture has reduced to about 1/4 the original volume and has thickened slightly. Pour the gravy over the quail. Serve promptly with black currant jelly.

BASTING SAUCE

1/2 cup pineapple juice
1/2 cup dry sherry
2 tablespoons vinegar
1 tablespoon honey
1 tablespoon grated orange peel
2 teaspoons juniper berries, crushed

Combine all ingredients in a 1-quart saucepan. Bring the mixture to boiling point, reduce heat, and simmer 2 to 3 minutes. Keep warm to use for basting quail.

MENU

Quail à la São Paulo
New Potatoes with Lemon and Chives
Buttered Broccoli
Lemon Ice

ROCK CORNISH HENS

Alas! my child, where is the Pen
That can do justice to the Hen?
Like Royalty she goes her way,
Laying foundations every day,
Though not for Public Buildings, yet
For Custard, Cake and Omelette . . .
No wonder, Child, we prize the Hen,
Whose Egg is mightier than the Pen.

OLIVER HERFORD

There is a restaurant in the Bois de Boulogne in Paris that has become my favorite. It's a pale chalet with outdoor tables overlooking a small lake. The service is impeccable and the food is prepared with the greatest of care. These plump little hens are only one of the gems that emerge from the tiny kitchen.

CORNISH HENS WITH SAUCE MADERE

(MAKES 4 TO 6 SERVINGS)

WINE SUGGESTION: *Red Bordeaux; Rochet (St.-Estèphe)*

Steps 2 through 4 may be prepared ahead of time. Do not stuff hens until time to prepare the meal.

4 ready-to-cook Rock Cornish hens (1 to 1½ pounds)
Salt and ground black pepper
3 tablespoons cooking oil
½ cup (1 medium) chopped onion
½ cup finely chopped celery
⅛ teaspoon ground nutmeg

1 cup raw wild rice, cooked according to package directions
2 raw egg yolks
Sauce Madère (recipe below)

1. Preheat oven to 350° (moderate).
2. Wash Rock Cornish hens and dry them thoroughly. Sprinkle them inside and out with salt and black pepper.
3. In a 2-quart saucepan, heat oil. Add onion and celery and cook, stirring frequently, until onions have browned lightly, 3 to 4 minutes.
4. Add 1 teaspoon salt, ½ teaspoon ground black pepper, nutmeg, wild rice, and egg yolks. Mix lightly, but well.
5. Spoon the stuffing loosely into the body and neck cavities of the hens. Close cavity openings with skewers and tie legs to the tails with twine.
6. Place hens on a rack in a shallow roasting pan. Roast, uncovered, 40 to 60 minutes, basting frequently with Sauce Madère.
7. Arrange hens on a large warmed platter. Serve 1 small hen to each person or split larger hens in lengthwise halves and serve ½ hen to each person. Serve with Sauce Madère.

SAUCE MADERE

Blend 4 to 6 tablespoons Madeira with 2 cups commercially prepared brown gravy. Heat and use for basting the hens while they are roasting. Serve the remaining sauce in a sauceboat to spoon over the hens at the table.

MENU

Cornish Hens with Sauce Madère
Zucchini and Corn Casserole
Broiled Tomato Halves
Fresh Peaches and Blueberries
with Brown Sugar and Sour Cream

Sesame seed comes from an annual East Indian herb which grows in many tropical and subtropical regions. It was valued by ancient civilizations as a source of oil and was first brought to America by African slaves. When sesame seed capsules are dry, they split open, as if by magic, and scatter the seed—a fact which may have given rise to Ali Baba's password "Open Sesame."

The pearly white seeds, used as a spice or flavoring agent in cooking, need to be browned either by baking or roasting to bring out their full, nutty flavor.

SESAME-RICE CORNISH HENS

(MAKES 2 TO 4 SERVINGS)

WINE SUGGESTION: *Vouvray*

This recipe may be prepared ahead of time. Reheat before serving.

1/2 cup raw brown rice
1 small onion, minced
3 tablespoons butter
1 cup chicken broth (fresh or canned)
2 Rock Cornish game hens (1 to 2 pounds each)
Salt and ground black pepper
3 teaspoons sesame seeds
Melted butter
Juice of 1/2 lemon

1. Preheat oven to 350° (moderate).
2. Sauté rice and onion in 3 tablespoons butter until onion is tender and rice begins to puff and change color.
3. Add chicken broth to rice mixture. Cover pan and simmer until all liquid is absorbed, about 15 minutes.
4. While rice cooks, sprinkle hens with salt and pepper.
5. When rice is tender, add sesame seeds and stir well.
6. Spoon rice stuffing into body cavities of hens; truss neck and body cavity.
7. Roast hens for about 1 hour or until very tender.

MENU

Sesame-Rice Cornish Hens
Batter Fried Onion Rings
Watercress and Plum Tomato Salad
Chocolate Torte

The smoky taste of Scotch makes this dish especially fine on a chilly evening, or after a football game, skiing, or ice skating on a frigid afternoon. Besides, it's a cinch to prepare.

SCOTCH CORNISH HENS

(MAKES 3 TO 6 SERVINGS)

WINE SUGGESTION: *Red Bordeaux; Château de Rouffiac (St.-Emilion)*

Steps 1 through 3 may be prepared ahead of time.

3 ready-to-cook Rock Cornish hens (1 to 1½ pounds each
2 tablespoons lime juice
2 teaspoons salt
1 tablespoon powdered mustard
¼ pound (1 stick) butter, softened
½ cup Scotch whisky
2 teaspoons Glacé de Viande (recipe below)
1 tablespoon Worcestershire sauce
1 tablespoon instantized flour
½ cup heavy cream and ½ cup milk, or 1 cup half-and-half

1. Preheat oven to 350° (moderate).
2. Wash Cornish hens and dry thoroughly. Rub the skin of each with lime juice and salt.
3. Blend mustard with butter and spread mixture over

the hens. Place them on a rack in a shallow baking pan and roast until tender, about 1¼ hours, basting at least 4 times with the pan drippings.

4. In a small saucepan, heat ¼ cup of the Scotch whisky, pour it over the hens and ignite. When the flame dies out, remove the hens to another pan or cutting board.
5. Cut the hens into lengthwise halves down the back, and place them on a large warmed platter. Keep warm while making the sauce.
6. Add the remaining ¼ cup Scotch whisky to the roasting pan, and scrape up all the browned bits from the bottom and sides of the pan.
7. Add Glacé de Viande, Worcestershire sauce, and flour. Mix well and simmer 5 minutes, stirring frequently.
8. Add milk and cream or half-and-half. Bring the mixture to boiling point. Remove from heat, adjust seasonings, and pour the sauce over the hens. Serve hot.

GLACE DE VIANDE

Put 2 cups (1 pint) canned beef bouillon in a 1-quart saucepan. Simmer about 15 minutes until the bouillon thinly coats a metal spoon. Pour the sauce over the Scotch Cornish hens. Glacé de Viande may be frozen to use as needed.

MENU

Scotch Cornish Hens
Fried Potatoes with Bacon
Marinated Sweet-Sour Tomato Slices
Butterscotch Parfait

The pungent, aromatic condiment called pepper consists of the dried, immature berries of a plant native to the East Indies. Black pepper is the product obtained when these dried berries, or peppercorns, are ground whole. White pepper, more subtle in flavor and often used in dishes primarily white in color, is obtained by removing the outer coating of the mature berries and grinding the whitish seeds inside.

CORNISH HENS WITH ORANGES

(MAKES 6 TO 12 SERVINGS)

WINE SUGGESTION: *Samuele Sebastiani Vin Rosé*

This dish may be made ahead of time. Reheat before serving.

6 ready-to-cook Rock Cornish hens (1 to 1½ pounds each)
2 teaspoons salt
¼ teaspoon ground white pepper
2 tablespoons fresh lemon juice
1 clove garlic, crushed
½ cup (1 stick) butter, melted
½ cup orange juice and ½ cup dry white wine, or 1 cup orange juice
2 cups Cointreau-Orange Sauce (recipe below)
Orange slices, cut ½ inch thick
Parsley

1. Preheat oven to 350° (moderate).
2. Wash and dry Cornish hens and rub the skin with salt, white pepper, lemon juice, and garlic. Pin neck skins to the back with skewers and tie legs to the tails with twine.
3. Place hens on a rack in a large shallow roasting pan. Spoon melted butter over them.
4. Place hens in the oven and roast 15 minutes. Then pour orange juice, or orange juice and wine, over them. Continue roasting until tender, about 45 minutes, basting 3 to 4 times with the orange juice or orange and wine.
5. Remove hens to a warmed platter and spoon Coin-

treau-Orange Sauce over them. Serve the remaining sauce in a sauceboat. Garnish platter with orange slices and parsley.

COINTREAU-ORANGE SAUCE

Roasting pan drippings
Orange juice
2 tablespoons butter
2 tablespoons flour
2 tablespoons Cointreau
Salt and ground black pepper to taste
2 unpeeled navel oranges, sliced ½ inch thick

1. Pour roasting pan juices into a 2-cup measure and add enough orange juice to make 2 cups liquid.
2. In a 1-quart saucepan, melt butter. Remove saucepan from the heat and stir in flour. Stir and cook until the mixture is smooth and bubbly.
3. Stir in orange juice and pan dripping mixture. Stir and cook until the sauce is hot. Add Cointreau and orange slices. Simmer 5 minutes. Add salt and black pepper to taste. Serve over roasted Cornish hens.

Apples are used in many stuffings. They are a natural mate to Calvados, and when this mixture is enriched with cream the result is delicious, if rich.

ROCK CORNISH HENS FLAMBE

(MAKES 4 TO 8 SERVINGS)

WINE SUGGESTION: *Beaujolais Saint Amour (Depagneux)*

Steps 1 through 6 may be prepared ahead of time.

4 ready-to-cook Rock Cornish hens (1 to 1½ pounds each)
1 cup (2 sticks) butter
4 small tart apples, pared and cut into wedges
1 teaspoon salt
¼ teaspoon ground black pepper
½ cup heavy cream
½ cup Calvados

1. Heat oven to 350° (moderate).
2. Wash Cornish hens and dry them thoroughly. Set aside.
3. In a large, deep, flameproof casserole, melt butter. Add apples, cover, and cook over moderate heat until almost tender.
4. With a slotted spoon, remove apples from the casserole and reserve them to use later.
5. In the same casserole and in the same butter, brown 2 hens at a time. Then put all 4 hens in the casserole, sprinkle with salt and black pepper, and add cooked apples.
6. Roast, tightly covered, 45 to 60 minutes or until the hens are very tender.
7. Pour cream over the hens, turn off heat, and leave them in the oven about 10 minutes which is long enough to heat the cream.
8. In a small saucepan, heat Calvados, pour it over the hens, and ignite. Allow the Calvados to burn a few seconds and then extinguish the flame. Serve promptly.

MENU

Rock Cornish Hens Flambé
New Potatoes in Lemon-Chive Butter
Chopped Spinach
Lemon Sherbet

On the highway between Rennes and St.-Malo there is an inn and restaurant in the town of St.-Brieuc that typifies what we all long to find when driving through France. The marvelous cooking of the chef-proprietor includes a variety of seafood and poultry dishes. This Cornish Hen recipe is one of the specialties.

STUFFED ROCK CORNISH HENS

(MAKES 6 TO 12 SERVINGS)

WINE SUGGESTION: *Red Burgundy; Pommard Épenots (Loubet)*

The hens and the ingredients for the stuffing may be prepared ahead of time. Do not stuff the hens until time to roast them.

6 ready-to-cook Rock Cornish hens (1 to 1½ pounds each
Salt and ground black pepper
Wild Rice Stuffing (recipe below)
½ cup (1 stick) butter, melted
½ cup dry white wine
6 to 12 canned peach halves
Cooked petits pois (little peas)

1. Preheat oven to 400° (hot).
2. Wash Rock Cornish hens, dry thoroughly, and sprinkle inside and out with salt and black pepper.
3. Spoon Wild Rice Stuffing loosely into the body and neck cavities of the hens. Close cavity openings with short skewers and tie legs to the tails with twine.
4. Place hens on a rack in a shallow roasting pan. Melt butter in a small saucepan, add wine, and brush the mixture over the skins of the hens.
5. Roast hens 1 hour or until they are tender, basting occasionally with the butter and wine mixture.
6. Remove skewers from the cavity openings, and arrange the hens on a warmed large platter. Garnish platter with well-drained peach halves filled with cooked *petits pois.* Serve promptly. If each hen is large enough to serve 2 persons, remove stuffing onto a large warmed platter. Split hens lengthwise and arrange them on top of the stuffing. Garnish the platter with peach halves filled with *petits pois.*

WILD RICE STUFFING

Giblets from 6 Rock Cornish hens
2 teaspoons salt
Cold water
3 cups giblet stock and water
1 teaspoon dried thyme
1½ cups raw wild rice
2 tablespoons butter
2 cans (4 ounces each) sliced mushrooms, drained

1. Wash giblets and put them in a saucepan with 1 teaspoon salt and enough cold water to cover them generously. Bring water to boiling point, reduce heat, and simmer giblets, covered, until they are tender, adding more water if needed.
2. With a perforated spoon, remove giblets from the stock, cool, chop, and set aside to use later.
3. Measure giblet stock and then add enough water to make 3 cups. Put stock into a 2½-quart saucepot. Add the remaining 1 teaspoon salt and the thyme and bring stock to boiling point.
4. Meanwhile, wash rice in 3 to 4 changes of cold water, drain well, and add to the boiling giblet stock and water. Simmer, covered, 25 to 30 minutes or until rice is tender and has absorbed all the liquid. Set aside.
5. In a 1-quart saucepan, melt butter. Add well-drained mushrooms and cook, stirring frequently, 5 minutes. Add to the rice along with the chopped giblets. Mix gently, but well, and cook over moderately low heat 5 to 10 minutes, stirring occasionally. Spoon the mixture into the body and neck cavities of the Rock Cornish hens.

MENU

Stuffed Rock Cornish Hens
Peach Halves Filled with Petits Pois
Salad Greens with Crumbled Bacon
Crème de Menthe Ice Cream

TURKEY

How blessed how envied, were our life,
Could we but scape the poulterer's knife!
But man, cursed man, on Turkeys preys,
And Christmas shortens all our days:
Sometimes with oysters we combine,
Sometimes assist the savory chine; *
From the low peasant to the lord,
The turkey smokes on every board.

JOHN GAY

Mexican cuisine is finally being recognized all over the world. It has emerged into its own as being extremely sensitive and imaginative. The varied ingredients in this dish meld beautifully and it is a very subtle treat.

GUAJALOTE A LA BALBOA

(MAKES 6 SERVINGS)

WINE SUGGESTION: *Red Burgundy; Clos St. Jacques (Gevrey-Chambertin)*

This dish may be prepared ahead of time. Reheat before serving.

1 turkey (8 pounds), disjointed
1½ teaspoons salt
1 teaspoon ground black pepper
1 teaspoon Hungarian or Spanish paprika
3 cloves garlic, minced
1 bay leaf
¾ cup white vinegar

* The saddle, or portion thereof.

1/4 cup olive oil
2 tablespoons butter
2 large onions, chopped
1 cup chicken broth (homemade or canned)
2 pimentos, sliced
12 green olives, pitted and sliced
1/2 cup capers, drained

1. Wash turkey and set aside.
2. Combine salt, black pepper, paprika, and garlic. Rub the mixture over the turkey pieces and put them in a large bowl. Add bay leaf and vinegar. Marinate 2 hours.
3. Remove turkey from the marinade and drain well.
4. In a heavy, deep, 12-inch skillet, or a very large flameproof casserole, heat 2 tablespoons of the oil and 1 tablespoon of the butter. Add turkey pieces, as many pieces at a time as the skillet or casserole will accommodate without crowding. Cook over high heat until browned on all sides. Repeat until all turkey pieces have browned, adding the remaining olive oil and butter as needed. Return previously browned turkey pieces to the skillet.
5. Add onions and chicken broth. Cover and cook over low heat 1¾ hours or until turkey is tender.
6. Add pimentos, olives, and capers. Mix gently and adjust seasonings. Turn into a large serving dish and serve hot over rice.

MENU

Guajalote à la Balboa
Rice
Honey Glazed Carrots
Cucumber Salad
Flan or Baked Custard

We have a Frenchman by the name of Jacques Coeur to thank for our Thanksgiving Day turkeys, our Christmas feasts, and all the other days of the year when we sit down to enjoy a succulent turkey dinner. Jacques Coeur was minister of France to King Charles VII, but fell into disgrace and retired to Turkey. He returned to France with a collection of curiosities; among them turkeys, which he planned to raise at his château. Curiously enough, it was also about that time that the apricot was introduced to France and it rapidly gained favor.

HOLIDAY TURKEY

(MAKES 12 TO 20 SERVINGS)

WINE SUGGESTION: *Red Burgundy; Bonnes Mares (Morey-St.-Denis)*

Ingredients for stuffing may be prepared ahead of time, but do not mix the stuffing until time to roast the turkey. Giblets may be cooked the day before and refrigerated until time to make the gravy.

1 ready-to-cook tom turkey (10 to 15 pounds)
Butter, softened
Salt and ground black pepper
Apricot or Oyster Stuffing (recipe below)
Giblet Gravy (recipe below)

1. Remove giblets from the turkey. Wash and refrigerate them until time to cook them for the gravy.
2. Rub the entire outer surface of the turkey with butter and refrigerate until time to roast it.
3. Then, sprinkle the body and neck cavities with salt and black pepper. Stuff the cavities loosely with Apricot Stuffing or Oyster Stuffing. Truss the turkey.
4. Rub the turkey skin with salt and black pepper and place it on a rack in a roasting pan. If desired, insert a meat thermometer in the center of the inside thigh muscle or in the thickest part of the breast, making sure that the bulb does not touch a bone.
5. Roast turkey in a preheated slow oven (325°) until the thermometer registers 185°, or if thermometer is not used, roast turkey 30 minutes per pound. The

turkey is done when the leg joints move easily and the flesh on the leg is soft and pliable when pressed with the fingers. If the breast and legs tend to brown too fast, cover these parts with foil.

6. If turkey appears dry, baste with Madeira or melted butter. To avoid diluting Madeira flavor do not baste with pan drippings.
7. Remove turkey to a warmed platter and let it stand 20 minutes for easier carving. Carve at the table.
8. Pass Giblet Gravy in a sauceboat at the table to serve over turkey and stuffing.

APRICOT STUFFING

3 large onions, chopped
2 cups celery, chopped
1/4 pound (1 stick) butter
2 cups diced, pared apples
1 cup chopped, dried apricots
1 1/2 teaspoons salt
2 teaspoons poultry seasoning
6 cups (about 12 slices) dry bread cubes

1. In a large saucepot, cook onions and celery in butter until soft. Stir in apples, apricots, salt, and poultry seasoning. Stir and cook 3 minutes.
2. Scatter bread cubes over the mixture and toss lightly until they are moist. Spoon the mixture into body and neck cavities of a 10- to 15-pound turkey.

OYSTER STUFFING

3 pints oysters
3/4 cup (1 1/2 sticks) butter
1 1/2 cups chopped celery
1 cup chopped onion
1 1/2 cups dry bread cubes
1/4 cup chopped parsley
3 teaspoons salt
1/2 teaspoon poultry seasoning
1/4 teaspoon ground black pepper

1. Drain and chop oysters, reserving the liquid to use later if needed.
2. In a large saucepot, melt butter, add celery and onion, and cook until soft, stirring frequently. Add oysters, bread cubes, parsley, salt, poultry seasoning, and black pepper. Mix lightly but well.
3. If the stuffing appears dry, add a little oyster liquid. Spoon the mixture into the neck and body cavities of a 10- to 15-pound turkey.

GIBLET GRAVY

Steps 1 through 4 of this recipe may be prepared the day before.

Turkey giblets and neck
½ cup (1 medium) chopped onion
Handful celery tops
1 teaspoon salt or salt to taste
1 small bay leaf
4 cups cold water
½ cup flour
⅛ teaspoon ground black pepper

1. In a 2-quart saucepan, put turkey gizzard and neck, onion, celery tops, salt, bay leaf, and water.
2. Bring water to boiling point, reduce heat and simmer, covered, 40 minutes. Then add liver and continue cooking 20 minutes longer or until giblets and neck are tender.
3. With a slotted spoon, remove giblets and neck from the broth and cool them until they can be handled. Pick meat from the neck and chop gizzard and liver. Refrigerate until ready to make the gravy.
4. Strain stock, measure, and add water to make 4 cups, if needed. Refrigerate until ready to make the gravy.
5. After removing turkey from the roasting pan, tip the pan, letting the pan drippings run in one corner. Pour off the fat or siphon it off with a baster and discard it or save for other uses.
6. Gradually blend flour with the juice which remains in the roasting pan. Scrape up all the browned bits from the bottom and sides of the roasting pan. Stir

and cook until the mixture bubbles.

7. Add stock, chopped giblets, and neck meat. Mix well. Stir and cook until the gravy thickens. Then cook 1 minute longer, stirring constantly.
8. Add black pepper and adjust salt. Serve hot over turkey and stuffing.

MENU

Holiday Turkey
Puréed Acorn Squash
Buttered Broccoli
Cranberry Sauce
Tossed Salad Greens with Tart Dressing
Christmas Plum Pudding with Brandy Sauce

This sophisticated dish was found in a very simple restaurant in Nantes and the recipe is an elegant solution for what to do with leftover turkey.

LEFTOVER TURKEY WITH MUSHROOM SAUCE

(MAKES 4 TO 6 SERVINGS)

WINE SUGGESTION: *White Burgundy; Chablis Côte de Fontenay Premier Crû*

2 cups diced cooked turkey meat
6 tablespoons butter
2 tablespoons flour
2/3 cup milk
1 3/4 cups turkey stock or beef stock (homemade or canned)
Salt to taste
1/8 teaspoon ground black pepper

1 tablespoon chopped parsley
½ teaspoon dried rosemary, tarragon, or thyme, or enough to taste (optional)
¾ cup fine dry bread crumbs
3 eggs, separated
Mushroom Sauce (recipe below)

1. Preheat oven to 325° (slow).
2. In a 2-quart saucepan, melt butter. Remove pan from heat and stir in flour. Cook, stirring, until the mixture bubbles.
3. Gradually add milk and turkey or beef stock, mixing well.
4. Add salt to taste, black pepper, parsley, and, if desired, rosemary, tarragon, or thyme. Mix well.
5. Stir in bread crumbs and diced turkey. Let the mixture cook over very, very low heat or over hot water.
6. Meanwhile, in a small bowl, beat egg yolks until they are thick and lemon colored. Gradually add to the cooked mixture. Mix well.
7. In a large bowl, beat egg whites until they stand in soft peaks, being careful not to beat them in stiff, dry peaks. Very carefully fold them into the cooked mixture.
8. Turn the mixture into a 4- or 6-cup ring mold or into 4 or 6 individual soufflé dishes, having only the bottoms buttered.
9. Bake 1 hour or until a knife inserted in the center comes out clean. Serve promptly with Mushroom Sauce.

MUSHROOM SAUCE

2 tablespoons butter
⅓ cup thinly sliced onion
1 can (10½ ounces) cream of mushroom soup, undiluted
1 cup milk
⅛ teaspoon ground thyme
½ teaspoon salt

1. In a $1\frac{1}{2}$-quart saucepan, melt butter. Add onion and cook, stirring frequently, until golden and soft, 3 to 4 minutes.
2. Add mushroom soup, milk, thyme, and salt. Mix well.
3. Cook, stirring, until hot. Serve over turkey soufflé.

MENU

Leftover Turkey with Mushroom Sauce
Foil Baked Potatoes
Asparagus Amandine
Boston Lettuce Salad
Lemon Chiffon Pie

This recipe was a gift from my dear friend Eloise. Pork sausage meat and chestnuts are go-togethers. Add them to black olives and a new flavor evolves. Purchase the chestnuts when they are in season and put them, uncooked, into the freezing compartment of the refrigerator. That way, you can have chestnuts all year round.

STUFFED ROYAL BIRD

(MAKES 6 TO 10 SERVINGS)

WINE SUGGESTION: *Red Burgundy; Chapelle Chambertin (Gevrey-Chambertin)*

The ingredients for stuffing may be prepared ahead of time, but do not mix them until ready to roast the turkey.

1 ready-to-cook turkey (6 to 8 pounds)
Salt and ground black pepper
*20 peeled chestnuts **

* How to peel chestnuts: With a pointed knife, cut a cross (+) in the shell of the flat side of each chestnut. Put chestnuts in a saucepan with enough water to cover them. Bring water to boiling

20 black olives, pitted and chopped
1½ cups (¾ pound) pork sausage, uncooked
4 strips bacon
Flour

1. Remove giblets from turkey and reserve them for another dish.
2. Wash and dry turkey. Sprinkle inside and out with salt and black pepper. Set aside.
3. Preheat oven to 350° (moderate).
4. Combine chestnuts, olives, and sausage. Mix well, but gently. Spoon the mixture loosely into the body and neck cavities of the turkey.
5. Truss the turkey and place it, breast up, on a rack in a roasting pan. Lay strips of bacon across the breast. If desired, insert a meat thermometer in the center of the inside thigh muscle or in the thickest part of the breast, making sure the bulb does not touch a bone.
6. Roast 1½ to 2 hours or until the thermometer registers 185°.
7. Remove turkey from the oven and discard bacon. Sprinkle a little flour over the skin of the turkey and baste with pan drippings. Continue roasting until the skin is golden brown and crisp, about 10 to 15 minutes, basting with pan drippings at intervals.
8. Cool turkey 20 minutes for easier carving. Spoon the stuffing into a warmed serving bowl. Cut turkey into slices and put the slices on a warmed platter.

MENU

Stuffed Royal Bird
Parsley Potatoes
Winter Squash with Cranberries
Cucumber and Mushroom Salad
Peaches in Port Wine

point and boil 20 minutes or until the shells can be easily pierced with a pointed knife. Keep chestnuts hot by leaving them in the hot water so they will be easier to peel. One at a time, remove from the water and strip off the shell and inner skin.

On a visit to England we rented a country house in Devon, complete with housekeeper, gardener, tennis court, and a cook who excelled in whatever she touched. She prepared Turkey Messina for one of our dinner parties and the guests almost swooned with delight when they tasted this magnificent feast.

TURKEY MESSINA

(MAKES 4 TO 6 SERVINGS)

WINE SUGGESTION: *Llords & Elwood Cabernet Sauvignon*

This dish may be prepared ahead of time. Reheat before serving.

1 ready-to-cook turkey (5 to 7 pounds)
Salt and ground black pepper
2 medium carrots, minced
2 chopped shallots or green onions (bulbs and tops)
1 bay leaf
1 clove garlic, chopped
2 ribs celery, chopped
1 leek (white part only)
1 sprig fresh thyme or 1 teaspoon dried thyme
1⅓ cups dry white wine
6 tablespoons (¾ stick) butter, melted
2 pounds small white onions, minced
1 pound walnuts, shelled and minced
2 tablespoons chopped parsley
2 egg yolks, beaten
¼ cup heavy cream, slightly heated

1. Wash and dry turkey and split it lengthwise, but not all the way through, so it will lie flat. Sprinkle both sides with salt and pepper. Set aside.
2. In a large roasting pan or casserole, combine carrots, shallots or green onions, bay leaf, garlic, celery, leek, thyme, and ⅓ cup of the dry white wine. In France, this is known as *mirepoix.*
3. Preheat oven to 350° (moderate).
4. Place turkey, skin side up, in a roasting pan or casserole on top of the vegetable mixture.

5. Pour melted butter over the turkey and roast, uncovered, 2 hours or until turkey is tender.
6. Place turkey on a large heated platter, leaving the *mirepoix* in the roasting pan. Keep turkey warm while making the sauce.
7. Combine minced small white onions, walnuts, parsley, and beaten egg yolks. Add to the *mirepoix* in the roasting pan and mix well.
8. Place roasting pan over low surface heat, add the remaining 1 cup dry white wine and cream. Stir and cook only until the mixture is hot. Do not boil. Serve in a sauceboat at the table to spoon over the turkey.

I don't know of anyone who has ever complained about having to eat leftover turkey. Even the carcass doesn't go to waste. The most flavorsome soup is made with the bones. Further on, there is a recipe for this savory broth. Meanwhile, here is a delicious way to serve turkey breasts.

TURKEY ALBERTO

(MAKES 4 SERVINGS)

WINE SUGGESTION: *White Burgundy; Chassagne-Montrachet (Morgeot)*

1 package (8 ounces) medium-wide noodles
4 tablespoons (½ stick) butter
1 cup freshly grated Parmesan cheese

1 egg
1 teaspoon dried oregano
¼ teaspoon salt
1/16 teaspoon ground black pepper
2 tablespoons water
8 slices cold roast turkey
1 cup fine dry bread crumbs
2 tablespoons cooking oil
Whipped Cream Sauce (recipe below)

1. Cook noodles according to package directions. Drain well and return them to the saucepan.
2. Add 2 tablespoons butter and Parmesan cheese and toss the noodles lightly. Then, turn them into a 2-quart oven-proof dish. Cover and put in the oven to keep warm while browning the turkey slices.
3. In an 8- or 9-inch pie plate, beat egg with oregano, salt, black pepper, and water. Put the bread crumbs in another pie plate.
4. Dip the turkey slices first in the egg mixture, then in the crumbs, coating them well. Arrange the slices on a piece of waxed paper or baking sheet and set aside 10 minutes to dry.
5. In a heavy, 12-inch skillet, heat the 2 tablespoons butter and the oil. Add the crumbed turkey slices and brown them on both sides over moderately high heat.
6. Arrange the browned turkey slices, slightly overlapping, on the noodles. Return the dish to the oven to keep warm while making the Whipped Cream Sauce.

WHIPPED CREAM SAUCE

2 tablespoons butter
2 tablespoons flour
1 chicken bouillon cube
½ cup milk
¼ cup heavy cream, whipped

1. In a 1-quart saucepan, melt butter. Remove from heat and add flour and bouillon cube. Mix well. Re-

turn the saucepan to the heat. Cook, stirring constantly and crushing the bouillon cube with the back of a wooden spoon, until the mixture bubbles.

2. Stir in milk. Continue cooking until the sauce thickens, about 1 minute.
3. Remove sauce from the heat, fold in whipped cream, and spoon the sauce over the turkey slices. Set oven control to broil. Place the dish under the broiler 4 inches from the source of heat. Broil 3 or 4 minutes until the sauce is golden and puffed, watching closely to prevent burning.
4. Bring the dish to the table immediately and serve promptly.

MENU

Turkey Alberto
Braised Endive
Compote of Spiced Fruits
Chocolate Soufflé
or
Orange Ice with Grand Marnier

The much used paprika is a condiment for flavoring and decorating foods. It is a fine, red powder made from the fruit of a variety of red pepper, ranging in pungency from very mild to quite hot. Hungarian paprika is considered to be the finest, and Hungarian cooking makes full and imaginative use of it in many dishes.

TURKEY IN CHAMPAGNE

(MAKES 8 TO 10 SERVINGS)

WINE SUGGESTION: *Champagne; Napoleon*

This dish, except for the sauce, may be prepared ahead of time. Reheat before serving.

1 ready-to-cook turkey (about 12 pounds)
2 teaspoons ground black pepper
1 teaspoon paprika
1 teaspoon salt
½ cup (1 stick) butter, melted
Champagne Sauce (recipe below)

1. Preheat oven to 325° (slow).
2. Remove and reserve giblets and neck for another dish.
3. Wash and dry turkey thoroughly, and press the black pepper into the skin. Then sprinkle with paprika and salt.
4. Truss the turkey. Place it on a rack in a shallow roasting pan, and pour melted butter over it.
5. Cover the pan loosely with foil and roast turkey 1 hour. Remove foil and continue roasting 3 hours, basting often with pan juices.
6. Transfer turkey to a warmed platter and let it stand 20 minutes for easier carving.
7. Spoon part of the Champagne Sauce over the turkey. Serve the remainder of the sauce in a sauceboat.

CHAMPAGNE SAUCE

1 cup roasting pan juices
1 cup champagne
½ pound mushrooms, thinly sliced
½ cup cream and ½ cup milk, or 1 cup half-and-half
2 tablespoons cognac

1. After turkey has been removed from the roasting pan to a warmed platter, pour the pan juices into a small bowl. Let the fat in the pan juices rise to the top and then spoon it off and discard it. Pour the juices left in the bowl into a 1-cup measure. If there is not enough to fill the cup, finish filling it with turkey broth. (The broth may be made from the giblets or canned broth may be used.)

2. Pour the 1 cup pan juices into a 1½-quart saucepan and heat until it begins to simmer, about 4 minutes.
3. Pour in champagne and add mushrooms. Bring the mixture to boiling point and boil rapidly 5 minutes.
4. Reduce heat and stir in cream and milk, or half-and-half. Heat only until the sauce is hot, about 5 minutes. Then add cognac. Serve piping hot over turkey.

MENU

Turkey in Champagne
Wild or White Rice
Braised Celery and Green Peas
Watercress in Vinaigrette Sauce
Blueberries and Peaches in Wine

My German grandmother created this recipe and it was handed on to me by my mother, who served it often. The *mirepoix* of sauerkraut-potato-onion is the flavorsome base for this turkey and served beneath the carved slices of meat, it is a most unusual variation. It is marvelously good the next day, served cold.

ROAST TURKEY LUCIEN

(MAKES 8 TO 10 SERVINGS)

WINE SUGGESTION: *Red Burgundy; Les Boudots (Nuits-St. Georges)*

This dish may be prepared ahead of time. Reheat before serving.

1 ready-to-cook turkey (about 10 pounds)
2 tablespoons butter
2 pounds sauerkraut
2 medium potatoes, peeled and grated
2 medium onions, grated

3 teaspoons ground black pepper
2 teaspoons salt
1 teaspoon sweet paprika

1. Wash and dry turkey and set aside.
2. Preheat oven to 325° (moderate).
3. In a 2-quart saucepan, melt butter. Add sauerkraut, potatoes, onions, and 1 teaspoon of the black pepper. Stir and cook over high heat for 5 minutes. Spread the *mirepoix* over the bottom of a roasting pan. Set aside.
4. Combine the remaining 2 teaspoons black pepper, salt, and paprika, and rub into the skin of the turkey.
5. Place turkey in the roasting pan over the *mirepoix*. Roast, uncovered, 2½ to 3½ hours or until the leg joint moves easily and the flesh on the legs is soft and pliable when pressed with the finger. Baste 3 to 4 times with pan juices the last 30 minutes of cooking time.
6. Remove turkey to a large platter or baking pan and let it stand 20 minutes for easier carving. Then cut it into slices.
7. Just before serving, reheat *mirepoix* and turn it onto a warmed platter. Arrange turkey slices over it.

MENU

Roast Turkey Lucien
Herbed Carrots and Onion Rings
Steamed Spinach with Walnuts
Stewed Red and White Cherries
Cookies

This recipe came about almost by accident. I didn't have enough leftover turkey for four, so I decided to prepare a type of Croque-Monsieur. It was a great success. These "sandwiches" are perfect for a late supper, a quick luncheon, or an easy dinner entrée, embellished with a cooked green vegetable. They may be prepared with boned chicken breasts as well.

ALMOND TURKEY SANDWICHES

(MAKES 4 SERVINGS)

WINE SUGGESTION: *White Burgundy, Clos-des-Mouches (Beaune)*

Steps 1 through 6 may be prepared ahead of time. Refrigerate and fry just before serving.

4 tablespoons (1/2 stick) butter
1/4 cup slivered, blanched almonds
1 cup fine dry bread crumbs
1 egg
1 tablespoon milk
8 slices raw turkey breast, about 1/4 inch thick
Salt and ground black pepper
4 slices cooked Smithfield ham, cut a little smaller than the turkey slices
4 slices American Cheddar cheese
1/2 cup flour

1. In a skillet, melt butter, add almonds and cook, stirring, over moderate heat until almonds begin to turn straw color. With a slotted spoon, remove almonds to a bowl. Reserve butter to use later.
2. Add bread crumbs to almonds and mix well. Set aside.
3. In another bowl, beat egg with milk. Set aside.
4. With the edge of a heavy saucer or a mallet, pound the turkey slices until they are 3 x 6 inches in size, being careful not to tear the meat. Sprinkle lightly with salt and black pepper.
5. Place a slice of ham and cheese between 2 turkey slices. Hold the sandwiches together with toothpicks.
6. Put flour in a pie plate and carefully dip each sandwich in it, coating it well. Now dip it into the beaten egg and milk and then into the almond-bread crumb mixture, coating it well.

7. Reheat the reserved butter in the skillet, add sandwiches and brown them on both sides over low heat. Serve very hot.

The mushroom is a flashy, umbrella-shaped fungus, some varieties of which are edible. It has not been determined whether or not mushrooms have any food value, but all good cooks agree that they certainly have culinary value, adding richness to a variety of dishes.

TURKEY WITH MUSHROOM DRESSING

(MAKES 12 TO 16 SERVINGS)

WINE SUGGESTION: *Red Burgundy; Clos de Thorey (Nuits-St. Georges)*

1 ready-to-cook turkey (12 to 15 pounds)
Salt and ground black pepper
2 loaves day-old white bread (1 pound each)
Water
2 eggs, lightly beaten
½ cup chopped parsley
1 raw turkey liver, chopped
2 tablespoons butter, melted
¾ cup finely chopped onion
½ cup finely chopped celery
2 cups chopped raw mushrooms
½ pound ground lean, uncooked pork

Sprigs of parsley (optional)
Unpeeled orange slices (optional)

1. Remove giblets from the turkey cavity, reserve liver for use in the dressing. Reserve gizzard and neck for another dish.
2. Wash turkey and dry thoroughly. Sprinkle inside and out with salt and black pepper.
3. Trim and discard crusts from bread. Tear bread into pieces, and soak it in only enough water to wet it. Using your hand, squeeze out the water. Add 2 teaspoons salt, eggs, parsley, and turkey liver. Mix well, but lightly.
4. In a large skillet, melt butter. Add onion, celery, and mushrooms. Cook, stirring, over moderate heat and add to the bread mixture.
5. In the same skillet, fry pork until lightly browned, add to the bread mixture and mix well, but gently.
6. Spoon mixture loosely into the cavities and truss the turkey. Preheat oven to 325° (slow).
7. Brush the skin of the turkey with a little extra melted butter and place it on a rack in a roasting pan.
8. Insert a meat thermometer into the center of the inside thigh muscle or in the thickest part of the breast, making sure the bulb does not touch a bone.
9. Roast until the thermometer registers 185°, or about 30 minutes per pound, if a thermometer is not used. Remove turkey from the oven and allow it to stand 20 minutes for easier carving.
10. Spoon stuffing into a warmed large bowl. Carve turkey and arrange slices on a large warmed platter. If desired, garnish the platter with sprigs of parsley and orange slices.

MENU

Turkey with Mushroom Dressing
Herbed Green Beans
Brussels Sprouts with Sliced Chestnuts
Raspberry or Cherry Tarts

Turkey is not a usual dish for the Chinese. This is one of only two turkey recipes I have heard of in Chinese cooking. I can only surmise that the birds are very expensive in the Orient, possibly because of the scarcity of land on which to raise them. I would venture to say that the turkey recipes were prepared in the United States.

LING'S MEMORABLE TURKEY

(MAKES 6 TO 8 SERVINGS)

BEVERAGE SUGGESTION: *Assorted beers*

This dish may be prepared ahead of time. Reheat before serving.

1 ready-to-cook turkey (8 pounds)
Hot water
2 teaspoons ground allspice
1 teaspoon sesame-seed oil
2 cups soy sauce
Peanut oil
Chinese noodles (optional)

1. Wash turkey in cold water, put it in a large, deep bowl and pour over it enough hot water to cover. Let the turkey stand in the hot water 2 minutes.
2. Remove turkey from the hot water, discard the water, and return the turkey to the bowl.
3. Combine allspice, sesame-seed oil, and soy sauce. Then pour the mixture over the turkey and marinate it ¾ hour, turning the turkey in the marinade frequently.
4. Preheat oven to 325° (slow).
5. Remove turkey from the marinade and place it on a rack in a roasting pan, reserving the marinade to use for basting the turkey.
6. Brush the skin of the turkey with peanut oil and cover loosely with foil. Roast 3½ hours or until turkey is very tender, basting occasionally with the marinade.
7. Remove the foil the last ½ hour of cooking time so the skin will brown and crisp. Let the turkey stand 20 minutes after removing from oven for easier carving.

8. Cut turkey into serving pieces and arrange them on a warmed large platter. Spoon some of the pan juices over the turkey slices. Serve very hot with fried Chinese noodles, if desired.

MENU

Ling's Memorable Turkey
Fried Chinese Cellophane Noodles or Steamed Rice
Batter Fried Green Peppers
Bean Sprout Salad
Melon Wedges

Mole de Poblano de Guajalote is a traditional Mexican holiday dish dating back to the sixteenth century. Mole is the Mexican word for a complicated sauce usually flavored with chili. Moles can be prepared from scratch or purchased in packages or cans in gourmet shops.

MOLE DE POBLANO DE GUAJALOTE

(MAKES 6 SERVINGS)

BEVERAGE SUGGESTION: *Beer; Dos Equis*

This dish may be prepared ahead of time. Reheat before serving.

1 ready-to-cook turkey (6 to 8 pounds)
1½ teaspoons salt
Water
½ cup cooking oil
3 medium green peppers, seeded and chopped
2 tablespoons sesame seed
6 cloves garlic, peeled
1 slice dry white toast
½ cup blanched almonds
8 medium tomatoes, quartered

1/2 teaspoon cinnamon
1/4 teaspoon ground black pepper
1 1/2 tablespoons chili powder
2 squares (2 ounces) unsweetened chocolate, grated

1. Wash turkey thoroughly and cut it into serving pieces. Put the pieces in a large saucepot with 1 teaspoon of the salt, and enough cold water to cover.
2. Cover the saucepot, bring water to boiling point, reduce heat, and cook, slowly, 1 1/2 hours or until the turkey is almost tender.
3. Remove saucepot from the heat and drain off all the broth, reserving 2 cups to use later. Dry turkey pieces.
4. In a heavy, 12-inch skillet, heat 1/4 cup of the oil. Add turkey, as many pieces at a time as the skillet will accommodate, and brown them on all sides. As the turkey pieces brown, transfer them to a large flameproof casserole. Pour the remaining 2 cups broth over the turkey.
5. In the electric blender,* put (in four batches) green peppers, sesame seed, garlic, toast, almonds, tomatoes, cinnamon, black pepper, chili powder, and the remaining 1/2 teaspoon salt. Blend a few seconds or until the mixture is smooth. Add grated chocolate and blend thoroughly.
6. In a 2-quart saucepan, heat the remaining 1/4 cup oil. Add the mixture from the blender. Cook over low heat 5 minutes, stirring frequently. Spread the hot mixture over the turkey. Simmer, covered, 2 hours, stirring frequently.
7. Bring the casserole to the table. Serve the turkey and sauce over hot rice if desired.

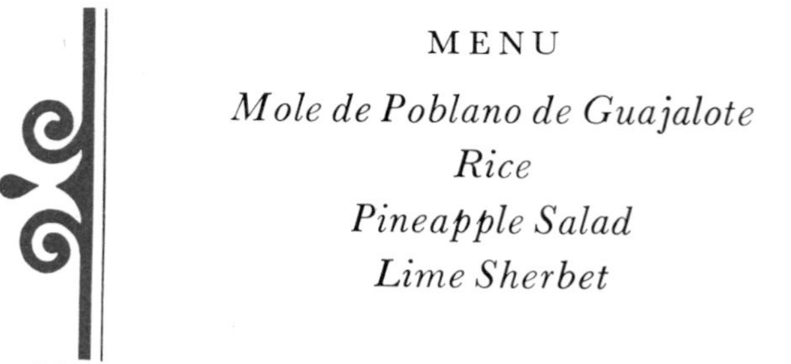

MENU

Mole de Poblano de Guajalote
Rice
Pineapple Salad
Lime Sherbet

* If blender is not available, chop ingredients finely.

No doubt, this is patterned after the famous Chicken Marengo masterpiece. I think turkey is even more delicious because the meat is richer. Chicken Marengo was created June 14, 1800, during Napoleon's Italian campaign. It was two o'clock in the afternoon. The French had lost two battles since eight o'clock that morning and General Desaix suggested engaging in a third. In the distance Austrian dispatch riders were dashing towards Vienna to announce their victory.

"Do what you please," Bonaparte told Desaix. "As for me, I am going to eat." He motioned his steward. "I fear," said the latter, "that the meal will not meet with your approval. Those cursed Austrians have intercepted our canteens and there is no butter in the kitchens." The First Consul sat down at the table. An hour later General Desaix was again on the road to victory and Chicken Marengo, sautéed in oil, had become history.

TURKEY MARENGO

(MAKES 6 SERVINGS)

WINE SUGGESTION: *Red Burgundy; Clos de Vougeot (Lamarche)*

This dish may be prepared ahead of time. Reheat before serving.

1 ready-to-cook turkey (5 to 6 pounds)
1 cup flour
2 teaspoons salt
1 teaspoon dried marjoram
½ teaspoon ground black pepper
¼ cup cooking oil
1 cup (1 large) chopped onion
1 clove garlic, minced
2 chicken bouillon cubes
1 cup water
4 medium raw tomatoes, peeled and chopped
½ pound raw mushrooms, sliced
Chopped parsley
1½ cups croutons (homemade or commercial)

1. Wash and dry turkey and cut it into serving pieces.

2. Into a medium-large brown paper bag, put flour, salt, marjoram, and black pepper. Put a few pieces of turkey at a time into the bag. Shake the bag enough to coat each piece well. Continue until all the turkey has been floured. Reserve flour mixture.
3. In a heavy, 12-inch skillet, heat oil. Add as many pieces of turkey at a time as the skillet will accommodate without crowding. Cook, over moderate heat, until the turkey has browned on both sides. As the turkey browns, remove it to a medium-sized roasting pan or to a 14 x 10 x 2-inch baking pan. Repeat until all the remaining turkey has browned. Set aside.
4. Preheat oven to 375° (moderate).
5. In the same skillet, unwashed, add onion and garlic. Cook, over moderate heat, until onion is soft. Stir in the reserved flour mixture and bouillon cubes. Cook, stirring and crushing the bouillon cubes with the back of a wooden spoon, until the mixture bubbles.
6. Add water and cook, stirring, 1 minute or until the sauce thickens.
7. Add tomatoes and mushrooms and bring to boiling point. Spoon the sauce over the turkey.
8. Cover the pan, place it in the oven, and cook 1 hour and 20 minutes. Remove cover and cook 10 minutes longer or until the turkey is slightly crisp on top.
9. Sprinkle chopped parsley and croutons over the top.

Prosciutto de parma is the most famous and most delicate of all hams. This delicacy is pale red and tender and sweet when mature. The early part of its curing includes a salting process, but its delicious flavor comes after the ham has been exposed to the air for six months in the hill town of Langhirano, which has the reputation for the best air for ham-curing. Hams from all over Italy are sent there to hang in the not too high and not too low altitude.

PERUVIAN TURKEY

(MAKES 6 TO 8 SERVINGS)

WINE SUGGESTION: *Red Bordeaux; Château de Rouffiac (St.-Emilion)*

This dish may be prepared ahead of time. Reheat before serving.

1 ready-to-cook turkey (about 8 pounds)
1 tablespoon salt
2 teaspoons ground black pepper
3 cloves garlic, minced
1 cup olive oil
4 medium raw tomatoes, cubed
4 medium green peppers, seeded and chopped
½ cup chopped parsley
½ cup white vinegar
1 pound thinly sliced prosciutto ham

1. Remove giblets from turkey cavity and reserve them for another dish.
2. Wash turkey and dry thoroughly. In a smaller bowl, mix salt, black pepper, and garlic to a paste. Rub the mixture inside the body cavity of the turkey. Place turkey in a large bowl or saucepot. Set aside.
3. In a 2-quart saucepan, combine olive oil, tomatoes, green peppers, parsley, and vinegar. Heat, stirring frequently.
4. Pour the hot mixture over the turkey. Marinate overnight or about 12 hours, turning the turkey in the marinade frequently.
5. Remove turkey from the refrigerator 4 hours before time to roast it. Let it stand at room temperature; baste frequently with the marinade.

6. Preheat oven to 350° (moderate).
7. Remove turkey from the marinade and place it on a rack in a shallow roasting pan. Pour marinade in the pan and roast, uncovered, 20 minutes per pound or until the leg joint moves easily and the flesh of the legs and thighs are soft and pliable when pressed with the finger. Baste with the marinade every 20 minutes of roasting time.
8. Remove turkey from the oven and let it stand 20 minutes for easier carving.
9. Slice turkey and arrange the slices on a large warmed platter, alternating each slice of turkey with 1 slice of prosciutto ham.
10. Pour pan drippings through a sieve. Serve in a sauceboat at the table to spoon over the turkey.

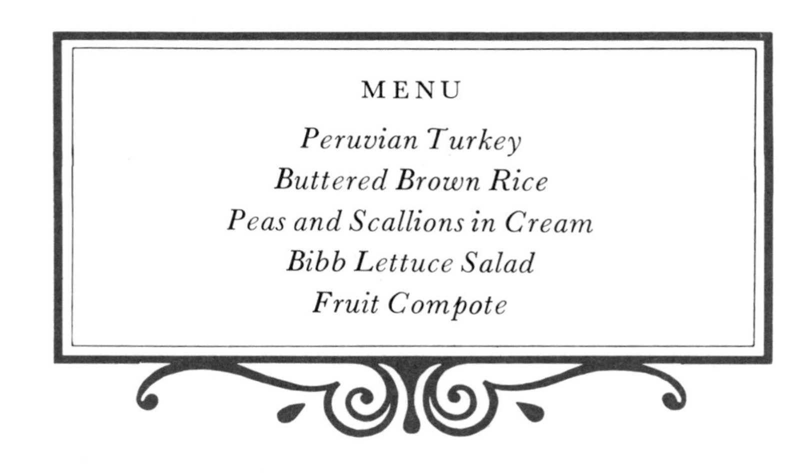

Please don't discard that turkey carcass! It makes one of the most elegant soups in the world. Even the carcass of a small turkey will make enough broth for a family. Besides, it is very good for you. Should you have too much soup left over, freeze it for another occasion. Thickened with flour, cornstarch or arrowroot, it makes a delectable base for sauces and may be used over any cooked meats or poultry to moisten.

TURKEY BROTH

(MAKES 1 OR MORE QUARTS OR 4 TO 5 SERVINGS)

1 turkey carcass (any size)
1 small bay leaf
½ cup (1 medium) chopped onion
½ cup chopped celery
½ cup chopped carrots
1 teaspoon salt or salt to taste
4 whole black peppercorns
Cold water
½ teaspoon dried basil
½ teaspoon dried marjoram
½ teaspoon dried thyme

1. Trim off all meat on the carcass and reserve it for other dishes.
2. Crack the carcass and break the large bones. Put them in a large saucepot. Add bay leaf, onion, celery, carrots, salt, peppercorns, and enough cold water to cover the bones.
3. Bring water to boiling point, skim off and discard scum which rises to the top of the water. Reduce heat and simmer, covered, 3 hours.
4. Add basil, marjoram, and thyme 10 minutes before removing broth from the heat. Adjust salt.
5. Cool broth slightly and strain. Refrigerate in a covered container until ready to use. Before using, remove all fat that may have risen to the top of the broth.
6. To store broth for a long period, pour it in sterilized jars, seal tightly, and freeze to use as needed.

WOODCOCK

The queen of the marshes. For its delicious flavor, its volatile principles and delicate flesh, it is sought after by all classes of gourmets. But it is eaten only during three or four months out of the year. Woodcocks on the spit are, after the pheasant, the most distinguished of roasts. This precious bird is so venerated that it is rendered the same honors as the Grand Lama: toast moistened with lemon juice receives its drippings and is eaten respectfully by the fervent gastronome. . . .

Though the flesh of the woodcock is excellent, it is not for the man with a weak stomach or one who is bilious or melancholy, but for those who exercise. Everything in a woodcock is good.

ALEXANDRE DUMAS

This recipe is not European but American, and was given to me by a woman from southern Georgia.

WOODCOCK AU NID

(MAKES 6 SERVINGS)

WINE SUGGESTION: *Red Bordeaux; Château Latour Montagne*

The ingredients for this dish may be prepared ahead of time, but neither mix nor cook until time to prepare the meal.

6 ready-to-cook woodcocks
Salt and ground black pepper
3 acorn squash
¼ pound (½ cup) ground chuck or ground round
½ cup crushed potato chips, cereal, or fine soft bread crumbs
1 teaspoon seasoned salt

1 teaspoon garlic salt
1/8 teaspoon ground black pepper
1 teaspoon poultry seasoning
3 tablespoons barbecue sauce
3 strips uncooked bacon, cut in half
Watercress
Whole egg tomatoes or medium small tomatoes
Green pepper rings

1. Preheat oven to 350° (moderate).
2. Sprinkle woodcocks, inside and out with salt and black pepper. Set aside.
3. Cut acorn squash in lengthwise halves. Remove seeds and fibers. Set aside.
4. In a bowl, combine ground meat, potato chips, cereal, or bread crumbs, seasoned salt, garlic salt, black pepper, poultry seasoning, and barbecue sauce.
5. Divide the mixture into 6 equal portions and shape each into a separate ball. Place 1 ball in the body cavity of each woodcock. Close body openings with small skewers.
6. Wrap 1/2 strip bacon around the body of each woodcock. Place one bird in the cavity of each half acorn squash.
7. Arrange squash in a shallow baking pan, and pour hot water in the pan to a depth of 1/4 inch. Cover pan with foil and bake 1 hour or until squash are soft and the birds are tender, adding additional hot water if needed.
8. Remove foil 20 minutes before baking time is up to allow birds to brown. Leave woodcocks in the squash nests and transfer them to a warmed platter. Garnish with watercress, whole egg tomatoes, and green pepper rings.

MENU

Woodcock au Nid
Straw Potatoes
Cucumber-Radish Salad
Lattice Crust Cranberry-Mince Pie

Whenever I have the opportunity to travel, I make a point of seeking out new and exciting specialties to enliven my collection of recipes. This woodcock recipe is enriched with all the ingredients that make for *haute cuisine:* cream, cognac, wine, and lingonberries, cream and cognac are the riches of all fine chefs. I found this recipe in Copenhagen at the lovely Hotel Hafnia Patio Dining Room.

WOODCOCK A LA PIERRE

(MAKES 6 SERVINGS)

WINE SUGGESTION: *White Burgundy; Chassagne-Montrachet "Grandes Ruchottes" (Picard)*

The Basting Sauce may be made ahead of time. The stuffing ingredients may also be prepared ahead of time, but do not mix the stuffing until time to cook the meal.

6 ready-to-cook woodcocks
Salt and ground black pepper
4 tablespoons butter
¾ cup soft, fine bread crumbs
½ cup canned lingonberries
2 tablespoons cognac
2 tablespoons heavy cream
Dry white wine
Basting Sauce (recipe below)
1 scant cup heavy cream

1. Preheat oven to 400° (hot).
2. Sprinkle woodcocks inside and out with salt and black pepper.
3. In a 1-quart saucepan, melt 2 tablespoons of the butter and add bread crumbs. Stir and cook, over moderate heat, until crumbs have browned.
4. In a bowl, combine browned bread crumbs, lingonberries, and cognac. Mix gently. Add the 2 tablespoons heavy cream and only enough dry white wine to moisten the stuffing.
5. Spoon the stuffing loosely into the body cavities of the

woodcocks. Close cavity openings with short skewers or toothpicks.

6. Melt the remaining 2 tablespoons butter and rub it over the skin of the birds.
7. Arrange woodcocks on a rack in a shallow baking pan. Roast, uncovered, 5 minutes. Reduce oven temperature to 300° (slow) and continue roasting 25 minutes or until birds are tender, basting often with the Basting Sauce, and adding melted butter if needed.
8. Remove skewers from cavity openings and place the birds on a heated platter. Keep warm.
9. Add the 1 scant cup heavy cream to the roasting pan drippings. Place the pan over low heat and stir until the sauce is smooth and has thickened slightly, scraping up the browned bits from the bottom and sides of the pan.
10. Add salt and black pepper to taste and pour the gravy over the hot woodcocks. Serve promptly.

BASTING SAUCE

1 rib celery with leaves, minced
1 scallion, minced
1/8 teaspoon dried chervil
1/16 teaspoon dried tarragon
1 cup dry white wine

1. In a 1-quart saucepan, combine all ingredients. Cover and simmer 10 minutes over low heat.
2. Strain the sauce into a small bowl to use for basting the woodcocks.

MENU

Woodcock à la Pierre
Glazed Carrots and Pineapple
Romaine Salad
Orange Sherbet *Marzipan Cookies*

Once you have tasted woodcock you won't want to make substitutions, but, unfortunately, these lovely little birds migrate only in the late fall and early spring. So if substitutions are necessary, one frying chicken or two Cornish game hens do very well for this delectable, pungent dish.

MARINATED WOODCOCKS

(MAKES 2 SERVINGS)

WINE SUGGESTION: *Red Burgundy; Paul Masson*

Steps 1 through 4 of this recipe may be prepared ahead of time.

2 ready-to-cook woodcocks
Marinade (recipe below)
1 strip uncooked bacon
1½ tablespoons lemon juice
2 tablespoons butter
1 cup sour cream

1. Wash and dry woodcocks, put them in a large bowl, and pour the hot marinade over them. Cover and cool the birds and marinade to room temperature. Then refrigerate 5 days, turning the birds in the marinade each day.
2. Remove birds from the marinade. With a sharp paring knife, make 2 to 3 slits in the skin over the breast of each bird.
3. Cut bacon into 4 to 6 crosswise strips and insert one strip in each slit. Fasten the neck skin to the back with skewers. Brush lemon juice over the skin of the birds.
4. In a deep saucepan, melt butter. Add birds and the marinade and simmer until birds are tender, about 30 minutes.
5. Preheat oven to 325° (slow).
6. Transfer birds to a casserole. Set aside.
7. Strain marinade. Then press the vegetables that were in the marinade through a sieve into a bowl and fold in sour cream. Discard the liquid. Spoon the mixture over the woodcocks. Roast them until they are tender, about 30 minutes. Serve with noodles or dumplings.

MARINADE

1 rib celery with leaves, sliced
1 medium carrot, pared and sliced
2 medium onions, thinly sliced
1 small bunch parsley, chopped
1 teaspoon salt
3 whole allspice
4 peppercorns (whole black peppers)
1 small bay leaf
1 slice lemon peel
1 cup water
3 cups dry red wine

In a 2-quart saucepan, combine all ingredients, bring the mixture to boiling point, and pour over the woodcocks.

MENU

Marinated Woodcocks
Apple Dumplings or Noodles
Orange and Onion Salad
Danish Cinnamon-Raisin Shortcake

It was only a week after we had returned from Europe that my husband, a complete novice, decided to try his luck at hunting. As luck would have it, he brought home two lovely woodcocks. I had so little in the larder that much had to be improvised and with good fortune this dish turned out magnificently. Two Cornish hens will do.

INSTANT WOODCOCK

(MAKES 2 SERVINGS)

WINE SUGGESTION: *White Burgundy; Beaujolais Blanc*

Steps 2 through 3 may be prepared ahead of time.

2 ready-to-cook woodcocks, split down the back
Milk
Salt and ground black pepper
2 to 3 tablespoons flour
1½ tablespoons butter
1 tablespoon cooking oil
About ½ cup sour cream
Parsley
Papaya slices sautéed in butter

1. Preheat oven to 350° (moderate).
2. Dip woodcocks in milk, sprinkle with salt and black pepper, and dredge in flour.
3. In a heavy skillet, heat butter and oil. Add floured woodcocks and cook until birds have browned on all sides.
4. Transfer woodcocks to a casserole and spread with enough sour cream to cover them. Bake 30 to 35 minutes until birds are very tender.
5. Arrange woodcocks on a warmed platter. Garnish with parsley and serve with sautéed papaya slices.

MENU

Instant Woodcock
Sautéed Papaya Slices or Baked Apple Rings
Mushrooms with Peas
Escarole Salad
Cannoli (available in Italian food markets)
or
Vanilla Cream Puffs

The
BOTTLES

WINE THROUGH the AGES

Man and wine have been having a love affair for centuries. Anthropologists maintain that man has been making wine for ten thousand years. It has been a very long and happy romance. Museums around the world are filled with examples of the art of goldsmiths, silversmiths, glassblowers and diamond etchers, patronized for their skills in making wine containers. Bottles and corks, however, didn't come into common use until the middle of the nineteenth century and wine was widely used as an anesthetic until the same time. Only a mere century ago did labels become common.

Today, with bottles, corks and labels to identify the whole pedigree of a wine—its native soil, vine type, maker, and age—there is little mystery left. It is easier now to find better wine to drink, with less happenstance and fewer disappointments.

Wine is one of the great treasures of the world. Today, as never before, wines are being enjoyed as a symbol of gracious living. Wine lends an aura of glamour and sophistication to a fine meal and enhances the flavor of good food. Of course, wine is good in itself, but as our taste for fine cuisine develops, our appreciation of fine wine increases.

What is wine? Basically, wine is uncomplicated. To make it you must have grape juice and that juice must ferment. The process of fermentation is organic. During the latter part of the summer, a sort of musty gray down appears on the grapes. Perhaps you have seen it on grapes in the market. This down is called *bloom* and it consists of innumerable minute living creatures. When grapes are pressed, the juice soon begins to foam and bubble, and a froth appears on the surface. The juice is then said to be fermenting. What is actually happening is that these living creatures, these ferments, are feeding on the grape juice, and, in doing so, they are transforming the sugar of the juice into alcohol. At the same time, carbonic acid gas is released in the air. At times, a sediment is formed which comes to rest in the bottom of the wine bottle. When the fermenting process comes to an end, the remaining liquid with its alcohol is known as wine. Always remember, fine wine is a living thing and a fine wine is not as simple to make as the process described above may make it appear. When wine is being bought, stored, and prepared for consumption, it is alive. Wine has a cycle of life. It has its infancy; it grows to maturity; it continues for a time at its best; and then it declines slowly or rapidly into decay; and finally, death.

It takes time . . . time . . . time and more time to make a fine wine. It takes time to make the oak casks, it takes time to make the corks exported from Portugal—rather it takes time for the cork oak trees to produce the cork, and more time under the strict Portuguese law which permits the careful hand stripping of the bark only once every nine years. A well-made cork permits a minuscule amount of air to enter the bottle and allows the wine to age slowly to perfection. Wine bottles are laid on their sides so that the wine may keep the cork moistened to prevent the cork from drying out and allowing air into the bottle. If too much air should seep through the cork, there is a swift transition from wine to vinegar.

TYPES OF WINE

The four principal classifications of wines are:

1) still table wines,
2) sparkling wines,
3) aperitif wines, and
4) dessert wines.

Still table wines are either red or white. The most widely known come from France, Germany, and Italy. The most popular are Bordeaux and Burgundy. These are imported from France and recognized as the finest of table wines.

Bordeaux wines are either red or white; the reds are known as clarets, which include Zinfandels and Cabernet wines.

The white Bordeaux are from the Graves district which produces many wines of medium sweetness entirely suitable for serving with both domestic and wild fowl. In its southern part lies the sub-district of Sauternes, where the great Haut Sauternes originate (see dessert wines).

Burgundy is a red or white wine with a rich, hearty bouquet. If it is an old Burgundy it will be slightly amber at the edges.

Lighter and drier than the white Bordeaux, Loire wines are full-flavored and have an excellent bouquet.

Rhine wines are clean white wines, extremely flavorful, traditionally bottled in brown glass.

Another favorite still table wine is the Rosé. These wines are delicately colored and noted for their freshness and fragrance. The better known Rosés include the French Tavel and Rosé d'Anjou and the Portuguese Mateus.

The second classification is sparkling wines. Authentic French champagne is produced only in the

Champagne region of France around the city of Reims, just east of Paris. Other well-known wines in this category include sparkling Burgundy and sparkling rosé.

The process that produces effervescence in champagne and other sparkling wines is a second fermentation which occurs in the bottle.

The third classification, aperitif wines, are of two types—sherries and vermouths. Vermouths are the most widely known of the aperitif wines. They differ from the other three classifications in that herbs, roots, barks, and other flavorings are added to produce unique vermouth characteristics. Vermouths may or may not be chilled. Many popular aperitif wines, such as Cassis, Positano, and Cinzano are also in this category.

The fourth classification, dessert wines, includes port and cream sherries. The sweeter Graves, including Haut Sauternes, Barsac and the great Château d'Yquem are usually served, well chilled, as dessert wines. Some are so rich that one glass at the end of a meal is sufficient.

Often, the word "fortified" is used in conjunction with dessert wines. This simply means that the alcoholic content of the wine has been increased by the addition of grape brandies. Perhaps the most famous of the fortified wines are sherries and port. Port and cream sherries are served at room temperature.

GENERAL INFORMATION ABOUT WINE

A vintage wine label denotes that the wine of a particular region is produced in a specific year. The term *estate-bottled* (*mise au domaine*) means that the wine is bottled at the vineyard by the owner. Therefore a wine of superior quality in Burgundy, Germany, and elsewhere, is equivalent to the château-bottled wines of Bordeaux. The words estate-bottled and *vintage year* are of great importance and a guide to the connoisseur as well as to the consumer who wants to order the very best in wines.

If the wine label includes the term *appellation contrôlée,* it means that the wine was produced under the French vineyard control laws. This phrase always appears in conjunction with the place name under whose laws the wine has been produced.

Appellation d'origine defines the limit of regions, districts, townships, and vineyards, as well as specifying what grapes can be grown, the ways they must be tended, and how the wines should be made. This label is a guarantee of an authentic wine, but not necessarily a guarantee of quality. However, it is the first to look for on a French wine bottle. If it does not appear, it means that the wine has not met any accepted legal standards. The more specific the label is, the more restricted are the control laws. For example, if a label simply reads *Burgundy* it merely indicates that the wine is from that region, and is entitled only to that appellation. A label that reads *Chambertin-Clos de Bèze,* indicates that the wine is from that specific vineyard in the Burgundy township of Gevrey-Chambertin. Both wines may come under the control laws, but the Chambertin is from a great vineyard, whereas mere Burgundy is certain to be nondescript. A wine takes the most specific designation it is entitled to under the control laws, and the above distinction is all-important in buying French wines.

A NOTE ABOUT SEDIMENT

Wines that mature in the bottle for a long period of time, such as red wines, will sometimes throw a deposit. In most cases, this simply indicates that the wine should be handled carefully and poured slowly. Sediment does *not* impair the quality of the wine. On the contrary, it indicates that the wine has developed. But the sediment is unpleasant to the taste. If there is much deposit in the bottle, bring the wine up from the cellar the day before and stand it upright so that the sediment will settle to the bottom of the bottle. Then pour the wine off into another bottle or decanter so that the sediment is left behind. The decanting is best done in front of a bright light, so as to detect the first particles of sediment which are about to emerge. As soon as the first particles reach the neck of the bottle, stop pouring. Usually, when this procedure is followed, the bottle from which the wine was decanted is placed beside the container holding the wine so that guests may see what they will be drinking.

UNCORKING THE WINE

Red wine is always uncorked about one hour before the meal is served. It is left to stand quietly, thus allowing any small amounts of sediment to settle. Red Burgundies and Bordeaux should be served at about 60°, or what used to be room temperature before central heating came into being. Many people give a red wine a quick chilling off on the window sill or even five minutes (but no more) in the refrigerator.

White and rosé wines must be chilled but not icy. These wines have a very delicate fragrance which would lose its freshness if they were exposed to the air for too long a time. Therefore, white Burgundies and rosés should be opened just before serving.

GLASSES

The use of many different types of glasses is becoming obsolete; they are completely unnecessary. Experts agree that one type of wine glass is perfect for all wines, including champagne. The perfect glass is long-stemmed and tulip-shaped, with a bowl the size of an orange. As a matter of fact, any large glass or goblet is better than the small, so-called "wine glass" that is in use in many homes and restaurants. Serving wine in a water goblet is a good idea when no regular wine glass is available.

SERVING THE WINE

Wine is poured as soon as food is brought to the table. It is the host, rather than the hostess, who serves the wine and sees to it that glasses are replenished during the meal. If a red wine is being served, its greater bouquet makes it desirable to fill the glasses about halfway to two thirds full. With white wines, and all sparkling wines, the glasses should be filled close to the top. The host should be justly proud of offering a good wine; he holds the bottle with the label up so that the guests may have a look at it. (Of course, he never wraps the bottle in a towel.)

ENJOYING THE WINE

Wine is made to be enjoyed by everyone. Anybody can become a connoisseur and once he has, his tastes are as valid as those of any expert. Tasting wines is always an enjoyable experiment, but a little knowledge helps one to get the most out of it.

The first step is to look at the wine in the glass. Tip the glass slightly to one side and look at the color of the wine; it should be bright and clear. The next step is to swirl the wine in the glass. This is done in order to let the wine "breathe" and come in contact with the air to develop its wonderful bouquet. It is for this reason that only a little wine is poured into a large glass, so that there is plenty of room for the perfume to expand and develop in the glass. Now that the swirling has brought out the bouquet of the wine,

VINTAGE WINE CHART

(Ratings: 1 to 20)

SUPERB—18, 19, 20
GREAT—16, 17
VERY GOOD—15
GOOD—14
PASSABLE—12, 13

POOR—11
VERY POOR—10 or under
A MINUS SIGN—the wine is too old
NV—nonvintage
R—Red

	1958	1959	1960	1961	1962	1963	1964	1965	1966	1967	1968
ALSACE	—	10	8	16	15	10	14	9	17	19	10
BEAUJOLAIS	—	—	—	—	—	—	16	10	18	19	11–14
BORDEAUX, Red (Medoc and Graves)	11	19	15	20	16	12	17	12	18	16	10–13
BORDEAUX, Red (St.-Emilion and Pomerol)	—	15	13	20	17	8	17	13	18	16	9
BORDEAUX, White (Sauternes and Barsac)	10	20	8	19	18	8	10	9	16	17	9
BURGUNDY, Red	17	18	8	20	17	9	18	8	19	10	8
BURGUNDY, White	11	14	14	18	16	10	17	12	18	15	8
CHAMPAGNE	11	17	NV	20	20	NV	20	NV	20	20	NV
COTES DU RHONE Red and Rose (Tavel and Châteauneuf-du-Pape)	15	13	15	19	17	8	14	15	18	12	14
LOIRE (Vouvray, Muscadet, Pouilly-Fumé, Sancerre, Anjou, Chinon)	—	17R	15R	15R	16R	8	17	8	16	19	8

NOTE: In some of the older vintages there will be considerable sediment; therefore decanting is in order. Wines of 1969 and 1970 are generally excellent, and some of them have received the highest possible rating.

sniff it. Smelling the wine in the glass is one of the greatest pleasures of wine-tasting, because the bouquet gives you a foretaste of the wine itself.

Next, sip the wine and roll it around with the tongue, then slowly let it trickle down your throat. Let a minute elapse before you take the next sip, repeating the sipping, rolling and trickling.

STARTING A WINE CELLAR

Wine cellars are no longer a luxury. They are becoming a source of enjoyment for all. While imported wines can often be costly, the pleasure to be derived from a fine bottle can often offset any qualms about an initial expenditure. An interesting collection of wines may comprise regional wines and only a few of the more expensive bottles. A wine cellar requires little room, but several factors must be taken into consideration.

First and foremost, it must be remembered that wine should never be subjected to sudden changes in temperature. Although constant heat is bad for wine, variations of heat and cold are, by far, the wine's worst enemy. The ideal temperature for a wine cellar is about 50°F. A difference of a few degrees in either direction is entirely satisfactory, if the temperature is kept fairly constant.

Secondly, wine should not be stored where it will receive too much light. Preferably, it should be kept in a fairly dark place away from direct sunlight or ultra-violet rays. (Ordinary light bulbs are better than fluorescent tubes.)

Finally, the location selected for a wine cellar should be a fairly quiet spot where the wine can rest and not be moved or shaken unnecessarily. Dryness or high humidity has little or no influence on the preservation of wine.

Racks can be purchased, the most common of which holds one case (12 bottles) of wine. Some racks are designed so that they can be stacked one on top of another on the floor of a closet, cupboard, cabinet, cellar, or garage. In lieu of racks, wine or spirit cartons can be used if they have, as many do, separate compartments for each individual bottle. If these cartons are used, they should be turned on their sides, so that the wine is stored in the proper position.

CATEGORIES OF WINE

Some wine experts have a set rule and believe in serving white wine with white meat birds, such as chicken, quail, and pheasant; and red wine with dark meated birds, such as duck, goose, dove, and woodcock. Others are more casual, but in general, the following guidelines apply.

Fish and Seafood: Simply prepared fish or seafood calls for a light, white dry wine such as a Pinot Chardonnay, Chablis, Pouilly-Fuissé, or Pouilly-Fumé.

Fowl and Game Birds: Light red wines usually accompany light-flavored game birds, such as pheasant or quail, depending on what type of sauce has been used in their preparation. Strong game birds such as wild duck require a rich, red Burgundy such as a Pommard, Corton, or Musigny. Chicken prepared in a light sauce is complemented by a dry white wine such as a Corton-Charlemagne or Meursault, or a chilled rosé, or a fine claret (Bordeaux). Chicken or any type of fowl prepared in heavy sauces or rich gravies are served with red Burgundies. Goose requires an assertive, full-bodied Burgundy, or some of the red Bordeaux.

Creamed dishes: All creamed dishes should be accompanied by a dry white wine, a light Bordeaux, a rosé, or a sparkling wine.

Spicy dishes: Curries, highly spiced foods and fried foods should be accompanied by a good beer. Even a stew, should it be so highly spiced as to overpower the wine, would be better served with beer.

Salads: Generally, wine is not served with salads; the acid dressing interferes with the true taste of the wine.

Desserts or Fruit: Serve sweet wines with soufflés, cake, or fresh fruit (except highly acid citrus fruits). Champagne may be served as a dessert wine but choose the extra dry, not the bone-dry brut.

Dessert Cheeses: If the entrée wine is being used to finish off the meal, and it happens to be a white wine, choose a light cheese such as *fontina* or Havarti. The strong cheeses overwhelm any wine.

NOTE: I have placed emphasis largely on French wines with regard to listings and specific recipe recommendations. It has obviously been impossible to name and list every good wine in Europe. There are many pleasant and even great wines from other parts of France, such as Châteauneuf-du-Pape (red) and Hermitage (red or white) of the Rhône district. In Germany the drier white wines of the Northern Rheinhessen district, such as Johannisberger, Niersteiner, Liebfraumilch, and a very light, wispy dry wine from the Rheinhessen district, a Hochheimer, are especially worthy of mention. From the Moselle, we would suggest Bernkasteler, Maximin Grünhaus, and Piesporter. Good Italian wines include the white Lacrima Christi, Soave, and the ubiquitous red Chianti, which may often be substituted for beer.

We suggest for the reader's enjoyment that from time to time he substitute these for the various menu suggestions.

IMPORTED WHITE WINES

Burgundy, White:

Bâtard-Montrachet (Puligny-Montrachet)
Beaujolais Blanc
Blagny (Meursault)
Chablis Chapelot Premier Crû
Chablis Côte de Fontenay Premier Crû
Chablis Fourchaume Premier Crû
Chambolle-Musigny Charmes (Meursault)
Chassagne-Montrachet Grandes Ruchottes (Picard)
Chevalier-Montrachet (Puligny-Montrachet)
Claivoillon-Montrachet (Puligny-Montrachet)

Clos Blanc de Bougeot (Chambolle-Musigny)
Clos de Chaniot
Clos-des-Mouches (Beaune)
Corton-Charlemagne (Aloxe-Corton)
Criots-Charlemagne (Aloxe-Corton)
Criots-Bâtard-Montrachet (Chassagne-Montrachet)
La Pièce-sous-le-Bois (Meursault)
Meursault Casse Tête
Meursault Les Perrières
Montrachet (Puligny-Montrachet)
Musigny Blanc (Chambolle-Musigny)
Pinot Chardonnay
Pouilly-Fuissé
Puligny-Montrachet "B.S.F."
Santenots (Meursault)

DOMESTIC WHITE WINES

Almadén Pinot Chardonnay
Almadén Sauvignon Blanc
Beaulieu Riesling Sylvaner
Château Beaulieu (Sauvignon Blanc)
Charles Krug Chenin Blanc
Christian Brothers Golden Sherry
Inglenook Chablis (vintage)
Inglenook Rhine Wine (vintage)
Korbel Grey Riesling
Louis Martini Pinot Chardonnay
Martin Ray Pinot Chardonnay
Paul Masson Rhine Castle
Paul Masson Emerald Dry
Samuele Sebastiani Green Hungarian
Souverain Pinot Chardonnay
Taylor New York White Tokay
Taylor New York Pale Dry Sherry
Taylor New York Cream Sherry
Taylor New York Rhine
Taylor New York Vermouth

Taylor New York Port and Tawny Port
Wente Brothers Pinot Blanc
Wente Brothers Sauvignon Blanc

IMPORTED RED WINES

Beaujolais:

Brouilly
Chénas
Côtes de Brouilly
Fleurie
Juliénas
Louis Latour
Morgon
Moulin-à-Vent
St.-Amour

Bordeaux, Red:
(Claret)

Château Angludet (Cantenac-Margaux)
Château Bel-Air-Marquis-d'Aligre (Soussans-Margaux)
Château Belgrave (St.-Laurent)
Château Beychevelle (St.-Julien)
Château Canon (St.-Emilion)
Château Clos de l'Amiral (St.-Julien)
Château Clos d'Estournel (St.-Estèphe)
Château de Pez (St.-Estèphe)
Château de Rouffiac (St.-Emilion)
Château de Figeac (St.-Emilion)
Château Haut-Batailley (Pauillac)
Château Haut-Brion (Pessac)
Château Haut-Cadet (St.-Emilion)
Château Lafite-Rothschild (Pauillac)
Château Lafleur (Pomerol)
Château La Lagune (Ludon)
Château Latour (Montagne)
Château Latour (Pauillac)

Château Léoville-Barton (St.-Julien)
Château Léoville-Las-Cases (St.-Julien)
Château Léoville Poyferré (St.-Julien)
Château Lynch-Bages (Pauillac)
Château Magdelaine (St.-Emilion)
Château Margaux (Margaux)
Château Montrose (St.-Estèphe)
Château Mouton-Rothschild (Pauillac)
Château Paveil de Luze (St.-Julien)
Château Pavie (St.-Emilion)
Château Prieuré Lichine (Margaux)
Château Rausan-Ségla (Margaux)
Château Robert (Côtes de Bourg)
Château Rochet (St.-Estèphe)
Château Trotanoy (Pomerol)

Bordeaux:
(Sauternes and Barsac)

Château d'Yquem (Sauternes)
Château Latour-Blanche (Bommes)
Château Lafaurie-Peyraguey (Bommes)
Château Haut-Peyraguey (Bommes)
Château Rayne-Vigneau (Bommes)
Château Suduiraut (Preignac)
Château Coutet (Barsac)
Château Climens (Barsac)
Château Guiraud (Sauternes)
Château Rieussec (Fargues)
Château Rabaud-Promis (Bommes)

Burgundy, Red:

Bâtard-Montrachet (Chassagne-Montrachet)
Beaune "Cent Vignes" (Chevillot)
Bonnes Mares (Morey-St.-Denis)
Caillerets (Volnay)
Chambertin (Gevrey-Chambertin)
Chambertin Lavaux (St.-Jacques)

Chambertin (Moillard-Grivot)
Chapelle Chambertin (Gevrey-Chambertin)
Château de Bellevue
Château Grèves (Beaune)
Château Margaux (Margaux)
Château Petrus (Pomerol)
Chevret (Volnay)
Clos de Chênes (Volnay)
Clos de Ducs (Volnay)
Clos de Jacques (Gevrey-Chambertin)
Clos St.-Jean (Chassagne-Montrachet)
Clos de Thorey (Nuits-St. Georges)
Clos de Vougeot (La Marche)
Corton Clos du Roi (Aloxe-Corton)
Dominode (Savigny-les-Beaune)
Fixin "Clos de la Perrière"
Givry (Thénard)
La Tâche (Vosne-Romanée)
Latricières Chambertin (Chambertin)
Les Boudots (Nuits-St. Georges)
Les Charmes Chambertin (Gevrey-Chambertin)
Les Porrets (Nuits-St. Georges)
Les St. Georges (Nuits-St. Georges)
Montrachet (Chassagne-Montrachet)
Musigny (Chambolle-Musigny)
Pommard Épenots (Loubet)
Pommard Rugiens (Pommard)

DOMESTIC RED WINES

Almadén Cabernet Sauvignon
Almadén Gamay Beaujolais
Beaulieu B. V. Burgundy
Beaulieu B. V. "Beaumont" Pinot Noir
Charles Krug Zinfandel
Inglenook Zinfandel (vintage)
Inglenook Burgundy (vintage)
Inglenook Pinot Noir (vintage)

Korbel Cabernet Sauvignon
Korbel Pinot Noir
Louis Martini Pinot Noir
Louis Martini Port
Llords & Elwood Velvet Hill Pinot Noir
Llords & Elwood Cabernet Sauvignon
Paul Masson Burgundy
Roma Claret
Roma Burgundy
Roma Zinfandel
Samuele Sebastiani Barbera
Samuele Sebastiani Burgundy

DOMESTIC ROSE WINES

Almadén Mountain Nectar Rosé
Charles Krug Rosé
Llords & Elwood Rosé of Cabernet
Souverain Grenache Rosé
Samuele Sebastiani Vin Rosé
Taylor New York Rosé

WHAT IS CHAMPAGNE?

A true champagne is always fermented in the bottle. It is a manufactured wine to the extent that the natural processes of fermentation have been interrupted. Champagne receives more care and attention than any other wine in the world.

Champagne is usually a combination of Pinot Noir and Pinot Chardonnay grapes. When the wine is blended in vats before bottling, the term *cuvée* is given to the batch. When a champagne is termed *vintage* it designates that it is a blend of wines from a single vintage. Nonvintage champagnes are from a few or several vintages blended to create balance, fullness, and bouquet. A champagne made exclusively from Pinot Noir grapes is called *blanc de noirs* (white of blacks). Champagnes made from the Pinot Chardonnay grape are termed *blanc de blancs,* and come from several provinces where light or white grapes are grown.

Champagne takes six years to mature in the bottle. The word *brut* designates the driest of the champagne types. *Extra dry* is the next driest, *sec* or *dry* is slightly sweeter, *demi-sec* is twice as sweet as *sec,* and *doux* is the sweetest of champagnes.

Brut champagnes are usually drunk without any food accompaniment, or if drunk with food it is usually with a *pâté de foie gras,* caviar, smoked foods, or any type of highly seasoned food. Extra dry and dry are excellent with all types of food, with oysters on the half-shell for a Sunday brunch or with elaborate dinner entrées, egg dishes, steaks, etc. The doux champagnes are drunk with desserts or by themselves. Pink champagnes may be served with most any food.

There are two confusing words that appear on a

champagne label: *cramant* and *crémant*. Cramant is the name of a town on the Côte des Blancs below Épernay from which some of the *blanc de blancs* come. *Crémant* is a type of champagne that is less effervescent, usually made from both red and white grapes.

Champagne bottles should be chilled between 40°F. and 45°F. Glasses are not chilled and should be shaped like a tulip, with the edges slightly turned in, not the saucer type which allows the bubbles to dissipate too rapidly. The glasses must be perfectly dry without a trace of moisture. Champagne is sipped slowly.

IMPORTED CHAMPAGNE

BLANC DE BLANCS	*Nonvintage*
BOLLINGER	*Extra dry; nonvintage*
CHAMPAGNE DE ST. MARCEAU	*Brut, blanc de blancs*
CHANSON	*Sparkling burgundy, sparkling rosé, and champagne*
CHARLES HEIDSIECK	*Brut*
CHATEAU ROYAL	*Brut*
CLICQUOT	*Brut and extra dry*
CUVEE GRAND SIECLE	*Brut champagne and French sparkling burgundy*
ILE DE FRANCE	*Brut champagne*
KRUG	*Usually nonvintage*
LANSON	*Champagne, extra dry and brut*
LAURENT-RODERER	*Brut and extra dry*
MERCIER	*Extra dry, brut, blanc de blancs, Reserve de l'Empereur blanc de blancs*
MOET & CHANDON	*White seal champagne, extra dry, dry imperial, brut imperial, Dom Pérignon*

MUMM'S	*Extra dry, Cordon vert, Cordon Rouge Brut, Cordon Rouge*
PERRIER-JOUET	*Cuvée and cuvée brut*
PIPER HEIDSIECK	*Cuvée des Ambassadeurs, brut, and extra dry*
POMMERY	*Brut*
RUINART	*Brut Traditions extra dry, Dom Ruinart, blanc de blancs*
TAITTINGER	*Brut, "La Francaise" champagne, blanc de blancs*
TROUILLARD	*Brut*

DOMESTIC CHAMPAGNE AND SPARKLING WINES

ALMADEN	*Brut, extra dry, sparkling rosé, sparkling pink and sparkling burgundy*
AMBASSADOR	*Champagne and sparkling burgundy*
BEAULIEU	*Brut, extra dry, rouge, sparkling burgundy, sparkling rosé*
BON SOIR	*Dry, extra dry, and sparkling pink champagne*
BUENA VISTA	*Brut champagne*
CHATEAU BOISSE	*Brut champagne*
CHATEAU CHEVALIER	*Champagne, sparkling burgundy, and pink champagne*
CHATEAU LOUIS CHAMPAGNE	*Pink champagne and sparkling burgundy*
CHATEAU MAURICE CHAMPAGNE	*Extra dry, brut, and sparkling burgundy*
CHATEAU NAPOLEON	*Pink champagne and sparkling burgundy*
CHATEAU PIERRE CHAMBERRY	*Gran spumante Malvasia and Wedding Day Champagne*
COOK'S IMPERIAL	*Extra dry champagne, sec, pink champagne, sparkling burgundy, and brut champagne*

CRESTA BLANCA	*Champagne, sparkling burgundy, pink champagne and brut*
CREBARI	*Pink champagne and sparkling burgundy*
CALWA	*Champagne and sparkling burgundy*
CUVALLE & CIE	*Champagne, pink champagne and sparkling burgundy*
CHRISTIAN BROTHERS	*Brut, extra dry champagne, sparkling burgundy, and pink champagne*
CUVEE D'OR	*Champagne, pink champagne, and sparkling burgundy*
GALLO	*Eden Roc Champagne, pink champagne, and sparkling burgundy*
GOLD SEAL	*Brut champagne*
GREAT WESTERN	*Extra Dry Champagne,* Special Reserve Champagne,† Brut Champagne,‡ Pink Champagne,‡ Sparkling burgundy †*
GREYSTONE	*Champagne, pink champagne, and sparkling burgundy*
HANS KORNELL	*Third generation: Extra dry and sec champagne, pink champagne, and sparkling burgundy*
INGLENOOK	*Brut champagne, vintage 1963*
JEAN LECOTE	*Extra dry champagne*
JACQUES BONET	*Champagne, sparkling burgundy, pink champagne, and cold duck*
KRUG	*Champagne, Brut Reserve*
KORBEL	*Korbel natural; Korbel brut, sec, extra dry, and rouge champagne and sparkling rosé*
LA VIE	*Extra dry champagne, sparkling burgundy, rouge and pink champagne and cold duck*
LA GRANGE	*Champagne and pink champagne*
LA RUE	*Champagne, pink champagne, and sparkling burgundy*

* Available in all sizes.
† Available in fifths and tenths only.
‡ Available in magnums, fifths, and tenths.

LE DOMAINE	*Extra dry champagne and sparkling burgundy*
LEJON	*Pink champagne and sparkling burgundy*
LLORDS & ELWOOD	*Extra dry champagne*
L'AMOUR	*Champagne, pink champagne, and sparkling burgundy*
MANISCHEWITZ	*Sparkling concord*
MARIE ANTOINETTE	*Champagne, sparkling burgundy, and pink champagne*
PAUL MASSON	*Extra dry champagne, brut champagne, pink champagne, sparkling champagne, and crackling rosé*
MEIERS OHIO STATE	*Brut champagne, sparkling burgundy, Château Reim, pink champagne, cold duck, and sparkling wine*
TAYLOR'S NEW YORK CHAMPAGNE	*Extra dry champagne, special reserve, brut champagne, pink champagne, sparkling burgundy, New York State Martinique*
POL D'ARGENT	*New York State champagne*
REGINA	*Champagne and pink champagne*
ROMA ESTATE HOLLOW STAR	*Champagne and pink champagne*
SONOMA	*Pinot champagne*
SAN MARTIN	*Demi sec, extra dry, brut champagne, pink champagne, and sparkling burgundy*
SARATOGA	*Champagne, pink champagne, and sparkling burgundy*
TOUR EIFFEL	*Champagne, pink champagne, and sparkling burgundy*
TRES BONNE	*Champagne and sparkling burgundy*
VERSAILLES	*Pink champagne*
WEIBEL	*Extra dry champagne, pink champagne, sec, brut sparkling burgundy, Chardonnay brut, crackling rosé, sparkling rosé, and Muscato spumante*

INDEX

A

Almanach des gourmands, 183
Almonds, 165–166, 249
Almond Turkey Sandwiches, 249–250
Aperitif wines 271, 272
Appellation contrôlée, 273
Appellation d'origine, 273
Apple brandy, 156
Apricot Stuffing, 236
Armagnac, 177
Artichokes, 185
Ashby-Sterry, Joseph, 162
Asian Chicken, 70–71
Aunt Fannie's Masterpiece, 23–24

B

Bacon-Wrapped Pheasant Livers and Sausage, 196–197
Baked Rice, 170–171
Basting Sauce
  for quail, 222
  for woodcock, 263
Beaujolais, 55, 67, 177, 208, 214, 282
Beaujolais Blanc, 59, 265
Beaujolais Saint Amour, 230
Beaulieu B.V. "Beaumont" Pinot Noir, 70
Beaulieu B.V. Burgundy, 156
Beaune "Cent-Vignes," 102
Beer, 25, 42, 63, 68, 73, 97, 108, 136, 205, 207, 211, 252, 253
Beychevelle, 114
Blanc de blancs, 286
Blanc de noirs, 286
Bloom, 269
Blueberry Chicken, 67–68
Bonnes-Mares, 154, 235
Bordeaux, 21, 23, 31, 34, 61, 78, 79, 83, 85, 86, 100, 101, 106, 114, 119, 121, 133, 138, 139, 145, 147, 149, 167, 179, 181, 192, 201, 212, 215, 219, 223, 226, 257, 260, 271, 282–283
Bouquet Garni, 90, 184
Braised Squab with Vegetable Salad, 88–89
Brandied Chicken, 50–51
Brandied Quail, 214–215
Brandy, 50, 204, 214
Brazilian Duck, 121–123
Bread Stuffing, 168–169
Breast of Guinea Hen Colbert, 175–176
Bressandes, 163
Brillat-Savarin, 92, 189
Broiled Grouse, 162–163
Broiled Spatchcock, 34–36
Broilers
  amount per serving, 17
  roasting timetable, 14
  stuffing for, 6
Brouillis, 113
Brown sauce, 50, 149, 150–151, 173, 174
Brut (champagne), 286
Buffet Chicken Crisps, 64–65
Burgundy, 18, 26, 28, 36, 39, 41, 45, 46, 50, 59, 77–78, 81, 82, 90, 92, 94, 98, 102, 104, 109, 111, 116, 117, 123, 124, 126, 127, 129, 131, 132, 135, 154, 156, 158, 160, 162, 163, 165, 172, 174, 175, 183, 187, 190, 191, 194, 195, 198, 199, 202, 204, 217, 218, 231, 233, 235, 238, 240, 243, 247, 249, 250,

Burgundy (*cont'd*)
255, 262, 264, 265, 271, 280–281, 283–284
Butler, Samuel, 145

C

Cabbage, with goose, 154
Cabernet, 271
Caillerets, 116
Calvados, 156, 190, 229
Canard à la Christophe, 124–126
Canard Côte D'Or, 92–94
Canard à la Montmorency, 117–119
Canard Moreau, 129–130
Canard au Vin, 106–107
Caneton à la Bergerac, 114–115
Caneton à la Chevalier, 102–104
Caneton à l'Orange, 123–124
Caneton en Ragoût, 94
Capons
  amount per serving, 17
  roast, 41–42
  roasting timetable, 14
  stuffing for, 6
Carême, Marie-Antoine, 218
Celery, 198, 205
Chablis Côte de Fontenay Premier Crû, 238
Chablis Fourchaume Premier Crû, 50
Chambertin, 124
Chambertin Lavaux, 81, 98, 174
Chambolle-Musigny, 28
Champagne, 49, 75, 209, 221, 245, 271–272, 286–290
  definition, 286
  list, 287–290
Champagne Sauce, 246–247
Chapelle Chambertin, 240
Charcoal Broiled Duck Breasts, 131
Charlemagne, 99–100
Charles VII (King of France), 235
Charles Krug Chenin Blanc, 47
Charles Krug Rosé, 38
Charles Krug Sauvignon Blanc, 71
Chassagne-Montrachet, 243
Chassagne-Montrachet "Grandos Ruchottes," 262
Château Angludet, 31
Château Beaulieu, 60
Château Bel-Air-Marquis-d'Aligre, 56
Château Belgrave, 167
Château Beycherelle, 23
Château Dauzal, 86
Château Figeac, 106
Château Greves, 90
Château Haut-Brion, 133
Château Lafite, 121
Château Lafleur, 219
Château La Lagune, 101
Château Latour, 149, 201
Château Latour Montagne, 260
Château Latour-Pomerol, 139
Château Léoville-Las-Cases, 179
Château Léoville-Poyferré, 147
Château Lynch-Boges, 34
Château Magdelaine, 145
Château Margaux, 83
Château Montrose, 198
Château Petrus, 135
Château Prieuré Lichine, 61
Château Rausan-Ségla, 181, 192
Château de Rouffiac, 226, 257
Château Trotanoy, 100
Cherry and Fig Sauce, 125
Chestnuts, 160, 240–241
Chevret, 160, 194

Chez Marcelle (restaurant), 138
Chianti, 25, 63, 68, 73
Chicken
  kinds of, 17
  recipes, 17–76
  roasting, 7
  roasting timetable, 14
  substituted for guinea hen, 169, 179
  substituted for pheasant, 190, 199
  substituted for turkey, 249
  used with leftover plum sauce, 209
Chicken Casserole and Things, 31–32
Chicken in Champagne Sauce, 75–76
Chicken El Paso, 25–26
Chicken with Green Noodles, 38–39
Chicken Mingsu, 63–64
Chicken Nero, 56–57
Chicken with Oysters, 47–48
Chicken Roquefort, 21
Chicken Salerno, 28–29
Chicken Soufflé, 30–31
Chicken Tuscany, 33–34
Chinese Doves, 83–84
Chinese New Year Duckling, 136–137
Chunking Inn (restaurant), 63
Cinnamon, 221
Claret, 271
Clos de l'Amiral, 21
Clos-des-Chênes, 217
Clos des Mouches, 78, 249
Clos du Roi, 36, 202
Clos St.-Jacques, 233
Clos de Thorey, 250
Clos de Vougeot, 41, 123, 131, 165, 255
Coconuts, 181
Coeur, Jacques, 235
Cognac, 113, 129
Cold Buffet Pheasant, 194
Cold Chicken Mexicali, 42–43
Cointreau-Orange Sauce, 229
Cornish Hens with Oranges, 228-229
Cornish Hens with Sauce Madère, 223–224
Corton Bressandes, 104
Corton Charlemagne, 39, 187
Corton Clos du Roi, 92
Cramant, 287
Creamed dishes, proper wines with, 278
Crémant, 287
Créqui, La Marquise de, 92
Curaçao, 129, 197
Cuvée, 286

D

Danish Roast Goose, 154–156
De Gouy, Louis P., 167
Demi-sec (champagne), 286
Desserts, proper wines with, 280
Dessert wines, 271, 272
Domestic birds
  cooking, 4–5
  definition, 3
  description, 3
  giblets, 8–9
  handling cooked poultry, 7–8
  handling and storing, 3–5
  proper wines with, 278
  stuffing and trussing, 5–6
  thawing, 4
Domestic Red wines, list, 284–285

Domestic rosé wines, list, 285
Domestic white wines, list, 281–282
Doux (champagne), 286
Doves and Squabs
  recipes, 77–91
Doves à la Madrid, 80–81
Doves in Red Wine, 79–80
Doves with Sweetbreads, 86–87
Doves in Wine, 78
Duck
  recipes, 92–144
  roasting timetable, 15–16
  stuffing for, 6
  used with leftover plum sauce, 209
Duck and Lentil Casserole, 116–117
Duckling Savannah, 132–133
Dumas, Alexandre, 183, 260

E

Eau de vie 113
Eloise's Stuffed Pheasants, 195–198
Epicurean, 34
Epulariò, 77
Estate-bottled, 273
Extra dry (champagne), 286

F

Faisan Nancy, 190–191
Faisan Oriental, 205–206
Faisan au Vin, 201–202
Fish, proper wines with, 278
Fixin Clos de la Perrière, 132
Francis I, 109
Fried Walnut Chicken, 73–74
Frosted Grapes, 157
Fryers
  amount per serving, 17
  roasting timetable, 14

Garlic, 183
Gay, John, 233
Gevrey-Chambertin, 199
Giblets
  gravy, 8–9, 237–238
  sauce, for duck, 112–113
  stock, for duck, 130
Glace de Viande, 115, 227
Glazed Duckling, 139–141
Golden Goose, 152–153
Goose
  recipes, 145–161
  roasting timetable, 15
  stuffing for, 6
Goose Piccadilly, 147–148
Grand Marnier, 123
Grapes
  Frosted, 157
  Thompson, 215
Gravy, for pheasant, 197
Green Beans Fiesta, 151
Green pepper, 201
Grouse
  recipes, 162–166
  roasting timetable, 16
Grouse Amandine, 166
Grouse in Tomato Sauce, 163–164

Guajalote à la Balboa, 233–234
Guinea Fowl
recipes, 167–182
substituted for pheasant, 190
Guinea Fowl in Coconut Milk, 181–182
Guinea Fowl Piedmontese, 167–169
Guinea Hen Blackhawk, 172–173

H

Hannah's Roast Wild Duck, 135–136
Haut-Cadet, 79, 85, 119
Herford, Oliver, 223
Holiday Brunch, 65–67
Holiday Turkey, 235–238
Hom, Robert, 63

I

Imported red wines, list, 282–284
Imported white wines, list, 280–281
Inglenook Chablis, 30
Inglenook Pinot Noir, 141
Instant Woodcock, 265–266

J

Juniper,172
Jurgensen's, 34, 116

K

Korbel Cabernet Sauvignon, 190
Korbel Pinot Noir, 143
Kowloon Roasted Chicken, 54
Krauted Grouse, 165

L

La Napoule Plage (restaurant), 71
La Pièce-sous-le-Bois, 46
La Tour d'Argent (restaurant), 98
Latricières-Chambertin, 172
Le Bistro (restaurant), 158
Leftover Duck, 101–102
Leftover Turkey with Mushroom Sauce, 238–240
Le Petit Auberge (restaurant), 45
Les Boudots, 247
Les Charmes Chambertin, 218
Les Porrets, 129
Ling's Memorable Turkey, 252–253
Llords & Elwood Cabernet Rosé, 33, 43
Llords & Elwood Cabernet Sauvigon, 52, 242
Llords & Elwood Velvet Hill Pinot Noir, 152
Loire, 58, 271
Longfellow, Henry Wadsworth, 211
Louis XIV (King of France), 94, 145, 214
Louis Martini Barbera, 82, 158

M

Madeira, 135, 152, 173
Madeira Sauce, 107, 224
Marinade
  for duck, 142
  for woodcook, 265
Marinated Duckling, 141–142
Marinated Woodcocks, 264–265
Marsala, 142, 171
Martin Ray Pinot Chardonnay, 204
Mateus, 271
Maximin-Grünhaus, 166
Meat thermometer, 4
Meek, Alfred, 79
Meursault Casse Tête, 45, 191
Mirepoix, 132, 149, 247
Mirepoix, Duc de, 132
Mise au domaine, 273
Mole de Poblano de Guajalote, 253–255
Montmorency, 117
Morgon, 177, 208
Moselle, 166
Moulin-à-Vent, 67, 214
Mouton-Rothschild, 215
Mushroom Sauce, 27, 239–240
Musigny, 127

O

Oie Normandy, 156–157
Oie au Sauce Maison, 149–150
Oie du Soir, 145–147
Oie St. Étienne, 158–159
Oie St. Malo, 160–161
Olive oil, 162
Onion Duck, 108–109
Oxford Chicken, 36–37
Oyster Stuffing, 236–237

P

Paloma de Sud America, 85–86
Paprika, 245
Partridge
  recipes, 183–188
  roasting timetable, 16
Partridge Chasseur, 187–188
Pato de Castellano, 119–121
Pato Español con Olivas, 143–144
Paul Masson, 264
Pavie, 212
Pecans, 202
Pepper, 228
Perdrix aux Artichauts, 185–186
Perdrix au Choux, 183–185
Peruvian Turkey, 257–258
Petit Norman (restaurant), 26
Pheasant
  number of servings, 13
  recipes, 189–210
  roasting timetable, 16
Pheasant Marguerite, 192–193
Pheasant with Pecans, 202–203
Pheasant Provençal, 199–200
Pheasant, Purple Plum, 209–210
Pheasant in Thick Cream, 191–192
Pigeonneau Sous Cloche, 82–83
Pilaf Stuffing, 52–53
Pineapple Duckling, 97–98

Pineapple and Orange Garnish, 197
Pinot Chardonnay, 26
Plum Sauce, 209–210
Pollo Cuernavaca, 43–44
Pollo Español, 61–62
Pollo Sevilla, 55–56
Pommard Épenots, 126, 231
Pommard Rugiens, 117
Port, 272
Pouilly Fumé, 58
Pouilly Fuissé, 18, 162, 183
Poularde Italienne au Pilau, 52–53
Poularde Sauté Régine, 68–69
Poularde aux Truffes, 19–20
Poularde Véronique, 60–61
Poule à l'Armagnac, 177–179
Poulet en Calvados, 18–19
Poulet Grand Marnier, 45–46
Poulet Sauté Lyonnaise, 22–23
Pressed Duck, 98–99, 100–101
Prosciutto (ham), 257

Q

Quail
  number of servings, 13
  recipes, 211–222
  roasting timetable, 16
Quail Baltimore, 217
Quail, Chinese Style, 211–212
Quail with Lichee Nuts, 212–213
Quail à la Margot, 219–221
Quail Montpellier, 218–219
Quail à la São Paulo, 221–222

R

Raisins, 133
Red Bordeaux, 21, 23, 31, 34, 56, 61, 79, 83, 85, 87, 100, 101, 106, 114, 119, 121, 133, 138, 139, 145, 147, 149, 167, 179, 181, 192, 201, 212, 215, 219, 223, 226, 257, 260, 282–283
Red Burgundy, 36, 41, 81, 83, 90, 92, 94, 98, 102, 104, 109, 111, 116, 117, 123, 124, 126, 127, 129, 131, 132, 135, 154, 156, 158, 160, 163, 165, 172, 174, 175, 194, 195, 198, 199, 202, 217, 218, 231, 233, 235, 240, 247, 250, 255, 264, 283–284
Red Graves, 185
Red Wines, lists
  domestic, 284–285
  imported, 282–284
Reynière, Grimod de la, 151, 183
Rhine, 65, 271
Rice, baked, 170–171
Richebourg, 109
Roast Breasts of Guinea Hen, 169–171
Roast Capon, 41–42
Roast Duck with Raisin Stuffing, 133–134
Roast Pheasant Marchand, 198–199
Roast Turkey Lucien, 247–248
Roasters
  amount per serving, 17
  stuffing for, 6
Roasting, 7
  timetables for birds, 14–16
Rochet, 223
Rock Cornish Hens
  amount per serving, 17

Rock Cornish Hens (*cont'd*)
recipes, 223–232
roasting timetable, 14
substituted for doves, 79
substituted for woodcocks, 264, 265
Rock Cornish Hens Flambé, 230
Rosé, 33, 38, 43, 88, 271, 285
Rosé d'Anjou, 271
Rugiens, 195

S

Saint Amour, 55
Samuele Sebastiani, 94
Samuele Sebastiani Vin Rosé, 228
Sauces
Basting, for quail, 222
Brown, 50, 149
Champagne, 246–247
Cherry and Fig, 125
Cointreau-Orange, 229
Colbert, 176
Diable, 35–36
Madeira, 107, 224
Maison, 149, 150–151
Mushroom, 27, 239–240
Plum, 209–210
Quick Brown, 173, 174
Soubise, 178–179
Tomato, 164
Truffle, 220
Whipped Cream, 244–245
Sauerkraut, 165
Sauerkraut-Stuffed Duckling, 111–113
Sauerkraut Stuffing, 112
Sautéed Quail Véronique, 215–216
Sautéed Wild Duck, 109–110
Sauternes, 271
Schloss Vollrads, 22
Scotch, 226
Scotch Cornish Hens, 226–227
Seafood, proper wines with, 278
Sebastiani Barbera, 175
Sec (champagne), 286
Sediment, 274
Sesame-Rice Cornish Hens, 225–226
Sesame seed, 225
Sherry, 272
Shih Meng, 136
Smith, Alexander, 17
Soused Duck, 126–127
South American Guinea Hen, 179–180
Sparkling wines, 271–272
Spatchcock, 34
Spicy dishes, proper beverages with, 278
Squabs with Pork, 90–91
Stewing hens or fowls
amount per serving, 17
Still table wines, 271
Stuffed Rock Cornish Hens, 231–232
Stuffed Royal Bird, 240–241
Stuffing for poultry, 6–7
Apricot, 236
Bread, 168–169
Oyster, 236–237
Pilaf, 52–53
Sauerkraut, 112
Tuscany, 33–34
Wild Rice, 96, 232
Summertime Pheasant, 207
Sunday Brunch, 39–40
Suprêmes de Caneton aux Noix, 127–128

Suprêmes de Poule de Guinée, 174
Suprêmes de Volaille Alphonse, 71–72
Suprêmes de Volaille Bernardo, 49–50
Suprêmes de Volaille Maurice, 26–27
Suprêmes de Volaille Régence, 59–60
Suprêmes de Volaille au Vin, 58
Suprêmes de Volaille Yvonne, 46–47
Sweet Red Wine Duckling, 138–139
Swiss Gruyère cheese, 46

T

Tavel, 271
Tipsy Pheasant, 204–205
Tomato Sauce, 164
Truffles, 219
  sauce, 220
Turkey
  recipes, 233–259
  roasting, 7
  roasting timetable, 14–15
  stuffing for, 6–7
  substituted for duck, 101
  substituted for pheasant, 199
Turkey Alberto, 243–245
Turkey Broth, 259
Turkey in Champagne, 245–247
Turkey Marengo, 255–256
Turkey Messina, 242–243
Turkey with Mushroom Dressing, 250–251
Turnips, 103
Tuscany Stuffing, 33–34

V

Vegetable Salad, 89
Venetian Pheasant, 208
Vermouth, 272
Vintage, 273, 286
Vintage Wine Chart, 276
Vol-au-vents, 39
Vouvray, 19, 169, 225

W

Water chestnuts, 211
Whipped Cream Sauce, 244–245
White Burgundy, 18, 26, 28, 39, 45, 46, 50, 59, 77–78, 162, 183, 187, 190, 191, 204, 238, 243, 249, 262, 265, 280–281
White Wines, lists
  domestic, 281–282
  imported, 280–281
Wild birds
  carving, 12–13
  cleaning, 10–13
  handling, 11–12
  number of servings, 13
  proper wines with, 278
  trussing, 12
Wild Duck in Marsala Wine, 104–105
Wild Rice Stuffing, 96, 232
Wine
  categories, 278–285
  cellars, 277–278
  definition, 269–270
  general information, 273–278

Wine (*cont'd*)
  glasses, 275
  serving, 275
  tasting, 275–277
  types, 271–272
  vintage chart, 276
Woodcock
  number of servings, 13
  recipes, 260–266
  roasting timetable, 16
Woodcock au Nid, 260–261
Woodcock à la Pierre, 262–263

Z

Zinfandel, 271

This book was set in
Baskerville type by
Brown Bros. Linotypers, Inc.
It was printed by
Halliday Lithograph Corp.,
and bound by
American Book-Stratford Press.
Illustrations and typography by
Loretta Trezzo